THE PROBLEM OF
MENNONITE ETHICS

The Problem of Mennonite Ethics

by

Abraham P. Toews, Th. D.

WIPF & STOCK · Eugene, Oregon

Wipf and Stock Publishers
199 W 8th Ave, Suite 3
Eugene, OR 97401

The Problem of Mennonite Ethics
By Toews, Abraham P.
ISBN 13: 978-1-62032-764-7
Publication date 11/15/2012
Previously published by Wm. B. Eerdmans, 1963

TABLE OF CONTENTS

Foreword vii
Abbreviations xii

PART ONE

1. Stating the Problem — 3
2. Definitions — 17

PART TWO

1. The Scripture and Mennonite Ethics — 35
2. Mennonite Adoption of Ethics — 54
3. Shaping of Mennonite Ethics — 62
4. The Philosophy and Theology of Mennonite Ethics — 81
5. Humanism and Mennonite Ethics — 101
6. Mennonite Ethics and Pietism — 123
7. Mysticism and Mennonite Ethics — 150

PART THREE

1. The Application of Mennonite Ethics to Others — 179
2. Mennonite Ethics in Relation to Self — 200

PART FOUR

Conclusion — 221
Appendixes I - III — 239
Bibliography — 256

FOREWORD

This writing has gone through three definite stages. Its embryo was deposited in the heart of a youth on a Manitoba farm flanked on the west by Steinbach, a solid Mennonite village; on the north by the early Clearsprings Settlement, almost exclusively Presbyterian; on the east by the first settlers in Canada, the French Canadians, totally Roman Catholic; on the south by Germans, stalwart Lutherans coming directly from Europe's Reformation arena. As if for good measure, the Slavic Greek Catholics in the background to the east and south filtered through with their nationalism and religious observances. The Presbyterian church with its organ, steeple and Gothic windows; the Roman Catholic church bells in nearby La Broqurie; and the Lutheran church in Friedensfeld with its *Posaunenchor* (brass band) and church bell, filled the youth with questions that had to wait almost half a century for their answers.

The desire to know why the different Mennonite way of life and worship was greatly intensified when this youth later attended Manitoba University, the United Church Seminary at Saskatoon, Canada, and the Evangelical and Reformed Seminary in St. Louis. Here he found that his fellow students and seminarians were equally pious and devoted to serve their Master with obedience and sincerity, and that in mutuality, Christian ideals and aspirations there was no difference. Their periodic Communion Services manifested a spirit of Christian brotherhood he was not even permitted to enjoy with other exclusive Mennonite denominations. There was a constant longing for a deeper understanding and appreciation of all denominations beyond the Mennonite pale. Without disowning the simple, literally biblicistic Mennonite way of life, their cold and unattractive Calvinistic church interior and worship, and at times, seemingly, an illogical nonconformity, an ever greater urge made itself felt to know just why Mennonites believe and behave as they do.

Intense graduate studies make thoughts jell. A good deal of inner satisfaction came when the "youth" came to Concordia Seminary (The Lutheran Church-Missouri Synod) in St. Louis. Under the wise counsel of Prof. Martin H. Scharleman, Ph.D., director of graduate studies, and Prof. Walter E. Buszin, Mus.D., professor of hymnology and liturgics, who took the student into his close guidance in acquiring a knowledge of expressions in worship, hymnody and religious inter-action, a pattern began to unfold that purported intelligent meaning. The result of these studies was the thesis entitled AMERICAN MENNONITE WORSHIP which can now be obtained in many bookstores. In this book is a partial answer to the questions the youth had when he heard the church bells ring to the east and to the south. In spite of this there remained with him the ever recurring query, "why are Mennonites and their kind always aware of their differences in language, religious expression and Christian living?"

As a rule graduate students are not satiated with partial answers. Prof. Alfred M. Rehwinkel, LL.D., at Concordia, a former Canadian Lutheran pastor and educator, dealt with Christian ethics in his seminars in a way that lured his Mennonite student to find the answers to the peculiar Mennonite faith and behavior. Dr. Rehwinkel and the other brethren at Concordia with their sympathetic understanding, patience and wise direction, gave the immediate impetus to put into concrete form what had been mulled over for decades. This book is the evidence of such effort. Since the field is so much larger than can be dealt with in one volume, the title, THE PROBLEM OF MENNONITE ETHICS, tells us that only one phase has been considered. Since the desire to know and make known is never stilled it is fondly hoped that others with like dreams and wonders will have the leading of the Lord to give their thinking also concrete form.

The author was very fortunate to have professors who were delightfully interested in philosophy and the Word of God. The first such was Prof. D. S. Dix, Ph.D., at the Seminary in Saskatoon. Dr. Dix capsuled the Word, philosophy and ethics in one prescription which made it most effective. At Eden Theological Seminary, Prof. Leonard Wernicke, Ph.D., applied the life in the Apostolic Church to the modern church and focused our attention on the very problems with which the Mennonites perpetually struggle. As an editor for many years of the *Abendschule,* a monthly church paper still found in many Mennonite homes, he knew many of my questions and answers. At Concordia Prof. Lewis Wm. Spitz, Ph.D., a most devoted teacher and servant of the Lord, sat with the student as his thesis advisor for many hours helping to integrate what had been observed during the years with that later taught in schools. Along with this, Prof. Albert Merkens, Ph.D., applied the resurrection of Christ philosophically to a modern setting of inter-denominationalism and Christian education. From all this the student came away with the conviction that Mennonite ethics and thinking are definitely a facet of the whole field of Christian philosophical endeavor.

But this was not all. Professor J. Theodore Mueller, Ph.D., Th.D., in his systematic theology classes referred time and again to the teachings of his personal friend, author and Mennonite leader, John Horsch, and convinced his students that it was absolutely essential that sound doctrine be the core of Anabaptism, Mennonitism and Lutheranism if they want to remain fundamentally sound. He left with every student the urge to make this truth known. Prof. Erwin L. Lueker, Ph.D., linked this interest with the Mennonites in the Atlantic States during and prior to the War of Independence and Prof. Carl S. Meyer, Ph. D., traced the Puritan movement from England through the Mennonite churches in Holland and finally as the earliest frontiersmen in New England. All of these studies reflected Mennonite reactions under various conditions.

No book comes into being without ample original source material. This was obtained through the kindness of Dr. Cornelius Krahn and Prof. John Schmidt at Bethel College Historical Library, Newton, Kansas. The author is indeed greatly indebted to these brethren for their untiring interest in the topic and making invaluable source material available. Last but not least is my good wife, who so nobly stood by at all times, especially when "the going was rough."

The author feels rather uneasy about the large number of footnotes and other impedimentia that are liable to hinder rapid reading. It is hoped that this will not prevent the procurement and distribution of the book especially among non-Mennonites who want just this kind of information to understand and appreciate their neighbors more fully. Mennonite publishers and churches should spare no effort to make all material of this kind known. To our knowledge the Mennonites have almost nothing on their ethics that they can put into the hands of an inquiring public. With a complete revision of the doctorate thesis it was still deemed essential that what is said be corroborated perhaps a little more than usual in popular and lighter reading.

The book is divided into four parts. Some parts are more difficult than others. It is perhaps not wise to put into one volume the difficult with the other but it was done this way for the sake of conserving financial outlay and facilitating the distribution among non-Mennonites most material for the smallest expense. Not only will Menonnites and non-Mennonites profit by these pages but also our own children, who want to know what their parents believe and why. Parents will do well to buy several books and present them to members of their family who have become estranged to the faith and way of life of our fathers. God will truly be pleased when parents, children and neighbors will come to greater realization of the Psalmist's words, "behold how good and how pleasant it is for brethren to dwell together in unity!" (Ps. 133:1).

The aim in this book is to set forth without reserve and in simple fashion the biblicistic belief of the Mennonites and their uncompromising nonconformity. Views expressed in places may be questioned but this still does not give any reason why the true Mennonite position should not be made known. It is hoped that these pages will help to clear up questions all of us, Mennonites and others, have been compelled to carry in our bosom without relief. Then, too, it has been painful to Mennonites when they acted in obedience to their convictions and were misunderstood. True Mennonite behavior must be, and is, just as beautiful as that of others. To keep it attractive and genuine, Mennonites cannot afford to rely only on tradition and custom. The only method of resisting this perversion is by bringing before the minds of men and women, in full force, the momentous realities and profound truths from which the Anabaptist movement drew back the Medieval veil. These realities and truths lie at the foundation of Mennonite spiritual life and moral force. The Mennonites will command confidence and respect in proportion to their teaching of these cardinal truths delivered unto them by those who were martyred for their faith.

In the following pages Menno Simons, Dietrich Philips, and many others will speak for themselves. Their main message is not necessarily Mennonite. It is a vital message that brings truths to the forefront that have been forgotten in many instances. The author is painfully aware that not all will agree with all the statements made here. Nevertheless, the question remains, why was this not done better long ago and let such attempt "degenerate into hands like mine?" This is not the issue though; the Mennonites owe it to the others to make known in an intelligent way who they are. May these pages clear up questions whose answers have long been overdue.

An attempt has been made to provide helps to make this reading as attractive as possible. The table of contents goes into some detail and the reader will find that most sections can be read independently. The bibliography is lengthy, but this again is in keeping with the aim to inform the public about the best literature available on the subject. It was not the purpose to list a number of references but to list those used, and which will stimulate further study and pave the way to good essays at our conferences and to good articles in our papers.

Above all, may God have the glory in that His own be drawn closer to Him in obedience, and to one another, in Christian fellowship.

A. P. Toews

ABBREVIATIONS

CWMS
: *The Complete Writings of Menno Simons* c.1496-1561. Translated from the Dutch by Leonard Verduin and edited by John Christian Wenger, with a biography by Harold S. Bender. Scottdale, Pa.: Herald Press, 1956.

EB
: *Encyclopaedia Britannica.* Edited by T. S. Haynes. Ninth edition. Chicago: R. S. Peale Company, 1892.

EoH
: *Enchiridion oder Handbüchlein,* von der Christlichen Lehre und Religion by Dietrich Philips. Uebersetzt in hochdeutsche Sprache. Lancaster: Gedruckt bey Joseph Ehrenfried, 1811.

GBvDV
: *Geschriftjes ten Behoeve van de Doopsgezinden in de Verstrooiing.* B. P. Plantanga, Secretaris der Vereeniging voor de Verstrooide Doopsgezinden, -te Haarlem, Holland, 1911.

ME
: *The Mennonite Encyclopedia.* Edited by Harold S. Bender and C. Henry Smith. Scottdale Pennsylvania: Mennonite Publishing House, c. 1956.

ML
: *Mennonitisches Lexikon.* Herausgegeben von Christian Hege und Christian Neff. Frankfurt a.M. und Weierhof (Pfalz), 1913ff.

MQR
: *The Mennonite Quarterly Review.* Editors Harold S. Bender et al. Goshen, Indiana: Mennonite Historical Society, Since 1927.

SAW
: *Spiritual and Anabaptist Writers.* Edited by George Hunston Williams and Angel M. Mergal. Volume XXV of *Library of Christian Classics.* Philadelphia: The Westminster Press, 1957.

PART ONE

CHAPTER I

STATING THE PROBLEM

THE DISCUSSION OF ETHICS

The Mennonites have never given much attention to the formal discussion of the problem of "ethics." The *Mennonitisches Lexikon* devotes only a few lines to it and the later *Mennonite Encyclopedia* has nothing at all. The *Mennonite Quarterly Review Cumulative Index Volumes 1-25* (1927-1951) directs us after "Ethics, Christian," to "Christian ethics." Turning to that topic we are told to refer to "Nonresistance." Under this topic we have thirteen articles dealing with "nonresistance" but none directly with the question of "ethics." In *The Mennonite Quarterly Review Cumulative Index Volumes 26-30* (1952-1956) we have no articles on "ethics." Nor is there any Mennonite book listed on "ethics" in Dr. Bender's list of Mennonite publications during 1727-1928. The Mennonite Historical Library at North Newton, Kansas, lists no volumes on "Mennonite Ethics." The problem of ethics again is treated in various articles under "nonresistance" as it is in *The Mennonite Quarterly Review*.

This disregard for a formal discussion of ethics indicates in no wise, though, that the Mennonites believe that they are perfect. To the question "Is the converted man perfect?" the Mennonite Brethren Catechism states: "No, he has only begun the race toward the goal of holiness; even the most holy men, as long as they are in this life, have their imperfections. Phil. 3:12-13; I John 1:8."

All who know the Mennonites have observed that they have unwritten ethics. Their ministers constantly exhort their church members to continue without wavering in their Mennonite doctrine, which is based largely on a literal interpretation of the Scriptures.

One of the earlier and very effective ministers to do this was A. Binnerts Sz., the preacher in the *Doopsgezinden* church in Haarlem, Holland. A very characteristic teaching of Mennonite conduct is his booklet *Wat Is Ons "Doopsgezind"?* This is

3

also the aim of the entire series of *Geschriftjes ten Behoeve van de Doopsgezinden in de Verstrooiing*. With the revival of Mennonitism in Europe after the First World War this question received wide attention in all the *Mennonitischen Blätter*. In order to coagulate the various opinions, *Was ist mennonitisch?* (what is Mennonite) was discussed on the rostrum and in print. In America for similar reasons, Harold S. Bender's article, "The Anabaptist Vision," appeared in special reprint.

The two great Mennonite ethical norms are pietism and biblical quietism. *The Mennonite Weekly Review* regrets that these are inadequately known in our day and adds that too many "try to live on a borrowed faith." For centuries the Mennonites have given themselves as a pious and quiet people, basing their piety on an avowed "biblicism." Their behavior regards the primitive and biblical organization and cultus as the ideal and has the constant urge to return to these forms. In matters of conduct Mennonites have always looked to the Bible, and the reason for their withdrawal from the Roman Catholic Church was that they wanted "to get back to the Bible."

THE RESPONSE TO THE WORD

The Mennonites from their inception have aimed to be biblical in their ethics and "faithful in response to God's demand." God's Word was to them at all times sharper than a two-edged sword. Compromising with the world even in times of gravest danger and loss of life was untenable to their tender conscience. Nothing less than the Word was recognized as having authority over them to judge their actions. Just this abhorrence of conceding to anything derogatory to God's requirements gave the first Anabaptists in Zurich that severe falling out with the Catholics, anti-Catholics and the state.

At no time seemingly did the persecuted spend much effort to determine what was "good or evil." The Bible revealed it and the consequences of their judgments in no uncertain terms. Dietrich Bonhoeffer of recent years speaks for them when he says,

> knowing good and evil, man is essentially a judge. As a judge he is like God, except that every judgment he delivers falls back upon himself.[1]

---

[1] Dietrich Bonhoeffer, *Ethics*, edited by Eberhard Bethge and translated by Neville Horton Smith from the German (first American printing; New York: Macmillan Co., 1955), p. 154.

Stating the Problem

All ethics depend on a fervent intimacy with deity for dependable guidance. Hans Denck, an early and influential Anabaptist, maintains that "the Word . . . had to become man in Jesus (so) . . . that people both in spirit and in flesh, from within and without, behind and before, and in all places might have testimony." Like the Stoics they said, "Man is a sacred object to man. All have God in themselves: the sacred spirit has its seat within us."[2] "I know very well," answers Menno

> that children have *spiritum vitalem* (that is, the spirit of life which God breathed into Adam and into all flesh that they might live, Gen. 2:7). But they do not have the *spiritum justificantem aut innovantem* (that is, the spirit which justifies or regenerates).[3]

This "sacredness of man," says Craandijk, makes itself felt in a pietism which is an "innige en toch zoo gezonde vroomheid" (innate tenderness with a sane devotion).[4] James Smart is of the opinion that under persistent suppression and martyrdom this piety in response to the Word "became" a sort of negative "reaction,"[5] the usual thing when all avenues of expression are blocked. For the Anabaptists, says Craandijk,

> it was not a matter of compiling a system of Christian principles, but an integration of the Gospel of Jesus Christ and Christian ethics. The result of this union was an ethic having a sound piety, a sincere Christian walk, an unfeigned love towards one another and a willingness to sacrifice everything for the sake of the faith. Neither from the church nor from the world could they expect any consideration. In neither had they any influence. They lived in the world but were not of the world. They did their daily work quietly with rejoicing in their souls.[6]

---

2 Reinhold Seeberg, *History of Doctrines*, History of Doctrines in the Ancient Church, translated by Charles E. Hay (Grand Rapids, Michigan: Baker Book House, 1954), I, 29.
Simons,
3 Menno Simons, "Christian Baptism, 1539," *The Complete Writings of Menno Simons c. 1496-1561*. Translated from the Dutch by Leonard Verduin and edited by John Christian Wenger, with a biography by Harold S. Bender (Scottdale, Pennsylvania: Herald Press, 1956), p. 271.
 Note: *The Complete Writings of Menno Simons c. 1496-1561* will have henceforth the abbreviation "CWMS."
4 J. Craandkijk, *Iets uit de Geschiedenis der Nederlandsche Doopsgezinden* (Arnhem: Harel F. Misset, 1889), p. 12.
5 James D. Smart, *The Teaching Ministry of the Church* (Philadelphia: Westminster Press, 1954), p. 174.
6 Craandijk, *op. cit.*, p. 14.

This withdrawal from the world bound them together by tradition, custom, kin, and "we feelings," which made a written ethics superfluous. Over the years this has resulted in "many shades of practice, which makes describing them accurately all the more difficult." As they advanced, each new problem gave additional reason for deviation from their former ways. The Mennonite "peculiar *Weltanschauung*,"[7] moored to tradition and pietism with an undiluted response to the Word, has at times radically affected their social and economic patterns.[8] This applies especially to the Amish and conservative branches, who prefer the foreign and outdated and give these religious significance. All of them when they accept a way of life that is not based entirely on a literal interpretation of the Scriptures "turn back as though they had forgotten something that had endeared their hearts." Many modern Mennonites agree with Gustave Aulèn when he says that it is an illusion to believe that any particular organization or cult today can produce a church based totally on original Christianity. It is difficult to understand why the early Mennonites did not see this. Nevertheless, time has since given us a better understanding of their conduct. Prof. J. W. Baum of the Reformed Theological Seminary at Strassburg, France, says: "Aside from a number of erroneous views and principles their only fault was that they lived three hundred years too early."

PERSECUTION

In Dr. Muralt's judgment there is another reason for the lack of a written ethical and philosophical treatise of the Mennonite life. "The whole Anabaptist movement," he says, "was persecuted from its very beginning. Never could they fully materialize their intentions. They had to flee into seclusion to save at least some of their members."[9] William the Silent truly had reason to say shortly before he died: "My God, have pity on my poor people." The result was that their leaders never could gather their beliefs and practices and issue a com-

---

[7] Henry E. Dosker, *The Dutch Anabaptists* (Philadelphia: Judson Press, 1921), p. 4.
[8] Roland H. Bainton, *The Reformation of the Sixteenth Century* (Boston: Beacon Press, 1952), p. 229.
[9] Leonard von Muralt, *Glaube und Lehre der Schweizerischen Wiedertäufer in der Reformationszeit* (Zürich: Kommisionsverlag Beer & Co., 1938), p. 30.

prehensive and uniform statement of their faith and ethics. Prof. Hoekstra points out that this made it difficult for the Mennonites as well as for their neighbors. That which usually creates authors could not come into its own among them. Since the earlier *Doopsgezinden* lived in seclusion and were separated from common knowledge which forms public opinion, it is not surprising to hear the well-known Mennonite minister and archivist at Deventer, Izaak Jan le Cosquino de Bussy, say: "Religion is a view of life and not a world view."

In all crisis experiences people think more about a way to live than definitions of conduct. Kierkegaard, for instance, nowhere presents "what might be termed a system of ethics," but confronts us with a way of life instead. With him the Mennonites subjectively determine that "an ethical life is not identical with a person's intellectual views and opinions,"[10] where for Hegel "the norm of ethics" was "objectively" constructed. For both ethics are a way of life which has to be taught. It was for this reason that the Mennonites "were among the most aggressive advocates of Christian day schools in the early part of the eighteenth century."[11] This acquisition of a dependable deportment came to them, as for Bonhoeffer in our own day, "not by astuteness, by knowing the tricks, but by simple steadfastness in the truth of God, by training the eye upon this truth until it is simple and wise" and then be taken in tow by experience and knowledge which give it "ethical reality."[12]

PRESENT CHALLENGE

The present age challenges the Mennonites as never before. We are in a post-liberal period which aims to piece the fragments of the immediate past together again. After half a century of unprecedented violence the world needs a revised "Bible" ethic and means of solving social ills with greater proficiency. To Mennonites the whole matter of peace, internally and externally, depends on the acceptance of the biblical teaching instead of violence and destruction of human life. In 1936 at the four hundredth anniversary of Menno Simons' renunciation of Catholicism the Mennonites wrote:

10 Reidar Thomte, *Kierkegaard's Philosophy of Religion* (Second Printing: Princeton: Princeton University Press, 1949), p. 38.
11 Edwin H. Rian, *Christianity and American Education* (Second Printing: San Antonio, Texas: The Naylor Company, 1951), p. 209.
12 Bonhoeffer, *op. cit.*, p. 4.

In the midst of economic distress and fearful rumors of war, the voice of Menno Simons can profitably be heard with its calm but convinced insistence upon a thoroughgoing practical Christianity making the whole of life subject to the lordship of Christ, and with its demand that men resolutely abandon all carnal strife and live together in peace and love.[13]

The question "Where are you going?" at this time seriously confronts all of society. The Mennonites uniquely refuse to view present national and international upheavals in the light of destruction and death. It has been their mission for centuries to preserve life rather than destroy it. They believe that the life Christ brought for all must be set in operation for all. They make it their business to reveal that "man was created by God that he might have life." What it may cost them to carry out this mission is a lesser matter to them. Conrad Grebel boldly admonished Thomas Müntzer (1524) when he heard that Müntzer was "willing to defend war,"

> By the common salvation of us all cease therefrom and from all notions of thy own now. . . . Stand by the others like a hero and champion of God. . . . If thou must suffer for it, thou knowest well that it cannot be otherwise.[14]

It is a common contention that no price is too high for the truth. Mennonites say, "While millions are giving their lives in sacrifice for error and to the god of war, should there be no martyrs to truth and the God of Heaven?" Times may be very hard and the future look hopeless but God will eventually be the victor, for He "is both invincible and magnanimous. In His magnanimity He corrects and proves all men." They believe that the world is in need of their faith today more than ever. It is their contention that "as long as we are in the will of God we have the promise of His approval, care and protection." God corrects man by letting him go his own way and destroy himself if he desires. In the midst of this conflict God "created the defenseless sheep as well as the long-horned cattle that can maim each other; and through thousands of years the sheep, typical of the defenseless Christian, are not extermi-

---

13 Harold S. Bender, "A Brief Biography of Menno Simons," *CWMS*, p. 3.
14 Conrad Grebel, "Letters to Thomas Müntzer," in *Spiritual and Anabaptist Writers*, edited by George Hunston Williams and Angel M. Mergal, Volume XXV of *Library of Christian Classics*. (Philadelphia: Westminster Press, 1957), p. 84.

nated."[15] How and why this is done is a part of the problem of their ethics. When they are tempted to compromise in their decisions they observe with Bonhoeffer that when man is seriously challenged he "lies to his own conscience to avoid despair."

FAITH AND ETHICS

The effervescing question for the Mennonites is "Why isn't it right for us to do what others are doing?" They understand that there must be some soundness in their norms seeing that they have outlived most severe deprivations and restrictions. None, except the Waldenses, were exposed to severer attempts to annihilate them. When it is said that the "faith of Luther is determined by his conception of God," mustn't we make allowance for the same motives to be inherent in the odd behavior of the Mennonites?

All ethics deteriorate in an atmosphere devoid of religious faith. Menno maintains that without religion man is like a branch without a trunk. As long as there is a healthy, living trunk not much attention need be given to the growth of the branches. They come naturally. For many years the Mennonites were kept so busy keeping the stem alive that little effort could be spared for anything beyond that. However, when the branches are stripped off the trunks, like they were during the last decades, concern arises over the main growth. Man is compelled to pay more attention to moral problems. Mennonites could get along without a formal ethics but not without a practical religion based upon God's Word.

As a result of this revival of faith and interest in the Word as it relates to ethics, the General Conference of the Mennonite Church appointed a special "discipline study committee" at its sessions in Winnipeg in 1956 to study and report on the many problems in the field of Mennonite social interests and behavior. The preface of this report speaks of sensing that the time has come in the General Conference Mennonite Church to address itself again to "this old and difficult problem."[16] Beyond the Mennonites the same thing is felt when George Forell points out that the "crucial question confronting our age is the question of ethics," and "rarely perhaps has any generation," says

---

15 George R. Brunk, Jr., *Ready Scriptural Reasons* (Scottdale, Pennsylvania: Herald Press, 1954), pp. 19, 129, 130.
16 Maynard Shelly, editor, *Studies in Church Discipline* (North Newton, Kansas: Mennonite Publication Office, c. 1958), p. v.

Dietrich Bonhoeffer, "shown so little interest as ours in any kind of theoretical or systematic ethics." When considering the Anabaptists and Menno Simons during and immediately following the Reformation we find manifested a form and manner of ethical enthusiasm all their own. It became partly theological and partly historical, making a satisfactory solution difficult. To those who look merely on the surface, extravagance and lawlessness, fanaticism and madness, credulity and imposture may provide a sufficient explanation of the whole Anabaptist movement. With a little deeper insight, however, one finds elements that are inconsistent with such supposition.[17]

Menno Simons, in whose teachings Mennonite ethics root, was a most outspoken opponent of fanatical Anabaptism.[18] When he withdrew from the Catholic Church in 1536 he made himself available to the brethren to expound the Word and serve as the shepherd of the flock. About a year after his conversion eight brethren approached him to be their minister since his reputation was irreproachable and he had the knowledge and the ability to convince disbelievers. They assured him at the time that they had nothing to do with the despised Münsterites. The reason for his acceptance, says Menno, were "the perils which daily surrounded" them "from the beginning." Later he points out that "many souls are deceived by false prophecies," such as those "with popes of Rome, with John of Leiden, with those of Münster and others."[19] Dietrich Philips, Menno's co-bishop later, wrote about the same when he said:

> There are those who persecute us with no consideration at all because of this baptism. They blaspheme, scold and compare us with the Donatists, Münsterites, and other erring spirits. They judge and proclaim that we are of

---

[17] T. M. Lindsay, "Anabaptists," *Encyclopaedia Britannica*, edited by T. S. Paynes (ninth edition; Chicago: R. S. Peale Company, 1892), I, 786.

[18] Menno Simons, "Meditation on the Twenty-fifth Psalm," c. 1537, *CWMS*, p. 64. Also pp. 129, 174, 215, 231 and Dietrich Philips, *Enchiridion oder Handbüchlein von der Christlichen Lehre und Religion*. Uebersetzt in hochdeutsche Sprache. (Lancaster: Gedruckt bey Joseph Ehrenfried, 1811), p. 388.
Note: From now on abbreviated *EoH*.

[19] G. K. Frerichs, "Menno Simons," in *Geschriftjes ten Behoeve van de Doopsgezinden in de Verstrooiing*. B. P. Plantanga, Secretaris der Vereeniging voor de Verstrooide Doopsgezinden (Haarlem, Holland), 1911, p. 311.
Note: From now on abbreviated *GBvDV*.

the same kind. This is before God a great wrong and we come far too short. . . .²⁰

Menno had concern that his followers should live a life "patterned after the teaching and example of Christ."²¹ Faith in the Word, God and man gave him visions of a perfect church based on a perfect conduct. He believed that the Reformers through their preaching "did not secure true repentance, regeneration and Christian living."²² Faith without any demonstration of regeneration was not true faith to him. "The Anabaptists," points out Fellman,

> looked mainly upon the daily walk of the Christian. Their only norm and guide for their faith and life was the Bible. They base their ethics more definitely than any of the other churches coming out of the Reformation upon the New Testament.²³

The Mennonites depended so much on the Scriptures that they did not even have a Prayer Book as did the Lutherans and others. For them the fear of the Lord was the beginning of wisdom, the foundation of faith from which they obtained rich peace and blessing. Sebastian Franck, a historian close to the earliest Anabaptists, said, "the Scriptures make one pretty wise."²⁴ They said, *Ethik ist Sittenlehre* (teaching of morals) and does not depend on philosophy but on religion. To them it was not the asceticism and pennance of Rome nor the proper faith of Augsburg²⁵ but the ideals of the Sermon on the Mount. It is striking how they agreed with the Catholics today when *The Commonweal* says, "The Gospel of Christ was not at all concerned merely with the avoidance of sin. . ., it was concerned to show the ideal of life which Christ set before His disciples."²⁶ None of Christ's words could be ignored, for they constituted a morality that arises within a person through faith and not a

20 Philips, *EoH*, p. 67.
21 Guy F. Herschberger, *The Recovery of the Anabaptist Vision* (Scottdale, Pennsylvania: Herald Press, c. 1957), p. 60.
22 *Ibid.*
23 Walter Fellman, "Ethik" *Mennonitisches Lexikon*. Herausgegeben von Christian Hege und Christian Neff. (Frankfurt a.M. und Weirhof [Pfalz], 1913ff.), I, 612.
Note: From now abbreviated: *ML*
24 Sebastiani Franck, *Ein Verantwortung/ und Reputation. Auf zween Send-Briefen/. Kürtzlich aus der Heil. Schrifft verfasset durch Dietrich Philips* (title p. missing).
25 Fellman, *op. cit.*, p. 612.
26 Edward S. Skillin, "Editorial," *The Commonweal*, LXII (Dec. 27, 1957), 327.

legality "that is placed upon the individual from without."[27] "The kernel of Anabaptism was an ethical urge and "if the Roman Catholic Church had improved its own morals," says Bainton, it might not have been too difficult for the Anabaptists "to return to her fold."[28] When the Catholics point out today that the command "resist not him that is evil" has almost become "a dead letter in the church,"[29] they state the major problem of Mennonite ethics.

IDEALS AND ETHICS

Mennonitism in its advance has had bright flare-ups but these have always soon faded away. It was always the main stream that prevailed through the storms. At all times did it gather the facts of life and mould them into their new way of life and ethic. Conduct always "as it arises from fact to ideal, becomes ethical" says T. V. Smith. To Mennonites the Christian ethic was the divine "judgment of human quality" and the Scriptures, especially the New Testament, were their authority and gave rise to discard everything not expressly stated in that basic collection of sources.[30] In their eyes the Lutherans and the Reformed needed a written code of ethics because their church membership included everyone in a given area. According to them a person has to have a religious experience and obey the Scriptures before he can become a member of the church. Instead of following an ethics set forth by the church he must obey the Bible. They observed that even at the time when the Nicene Creed was formulated "ethics had no place."[31] There was an understood scriptural principle that satisfied all ethical demands. Their Christian ideal was "much more radical than either Lutheranism or Calvinism."

T. M. Lindsay remarks that Anabaptism as a system may be looked upon as "the Reformation doctrine carried to its extreme limits." This radicalism defied the "definition of the

---

27 Werner Elert, *The Christian Ethos*, translated by Carl J. Schindler (Philadelphia: Muhlenberg Press, 1949), p. 3.
28 Roland H. Bainton, *The Reformation of the Sixteenth Century* (Boston: Beacon Press, 1952), pp. 96f.
29 Skillin, *op. cit.*, cf. p. 328.
30 Kenneth Scott Latourette, *A History of Christianity* (New York: Harper & Brothers, c. 1953), p. 776.
31 Edwin Hatch, *The Influence of Greek Ideas on Christianity* (Harper Torchbooks, first edition; New York: Harper & Brothers Publishers, 1957), p. 1.

Christian faith more than the others."³² It is especially difficult to arrive at any statement of ethics when taking into account their views on "personal faith in religion," the relation of the church and state, and the "doctrine of the sacraments or political reasonings."³³ In spite of such difficulty we must "recognize in the Radical Reformation a major expression of the religious movement of the sixteenth century." It is one, points out George H. Williams, "as distinct as Lutheranism and Calvinism," and one breaking away from the mystical past. It was not concerned with Eckhard's *Entwertung* (self-depreciation) and mystical annihilation, Calvin's obedience or Luther's firsts in religion. The whole man was its person-centered and ethical ideal.³⁴

One of the main pillars of this third branch of the Reformation was, in the words of Kierkegaard, an "intensity of duty," expressed in a peaceful relationship of man to man. There was no need to formulate it again since the Scriptures did this most clearly and effectively. God operating in the hearts of man was at all times the supreme ruler and judge. This thinking was in direct opposition to Tillich's contention today when he says that "man wants to gain power over the divine." God was their judge and they had to overcome sin in themselves and others through non-resistance. They were not permitted to use the weapons of the world but those provided for in the Scriptures which were much more powerful and effective.³⁵ In this ideal of their ethic was a great deal of Bergson's "self-creativeness and originality akin to all creative act,"³⁶ with a "program of definitiveness and power."³⁷ Even those who know the Mennonites only superficially will agree with John Horsch that they are creative and original in their "ways, manner of life and conduct."

---

32 Latourette, *op. cit.,* p. 778.
33 Lindsay, *op. cit.,* p. 787.
34 Paul Tillich, "The Relation of Religion and Health," in *Religion and Health,* edited by Simon Doniger (A Symposium, Reflection Book; New York: Association Press, 1958), pp. 17-18.
35 Ernest J. Bohn, *Christian Peace According to the New Testament.* "Peace Teaching Outside the Gospels," one of a series of Peace Pamphlets issued by the Peace Committee of the General Conference of the Mennonite Church of North America (Souderton, Pennsylvania, 1938), p. 35; and Bender, "The Anabaptist Vision," *op. cit.,* p. 13.
36 Henry Bergson, *The Two Sources of Morality and Religion* (Garden City: Doubleday & Co., Inc., 1956), p. 53.
37 Bender, "The Anabaptist Vision," *op. cit.,* p. 4.

The big problem of the faith of this ideal is the translation of the ethics "of love and nonresistance into action." It is an ethic which is "deeply personal" and different in that its "new conception of the church is a brotherhood," composed neither of "Jew nor Greek."[38] In it is "no systematic array of ethical concepts" but everywhere application is directly made from the Scriptures.[39] As a member of this society a person knows that he is not to close his heart against others, making the love act a social obligation.

Modern Theology and Ethics

A further appreciation of the problem of Mennonite ethics can be obtained through the comparison of their thinking with that of present-day theologians. The Mennonites maintain that ethics originating with God through His Word strike vertically through faith and revelation. The Bible as the inspired Word of God has divine authority and must be literally obeyed. They are "biblicists" and their daily acts must conform to the demands of the Scriptures.

Such attitude to the Bible and faith in God produces good works to friend and foe alike. No misinterpretation of their motives may deter them in their God-given objectives. In Aulèn's words the "heavenly world is in relation to men, not men in relation to heaven"; they represent God to men and not men to God. Their Christ can do all things. The accounts of their earlier tortures are replete with proofs of the Lord's statements: "to me is given all power in heaven and on earth," or "the earth is the Lord's and all that is in it."

Modern theologians reverse this process. They say society strikes the individual Christian after which he responds to satisfy its moral needs. The Word and physical aid implement the moral doctrine resulting in reaching up to God. Kierkegaard was struck by God as the Anabaptists but he failed to reach out into society. God's message remained isolated. According to Williams, Aulèn argues for the Lutheran view "that out of the new relationship of the sinner justified by faith,

---

[38] Guy F. Hershberger, *Mennonites and Their Heritage*, number V in series of *Christian Relationships to State and Community* (Second edition; Akron, Pa.: The Mennonite Central Committee, 1942), p. 68.

[39] S. Hoekstra, *Beginselen en Leer der Oude Doopsgezinden*, vergeleken met die van de overige Protestanten (Amsterdam: P. N. Van Kampen, 1863), p. vi.

there must flow constructive Christian action into society." It is an action for God upon the individual who then reaches out for his neighbor. The Anglican has a "synthesis of faith and reason" motive. Nevertheless, says Williams, the *Logos* incarnate in Christ fulfills and incorporates the highest human reason. Social ethics is a natural result from a faith in Christ. God does not act directly contacting man, nor is man "sufficient to meet God in His ultimate truth."

Among moderns is a division as to the way that God elicits ethical expressions. Nygren, Niebuhr, Ramsey and Brunner say that "God's love is sacrificial" and when this love comes over us we will also sacrifice in such hour of crisis. A second view is found in Macmurray, Vlatos, Wieman and others who say that the love of God shed abroad in our hearts wants to include everyone. Both views arrive in defense of fundamental democratic rights and freedoms.[40]

Tillich has "a free reciprocity between God and man" and this is with him "the root of the dynamic character of religion."[41] He steers clear of metaphysics when he speaks of "respecting man's freedom and his personal self-relatedness." His approach to social ethics is through the Word as man's word. Here the Mennonites most definitely disagree with him, for they speak of the Word of God, the unshakable and solid foundation of the truth. Ethics for them are of divine origin, for Tillich of human origin and of non-metaphysical essence. For Ritschl "religion must not be theoretical."[42] To the question, How can a person be saved?, he answers, "What must I do to be saved?" Mennonites do not equate salvation and doing, but doing is the result of salvation.

Nor do the Mennonites agree with Harnack in his emphasis on man's divinity. To him the human soul is too precious to be eternally lost. The Mennonites believe that the human soul is already lost without Christ and doomed to eternal judgment if not saved by Him. No human being can do this; God must do it through His Son and the Holy Ghost. Jesus has become flesh through incarnation effected by God and the Holy Spirit,

---

[40] Daniel Day Williams, *What Present-Day Theologians Are Thinking* (New York: Harper & Brothers, Publishers, 1952), pp. 78, 82, 88.
[41] Paul Tillich, *Biblical Religion and the Search For Ultimate Reality* (Chicago: The University of Chicago Press, 1955), p. 30.
[42] William Hordern, *A Layman's Guide to Protestant Theology* (New York: The Macmillan Company, 1957), p. 51.

and His miracles and teaching are a witness to His divine sonship. They totally disagree with him when he sets the human soul above the Son, His miracles and divinity. All man can do about his salvation is to present himself humbly to God. His ethics are God's ethics, created when man was created. Mennonites do not practice their ethics because they want to be saved but because they are saved. Their ethics are an expression of obedience to their Saviour, Jesus Christ.

Never have the Mennonites been much concerned about producing a detailed plan of reconstructing human society. What they had was an extremely simple pattern of Christ's Kingdom on earth. The literal interpretation of the Scriptures supplied all the information they needed to produce such a plan.

PRESENT NEEDS

In our day with much more social inter-action Mennonites need to re-examine this plan of a new society. It is imperative that they know their neighbors and as soon as they will supply their neighbors with the essential information about themselves they will be understood and judged more correctly. It is their desire to have a happy relationship with the many much larger religious groups with which they daily mingle. They are peremptorily reminded that they must have a modern Mennonite vision. The early Anabaptist vision can and must serve only as a foundation and direction of their present thinking and efforts. The "Anabaptist vision," Bender points out

> was not a detailed blueprint for the reconstruction of human society, but the Brethren did believe that Jesus intended that the Kingdom of God should be set up in the midst of the earth, here and now, and this they proposed to do forthwith. We shall not believe, they said, that the Sermon on the Mount or any other vision that He had is only a heavenly vision meant but to keep his followers in tension until the last great day. But we shall practice what He taught believing that where He walked we can by His grace follow in His steps.[43]

[43] Bender, "The Anabaptist Vision," *op. cit.*, p. 22.

CHAPTER II

DEFINITIONS

ANABAPTISM

Denominations like "Anabaptists," "Mennonites" and "Doopsgezinden" imply a considerable amount of ethical connotation. Before proceeding with this discussion these require more definitions.

Besides the Lutheran and the Reformed there was a third general Reformation movement, that of the Anabaptists, who believed their kind had existed "through every century from the days of Christ."[1] Others said this movement belonged to the *schwärmerischen Bewegungen im Reformationszeitalter*[2] (enthusiastic stirring during the Reformation). "They were separatists who had the courage to put instant obedience to conscience above obedience to the magistrate and so . . . incurred the epithet Anabaptist, an ill name. . . ."[3] Their aim was to get "acquainted with the ethics of Christianity as applied to conduct."[4]

The ideal of the Anabaptists was to form societies of truly converted Christians. This ideal implied a self-governing congregation composed of regenerate persons independent of state or episcopal control, who had the Bible as their law and an "ascetic life of strict conformity to a literal interpretation of supposedly Biblical requirements."[5] These "holy" societies were intended to be "the promulgation of a new law of con-

---

1 J. Thieleman van Braght, *Martyrs Mirror*, translated from the original Dutch edition of 1660 by Joseph F. Sohm (Scottdale, Pa.: Mennonite Publishing House, 1938), p. 15.
2 Friedrich Gehninger, *Geschichte des Christentums* (Elftes bis zwanzigstes Tausend; Konstanz: Verlag von Carl Hirsch, 1897), p. 323.
3 William Haller, *The Rise of Puritanism* (Harper Torchbooks; New York: Harper & Bros., Publisher, 1957), p. 366.
4 Ernest J. Bohn, *Christian Peace According to the New Testament Peace Teachings Outside the Gospels* (One of a Series of Peace Pamphlets Issued by the Peace Committee of the General Conference of the Mennonite Church of North America; Souderton, Pennsylvania, 1938), p. 12.
5 Williston Walker, *A History of the Christian Church* (New York: Charles Scribner's Sons, 1945), p. 368.

duct."[6] Dietrich Philips, one of the first Mennonite elders, wrote: "First of all they must have become children of God through faith." Those who joined their societies were not baptized in infancy but upon their own confession of faith and conversion. "To them baptism, as a symbol of being a Christian, was meaningless."

The Anabaptists (re-baptizers) were thus named by their opponents. The *Encyclopaedia Britannica* defines "Anabaptists" as "rebaptizers (from the Greek *ana* and *baptizo*)." The great majority to whom it was applied repudiated it. Infant baptism to them was not valid and therefore, an "administration of the rite" during the years of inaccountability was not baptizing, only a "dipping in the Romish bath."[7]

In German the term *Wiedertäufer* is used. Its use is also often avoided because it is considered a *Schimpfname*[8] (name-calling). A much more accepted name is *täuferisch* (baptizingly). The former implies defiance, "civil disobedience and rebellion."[9] The term "Anabaptists" is a Latin derivative meaning "one who re-baptizes (German *Wiedertäufer*). Lutherans and Zwinglians applied it in the beginning to those who separated themselves from the main body of the state church. It was common practice to give them names that described their ethics as interpreted by others. Philips writes: "When they call us Anabaptists that is not the truth. Our baptism is spitefully misinterpreted. But we know that all the devout were always treated that way. Slander and lies have been used to disgrace them."

In a discussion of Mennonite ethics it is important to note

---

6 Edwin Hatch, *The Influence of Greek Ideas on Christianity* (First edition; Harper Torchbooks: New York: Harper & Brothers Publisher, 1957), p. 1.

7 Roland H. Bainton, *The Travail of Religious Liberty* (Nine Biographical Studies; Philadelphia: The Westminster Press, c.1951), p. 18.

8 Gerhard von Beckerath, *Die Wirtschaftliche Bedeutung der Krefelder Mennoniten und Ihrer Vorfahren im 17. und 18. Jahrhundert* (Abhandlung zur Erlangung des Grads eines Doktors der wirtschaftlichen Staatswissenschaften der Rechts und Staatswissenschaftlichen Fakultät der Rheinischen Friedrich-Wilhelms-Universität zu Bonn, 1951), p. 2.

9 Hans J. Hillerbrand, "The Anabaptist View of the State," *The Mennonite Quarterly Review*. Editors Harold S. Bender, et al. Goshen, Indiana: Mennonite Historical Society, Since 1927 (April, 1958), XXXII, 83; and Menno Simons, "Foundation of Christian Doctrine," CWMS, p. 220.

Note: From now on *The Mennonite Quarterly Review* will be abbreviated *MQR*.

that their "later interpreters, hostile and friendly, have read into their movement their own stereotypes such as, 'revolutionaries,' 'individualists,' 'liberals,' 'Biblicists,' 'enthusiasts' (*Schwärmer*), 'Bolsheviki,' 'Bible Christians.' When they left the Roman Catholics they were called *Schwärmer*, 'Antitrinitarians,' 'spiritualizers,' and 'religious individualists.' "[10] It is quite reasonable to believe that at times there were reasons for such names. It is difficult to believe, however, that their whole movement was only *Schwärmerei*. Much more was required to continue to exist under unheard-of opposition.

After the Peasants War, into which several so-called Anabaptists unfortunately blundered, the name designated a good deal of unethical behavior. After this uprising the "name 'Anabaptists' stood for sectarians, separatists, or those having a fanatical spirit. It was said that these people disdained the sacraments and were Anabaptists, enthusiasts, fanatics and the like."[11]

The term 'Anabaptism' "designates a movement which by no means was homogeneous in its early stages. . . ."[12] It embraced a wide variety of religious opinions and each "leader in general," says Newman, had "marked idiosyncrasies." Of the ten different groups he mentions, chiliastic enthusiasm was perhaps the most influential. Each group aggravates the discussion of the problem of Mennonite ethics.

"Menno Simons says correctly that the differences among the Anabaptists were even greater and more radical than those which separated the infant baptist parties from each other."[13] "The mutinous Münster and their followers have," says Menno, "taken up the sword contrary to God's Word. We have to hear continually as if we were one with them. . . ." Obbe Philips, who baptized him, he said later, "has become a Demas." About controlling his members he remarked, "So long as they do not repent they are dismissed and no more counted among us."

10 Franklin Hamlin Littell, *The Anabaptist View of the Church* (Second edition, revised and enlarged; Boston: Starr King Press, 1958), pp. XV, XIV, 1.
11 Johann Loserth, *Doctor Balthasar Hubmaier und die Anfänge der Wiedertaufe in Mähren* (Herausgegeben von der historisch-statistischen Section der k. k. mähr. Gesellschaft zur Beförderung der Landwirtschaft, der Natur- und Landeskunde; Brün: Verlag der hist.-statist. Section, Druck von Rudolf M. Bohrer, 1893), p. 7.
12 Erland Waltner, "The Anabaptist Conception of the Church," *MQR*, XXV (Jan. 1951), 6.
13 John Horsch, *Menno Simons* (Scottdale, Pennsylvania: Mennonite Publishing House, 1916), p. 41.

Certain trends in Anabaptism gave Menno Simons much concern. He was more severe and outspoken in his opposition to some Anabaptists than to the great churches. He held Martin Luther in high esteem and denounced the Münsterites and Batenburgers who took the sword. They seem to have been much closer to the Zwinglians than to Menno. A major ethical difficulty arose for the Mennonites later when all those who rejected infant baptism were called "Anabaptists." The name commonly used in English today includes the entire left wing of the Reformation, a motley collection of no common faith. In German the term *Täufer* is gradually coming into use to describe the peaceful, evangelical Anabaptists. *Täufer* has "no comparable English term." Perhaps closest to its real meaning is the Dutch *Doopers* or *Doopsgezinden*.[14] To the Dutch the designation meant that he belonged to the Christians.[15] Dosker thinks that this does not describe them correctly. He stresses the "baptizing" and not the "belonging together." "*Doopsgezinden*," he says,

> stands for those inclined to baptism or Baptists. The derivation of the word *Doopsgezinde* may be from *gezind* (inclined to) or from *gezindte* (an association of believers of a fixed doctrinal basis). In the latter case adult baptism would be such a basis. The former derivation seems, however, more likely correct inasmuch as the Anabaptists never formed a *gezindte* in the true sense.[16]

Franklin Littell has another viewpoint when he says "the Anabaptists (were) most concerned for the nature of the 'church' (*rechte Kirche*) upon the apostolic pattern as they understsood it."[17] Friz Heyer agrees with the latter. "The ultimate significance of the Anabaptism (*Schwärmertum*) of the sixteenth century," he says, "is grounded in the concept of the church." Discriminating between the *Schwärmer* and evangelical Anabaptists occupied most of Menno's efforts. For him and his

---

14 Robert Friedman, "Anabaptists," *The Mennonite Encyclopedia*. A Comprehensive Reference Work on the Anabaptist-Mennonite Movement (Scottdale, Pa.: Mennonite Publishing House, c.1955), I, 114, col. 2; and C. Henry Smith, *The Story of the Mennonites* (Berne, Indiana: Mennonite Book Concern, c.1941), p. 19.
Note: From here on this work will be abbreviated *ME*.
15 A. Sz. Binnerts, "Wat is ons 'Doopsgezind'"? No. 36 in *GBvDV*, p. 4.
16 Henry Elias Dosker, *The Dutch Anabaptists* (Philadelphia: The Judson Press, c.1921), p. 5.
17 Littell, *op. cit.*, p. XVII.

Definitions

followers the real issue was the question of the type of Church which should take the place of the Old Church. The noted Mennonite historian, Peter M. Friesen, gives perhaps a most authoritative statement when he says:

> A considerable number of evangelical fathers in Germany were called Anabaptists, Again-baptizers or Baptists. Since these names bear a spiteful connotation it is safer to call them Mennonites after their gentle and worthy leader, Menno Simons.[18]

These radicals wanted to be known only as *Brüder* (brethren) since they had a common social and economic background. "They were drawn largely from the peasants and artisans who were suffering injustices" together. They were *Bejaarddoopers* (adult baptizers) and their

> baptism became important only because it was the most obvious dividing line between two patterns of church organization. . . . "Anabaptist" was a popular term with the authorities because it afforded them an excuse for forcefully suppressing the radicals.[19]

"When referring to the radical Reformers," says Dr. Bender, "we can either use 'Swiss Brethren,' 'Anabaptists,' or 'Mennonites.' " The last though could not be applied until 1544 when "Menist" (followers of Menno Simons who became openly an Anabaptist in 1536) was first used. Only in the Dutch-North German group of evangelical Anabaptists was it applied. The "Swiss Brethren" leader, Conrad Grebel, never was "connected with Menno Simons."[20]

The early Anabaptists who became the stock of later Mennonites preferred to go nameless. They felt the injustice when they were called *Wiedertäufer*. They never used the term themselves "because of the *approbrium* and criminal character attached to the name." *Wiedertauf* was likewise unacceptable because of the "old imperial edict connected with it."[21]

In view of the many early Anabaptist groups Littell thinks that "a reassessment of the entire movement is timely." Prof.

---

18 Peter M. Friesen, *Die Alt-Evangelische Mennonitische Brüderschaft in Russland (1789-1910) im Rahmen der Mennonitischen Gesamtgeschichte* (Halbstadt, Taurien, Russland: Verlagsgesellschaft "Raduga," 1911), p. 1.
19 Littell, *op. cit.*, p. XV.
20 John Christian Wenger, *Glimpses of Mennonite History and Doctrine* (Third edition; Scottdale, Pennsylvania: Herald Press, 1949), pp. X-XI.
21 Friedmann, *op. cit.*, p. 113, c.1.

S. Hoekstra of the Doopsgezind Seminarie at Amsterdam points out that when this is done we must not forget that ethics and doctrine go together. He selects the heading for his chapter discussing the faith of the Mennonites and their ethics:

Die Sittlichkeit allein ersetzt den Glauben nicht;
Doch weh' dem Glauben, dem die Sittlichkeit gebricht.

(Morality alone cannot take the place of faith; but woe unto that faith which has not morality).[22]

In a re-examination of the motives and ethical implications of the various Anabaptist groups we canont afford to ignore the fact that their ethics are lifted directly from the Scriptures. It was not difficult for the *geestdrijvers* (fanatics) and the *gematigde geestesrichting* (moderates) to use the same text with different effects. What led to open rebellion in one group produced *die Stillen im Lande* (the quiet in the land) in another group. Pertaining to the perverse interpretation of the Scriptures the Lutherans and Mennonites felt the same. Obbe Philips laments that the fanatics (*Schwärmer*) even swore to kill him and others of the conservatives.

No fanatical movement lasts very long. In Central Europe this sort of radical Anabaptism died in various ways. "In some cases," says Robert Friedmann,

> it returned to the national church of the land, in others it led to indifference or rationalistic attitudes, in some it brought a thorough moralization of religion, in others it resulted in a freezing into a narrow sectarian system, and in still others finally it was transformed into pietistic subjectivism.[23]

But this was not, as it may seem, the end of Anabaptism. After Münster (1534) persecution and oppression drove the extreme factions "under cover." The conservative wing, "the Obbenites. . . . gained at the expense of all the others."[24] "The peaceful and soundly Biblical wing of the Anabaptist movement in the Netherlands," continues Smith, "was sometimes called by the name 'Obbenites' after their leaders; and was the group with which Menno Simons later affiliated."

---

22 Hoekstra, *op. cit.*, p. II.
23 Robert Friedmann, *Mennonite Piety, Through the Centuries, Its Genius and Its Literature* (Goshen College, Goshen, Indiana: The Mennonite Historical Society, 1949), p. 9.
24 C. Henry Smith, *op. cit.*, p. 91.

MENNONITISM

One error the historians have made was putting "totally incompatible and dissimilar groups" into one category under the common heading of "Anabaptists and *Schwärmer.*" Against this, says Joachim Wach, "justifiable protests have recently been levied," and Littell says, "the movement of the Anabaptists cannot be a facile interpretation. The True Church was always dominant." It was when George Blaurock baptized Conrad Grebel in 1525 that the true Mennonite faith as a branch of the True Church came into open existence.

For a decade, from the time of this first open adult baptism in the Anabaptist sense to Menno Simon's baptism in 1536, the true core of the whole movement was obscured. Its adherents were called "radicals" which term embraced a wide variety of religious opinions. The followers of Menno Simons protested against such indiscriminate lumping, "for without newness of life, they held, faith was hypocritical." Mennonites today agree with them when they say "Anabaptist" has "precise meaning only by limiting its use to those numbered among the Swiss Brethren, Hutterites, South German Brethren, and Dutch Mennonites."[25] Peter M. Friesen reminds us that "the definitely pro-Lutheran *Kirchliches Handlexikon* von Dr. Karl Meusel," states that "one cannot say that the Mennonites were descendents of the Münsterites because there is definite evidence that their beginning was earlier. Both movements can be traced independently to the same source."[26] It was against "these immoderate forms of spiritualism that Luther took such decided stand."

The Mennonite "lineage is Anabaptist," says Qualben, "but they departed from the early apocalyptic and revolutionary elements of Anabaptism." From the year 1545 when Menno's followers for the first time were called "Menists" the name "Anabaptism" became an ignominy.[27] Niebuhr points out that

---

25 Littell, *op. cit.,* p. 45.
26 Friesen, *op. cit.,* p. 3. *Kirchliches Handlexikon* von Dr. Karl Meusel, IV, 549; Brockhaus, "Menno Simons" in *Konversations-Lexikon* (14. Auflage: Leipzig: F. A. Brockhaus in Leipzig, 1894), XI, 770; and H. Richard Niebuhr, *The Social Sources of Denominationalism* (Living Age Books: New York: Meridian Books, 1957), pp. 34-39; and Harold S. Bender, "A Brief Biography of Menno Simons," *CWMS,* p. 24; and Menno Simons, "Reply to Callius Faber, 1554," *op. cit.,* pp. 630; etc.
27 Walker, *op. cit.,* p. 175.

the Mennonites were ethically not Münsterites nor revolutionists but from violent revolution their path of development led through stubborn nonresistance and unyielding assertion by non-assertion of the principles of causality and love to an accommodating quietism.[28]

Menno's leadership marks the final elaboration of a mature Anabaptist church view. Obbe Philips defected because he did not see clearly the picture of the future church, and dropped completely out of Anabaptist history.

Menno's life was filled with hardship and distress. Edicts of the time indicate "the intensity of the persecution which he and his followers" had to endure. In all this turmoil and martyrdom, says Nippold, the Mennonites settled down as again-baptizers (*die Mennoniten die nachreformatorischen, zur Ruhe gekommenen Täufer*).[29] Anna Brons in the title of her book, *Taufgesinnte oder Mennoniten* (Baptists or Mennonites) has for the subtitle: *Ursprung, Entwickelung und Schicksale der altevangelischen Taufgesinnten oder Mennoniten in kurzen Zügen übersichtlich dargestellt* (Origin, Development and Experiences of the Old Evangelical Baptists or Mennonites Portrayed in Brief Overview). In this caption we have the whole process and definition of Mennonitism. Van der Smissen does the same in his *Kurzgefasste Geschichte und Glaubenslehre* (Brief History and Doctrine) where he makes no distinction between the Mennonites and the *"altevangelischen Taufgesinnten"*[30] (Old Evangelical Anabaptists or Baptists — the early 15th century Evangelicals in Switzerland and surrounding area that broke away from Rome).

According to these historians the principles of the early Anabaptists in Switzerland and the Mennonites in Holland later, were the same. Not all *altevangelische Taufgesinnte* nor the Mennonites, but the so-called *Wiedertäufer* (Anabaptists) of the radically revolutionary sort gave and still give the Mennonites trouble when discussing their ethics. What the Old-Evangelical Anabaptists stood for is accepted today without question. Their ethics are, and were, those of their Dutch

---

28 Niebuhr, *op. cit.*, p. 38.
29 Friedrich Nippold, "Beiträge vermehrt und herausgegeben," *Berner Beiträge zur Geschichte der Schweizerischen Reformationskirchen* (Bern: Druck und Verlag von K. J. Wyss, 1884), p. 235.
30 Carl H. A. van der Smissen, *Kurzgefasste Geschichte und Glaubenslehre der Altevangelischen Taufgesinnten oder Mennoniten* (Summerfield, Illinois: Im Selbstverlag des Verfassers, 1895), p. 1.

brethren, the Mennonites, who, according to Smith and many others, "are their lineal and spiritual descendants" and formers of the "liberal wing of the Reformation." Radicalism in its metamorphosis into Mennonitism, according to Dr. Hoekstra, had to perform its act before the curtain could be drawn. When the next act appeared, to give it more spirit, it took on the role of a prophet. Saner Anabaptists did not have the courage to rise against their brethren because of doctrine. Numerous history-making events crowded out clear lines of dependable Christian norm. Creating such norm required time. The popular *Wederdoopers* had to make a few serious mistakes before they were known.

This situation was more difficult for the Mennonites than for the organized state churches. The former were of the same faith outwardly where the latter were not. The fanatics agreed with the Evangelical Anabaptists in some of the direct teaching of the Scriptures but disagreed radically in their actions. In the matter of non-resistance they were opposed to the Mennonites and in full agreement with the state churches. Menno tried to transmit his ideal of practical holiness and peace to his followers in unmistakable terms. Since his conversion in 1536 his teaching stood for the high ideal of the church in the cause of Christ. In counteracting David Joris' ecstatic, fanatic and visionary interpretations of the Scriptures Menno's services to the "cause of the evangelical Anabaptists were of the greatest importance."

Before Menno and even as late as 1555, says Sebastian Franck, the Strassburger *Doopsgesgezinden* did not make much difference between the *Hofmanschen* and the brethren in the Netherlands. The great differences in the Anabaptist camp came into relief in response to Menno's doctrine. Those who differed were spoken of as the "erring Zwinglians, dropping-out brethren and Popists." The fanatics were related to their brethren as Judas to the Twelve.[31] They were said to know better but were looked upon as weak, discouraged and tempted by various sects. "For it is the custom of all the sects," says Menno in his *Fundamentboock*

> who are outside of Christ and His Word to make valid their positions, faith, and conduct with the sword. The

---

[31] Hoekstra, *op. cit.*, p. 19.

Roman Catholics, the Arians, the Circumcellions, the Lutherans, the Zwinglians, and the Münsterites are our witnesses. But Christ, and these who are His, bear and suffer.[32]

In listing these groups Menno had in mind all factions that in his judgment did "not take their stand firmly and exclusively on the Word of God but established their respective systems of doctrine partly on human authorities."[33] In his writing "To the Corrupt Sects" he lifts out Mennonite ethics when he speaks about "our dear brothers and sisters who have erred unknowingly." In expounding his doctrine he says,

> O you apostate, erring children if you had received Him as the true and living Son of God, then you would never have allowed yourselves to be led so far from his ways, nor would you have given in to such frightful errors. . . Is it not a grievous error that you suffer yourselves to be so woefully seduced by such worthless persons, and so sadly misled from one unclean sect to another? You are ever learning but never able to come to the knowledge of the real truth. You suffer yourselves to be led about by every wind of doctrine. You choose out a way for yourselves as do also the priests and monks, and hold not to the head, Christ, from which all the body, fitly joined together, cometh unto a perfect man, unto the measure of the stature of the fulness of Christ.[34]

The Mennonites and Anabaptists did not walk side by side but against each other. Hoekstra says that the Anabaptists put shame on the *Doopsgezinden* and always contended with them as they did with the Lutherans and Reformed. There was this difference though, they disagreed with the former because of conformity with that which was above the world and with the latter because of conforming to that which was in the world. The first had visions and the latter the world in the Scriptures. By their own means both aimed to bring about the perfect church upon the earth.

The extremely high standard of ethics that Menno demanded of his followers originated in his radical change of heart at the time of his conversion. His becoming a "Mennonite" was a change

> so deep, so thorough, so complete, and gave him such sense of divine mission, that he was enabled by the grace of God

---

[32] Menno Simons, "Foundation of Christian Doctrine," *op. cit.,* p. 175.
[33] *Ibid.*
[34] Menno Simons, "Foundation of Christian Doctrine," *op. cit.,* p. 215.

to be an inspired leader, a mighty tower of strength to his bitterly persecuted people, for more than twenty-five years.[35]

To him Christ was king and not John of Leiden and other fanatics. The ethics of his followers were authorized by none else than Christ, the creator of man. When Faber sneeringly told Menno that his church was only sixteen or seventeen years old he did not answer but left it to others to judge by the Word of God whether he promoted the true church established ages ago by Christ and the Apostles. To him the ethics of the true church were spiritual, not carnal. "It is a small matter to us," he goes on to say,

> to be called sect-makers by the world; for the children of God from apostolic time were called that. Notwithstanding, we in our simplicity would say this in regard to this matter, that we point to Christ Jesus, God's eternal Wisdom, Truth, and Son, for He is the One whom it concerns, and we appeal to His doctrine, ordinance, and usage with confidence. If anyone under heaven can convince us with the infallible Word that we are wrong and act contrary to His Word, then we will gladly hear and obey the truth.[36]

In the movement from Anabaptism to Mennonitism the Anabaptists' doctrine prevailed but its application was clarified. The name "Anabaptists" was accepted by the Mennonites not "by choice or desire but of necessity."[37] Before the fanatical Anabaptists emerged "there was not much difference in their ranks." It is striking that even Joachim Wach recognizes them now as separate among our Christian minimum groups.[38] The Mennonites accepted the name "Anabaptists" more for what it expressed than what it might imply. To them it meant being "Christ-minded, Apostle-minded or Gospel-minded (Gal. 3:26, 27, 29)." They aimed to produce a doctrine that was Scripturally sound.

The old Anabaptists practiced baptism upon confession, repentance and faith in Christ Jesus, their Redeemer. This was done openly in the face of martyrdom in obedience to their Saviour. Where Mennonites in recent years again have used the name "Anabaptist" they have done so to lay renewed stress on

---

35 Bender, "A Brief Biography of Menno Simons," *op. cit.*, p. 12.
36 Menno Simons, "Reply to Callius Faber, 1554," *op. cit.*, pp. 732-33.
37 Braght, *op. cit.*, p. 16.
38 Joachim Wach, *Sociology of Religion* (Phoenix Books. Chicago: University of Chicago Press, 1944), p. 147.

the original confession and obedience involved in adult baptism. "It is evidence of a concern for the restriction of the 'True Church.' "[39] They disagree with the Baptists, Amish and Hutterites when they emphasize the expressions and modes of the "true church." The former looked at the church from the outside in and the latter from the inside out. The Anabaptists were not concerned about the mode of baptism,[40] and paid no attention to the apostolic succession of their church. The Mennonites claimed that they had always been a part of the "true church," even when they were still in the Catholic Church. Since many of its founders and members had been former priests this made this still more so. Where the Baptists dwell on the mode of baptism and the Amish and Hutterites on previous cultures the Mennonites developed a religious ethic from the Scriptures and a life within the church which evolved a *Nachfolge* (obedience) deducted from "the Sermon on the Mount."

George W. Forrel points out that Christians make their way of life more acceptable to human reason by way of the Scriptures. C. Henry Smith does the same for the Mennonites when he says that their ethics are not necessarily Christian, but a philosophical expression of "physical solidarity." The literal acceptance of the "Sermon on the Mount" has resulted in an ethics with peculiar racial qualities. "I say race deliberately," Smith reminds us,

> for like the Jews, and unlike most other religious and social groups, Mennonites were not only a group of people having a common religious faith but, possessed with a strong spirit of nonconformity to prevailing religious doctrines and social practices engendered through centuries of relentless persecution, they had developed in course of time not only a spirit of homogeniety, but a physical solidarity as well, which through a process of inbreeding, had accumulated many of the characteristics of a distinct human type. By the middle of the sixteenth century Mennonitism ceased to expand.[41]

In spite of Mennonite peculiarities being puritanical they were not Puritans. The Puritans were Protestants of an in-

---

39 Littell, *op. cit.*, p. XVI.
40 Cornelius Krahn, *Menno Simons. Ein Beitrag zur Geschichte und Theologie der Taufgesinnten* (Karlsruhe: Druck und Verlag: Heinrich Schneider, 1936), p. 137.
41 C. Henry Smith, "The Education of a Mennonite Country Boy," *op. cit.*, p. 1.

tensely aggressive type made thus through generations of conflict with the Church of Rome.⁴² Their preachers prepared. "that state of mind (from) which the civil wars, the Puritan Commonwealth, the Westminster Assembly and sects" came.⁴³ Zwingli for them "had decided that the Protestant church should, in its relationship to the state, take the place which hitherto the Roman Church had held." After the new Protestant churches had been established Luther and Zwingli "asserted that they had not forsaken the Roman Church, but had reformed it"; the Anabaptists "on the other hand . . . had withdrawn from the true church."

"The early Swiss Brethren and Mennonites held that a true Christian church consists of those who by their own choice accept Christ and bid adieu to the world. . . . Believers are those 'called out' from the world . . . distinct and separate from the world."⁴⁴ They did not become members of Parliament, agitate and protest for more rights. Carter even goes so far as to say that they were not Protestants, for they were by edicts totally disowned. The Protestants had enough left to be able to speak of "God's Word to be the only rule, and worship services were not to be prescribed."⁴⁵ The Mennonites existed separately . . . and said that "the true church is conformed to the nature of Christ." In the world they had nothing left about which they could protest and were therefore not Protestants.

As pacifists, the Mennonites took only to pacifistic resistance, which the fanatical Anabaptists and Baptists did not. "Balthasar Hubmaier in particular has become the Baptist hero, no doubt because he alone of the Anabaptists took a position on the magistracy and war which agrees with the present Baptist position." Smith goes on to compare this Mennonite ethic with that of the Quakers who some years later, like the Anabaptists, made

> much of love as a solvent of such social ills that result from human passions. Life was too sacred to be snuffed out at the hands of an individual seeking vengeance, or by state authority, either by courts of law or by force of arms. War, especially, to them seemed unchristian. Men-

---

42 Ezra Hoyt Byington, *The Puritans in England and New England* (Boston: Roberts Brothers, 1896), p. 282.
43 Haller, *op. cit.*, p. 18.
44 Horsch, *op. cit.*, pp. 338, 344, 345.
45 Hoekstra, *op. cit.*, pp. 25, 26.

nonites were often called the Revengeless Christians. Even their worst enemies recognized their sober character, peaceful and upright life, and moral integrity. Their whole social program, in short, was the Sermon on the Mount completely and literally accepted.[46]

The Mennonites are non-conformists. The Mennonites (Old) teach that the "Church" is the body under the leadership of Christ and the "world" under the author of all iniquity. In the light of this definition they apply the Scriptures of Romans 12:2 to their daily life, to business methods, to amusements, to dress, to speech, to everything in which the standards of the world are in conflict[47] with the standards of the Gospel. Very frequently they were designated as "separatists." Their motives for not assisting in the formation of a state church were often not understood and sometimes harshly interpreted. Johann Heinrich Kurtz treats the history of the Anabaptists under the caption "The Deformation of the Church, classing them in point of orthodoxy beneath Romanism."[48]

This seeming lack of Mennonite cooperation has its origin in their desire to be consistent in their teaching and actions. It is an "earnest effort" to render absolute obedience to the text of Scripture and speak sincerely and without guile. It also seems to have had its root in the nature of decision, involving equality and freedom of choice. There must be both to make it decision. Neither can it be merely the repetition of tradition and custom to be genuine. This truthfulness made Menno Simons the successful Mennonite.[49] They could not afford to confuse custom and decision. Menno did not refrain from open confession even when grossly misunderstood. In the matter of freedom of conscience, equality, and separation of church and state he was just ahead of the thinking of his day.

---

46 C. Henry Smith, "The Education of a Mennonite Country Boy," *op. cit.*, pp. 1, 2.

47 Church Polity Committee of the Mennonite General Conference, compiler *Mennonite Church Polity*, S. F. Coffman, editor (Scottdale, Pennsylvania: 1944), pp. 92, 93.

48 John Horsch, "The Rise and Early History of the Swiss Brethren Church." *MQR* (July 1932), VI, 169.

49 Menno Simons, "Foundation of Christian Doctrine," *op. cit.*, p. 105; under different titles in his works on the following pages: 544, 101, 609-10, 668, 670, 294-95, 268.

Note should be taken that this is in direct opposition to Spencer's ethics as described by Charles A. Ellwood in *A History of Social Philosophy* (New York: Prentice-Hall, Inc., 1938), pp. 460-61.

Mennonite ethics are both Mennonite and Anabaptist where Mennonite doctrine is not violated. The Anabaptist movement for itself ended when it came, especially in the Netherlands, under the wise, peace-loving and anti-fanatical leadership of Menno Simons (1492-1561), to whom its worthy reorganization was primarily due."[50] This thesis uses the terms "Anabaptist" and "Mennonite" indiscriminately where doctrine and adherence to doctrine are the same. This agrees with Smith when he says: "Under whatever name these descendants of the peaceful Anabaptists went they were essentially of one faith, and ultimately recognized each other as members of a common branch of the church, as fellow Mennonites."

At present there is a renewed emphasis on Mennonite ethics. The public speaks of Mennonites rather than Anabaptists. It has ceased to interpret Anabaptist ethics in other than Mennonite terms. Wach points out that there is a renewed intensified interest in devotional practices among Christians in general and that for the Mennonites and similar groups it expresses itself in the kiss of peace, the right hand of fellowship, the love feast, and the washing of the feet."[51]

One factor that gives Mennonite ethics more attention and recognition today is that they are steadily fitted together over the Scriptures as their common denominator. Coffman Shenk in *The Christian Ministry* recommends Dr. L. Fuerbringer's book *The Eternal Why* as "a worth-while addition to any Bible student's library."[52] On the same page Melvin Gingerich in his review of the book *Byways in Quaker History, A Collection of Historical Essays* says: "the Quakers treated in the essays had one quality in common . . . the authority of the 'Inner Light.'" He goes on to say that Mennonites and others who hold to the belief in the finality of God's revelation of the Scriptures will not be able to follow the writer to the conclusions he draws in his essay. Dietrich Philips, Menno's co-laborer, (1568) poignantly alludes to the Scriptures being the sole guide of Mennonites in their behavior when he says,

50 Walker, *op. cit.*, p. 375.
51 Wach, *Sociology of Religion, op. cit.*, p. 178.
52 Coffman Shenk, book review of "The Eternal Why" by L. Fuerbringer and the book review by Melvin Gingerich of "Byways in Quaker History, A Collection of Historical Essays," in *The Christian Ministry*, II (April 1949), pp. 127-28.

we must consider Christ's general behavior and note His complete obedience to the Father (Phil. 2, a. Hebr. 5, b), how His word agreed with His fulfillment of all righteousness in the Old and New Testaments. In like manner, He as the true Mediator, has also given us the way in which we are to walk.[53]

[53] Dietrich Philips, *EoH*, p. 276. "Darum so müssen wir den ganzen Handel und Wandel Christi wohl anmerken und bedenken, wie gehorsam dass er seines Vaters Willen gethan (Phil. 2, a.; Hebr. 5, b), und sein Wort gesprochen hat, wie dass er alle Gerechtigkeit beide des Alten und Neuen Testaments vollkommenlich erfüllt hat . . . Darüber so hat Christus auch als ein rechter Mittler des Neuen Testaments uns den Weg gebahnet den wir wandeln sollen. . . ."

PART TWO

CHAPTER I

THE SCRIPTURES AND MENNONITE ETHICS[1]

SCRIPTURAL AUTHORITY

The basis of all Mennonite ethics is the New Testament concept of obedience.[2] The sixteenth century Mennonites, says Wenger, withdrew from the Roman Catholic Church because "they were determined by God's grace to get back to the faith of the church of the New Testament."

For the Mennonites ethics and worship have the same ingredients. For them religion and morality go together, and in order to be moral they must know the Scriptures. "It is therefore somewhat arresting, if not actually shocking," to them, "to discover that many writers are sharply distinguishing worship from ethics and that the process of again separating religion and morality"[3] makes its appearance. They feel that they cannot relax in the attempt to keep the two together.

Mennonites believe that according to the Scriptures the believers differ in conduct from the "unconverted."[4] During the years of most inhuman persecutions no lesser authority than the Scriptures could induce them to endure such brutalities. The Scriptures, and especially the New Testament, were their sole authority,

> and tended to discard all that they could not find expressly stated in that basic collection of sources. They wished to return to the primitive Christianity of the first century. They thus rejected much more which had come through the Catholic Church than did Lutherans and the Reformed. They believed in "gathered churches," not identical with

---

1 See appendix I.
2 John Christian Wenger, *Introduction to Theology* (Second revised edition; Scottdale, Penn.: Herald Press, 1956), p. 376.
3 Illion T. Jones, *A Historical Approach to Evangelical Worship* (New York: Abingdon Press, 1954), p. 177.
4 Church Polity Committee of the Mennonite General Conference, *Mennonite Church Polity*, S. F. Coffman, editor (Scottdale, Pa.: Mennonite Publishing House, 1944), p. 47.

the community at large, but composed of those who had the experience of the new birth.[5]

Whenever they were nicknamed "Anabaptists" that did not apply, for their ethics depended not on baptism but on the acceptance of the Lord Jesus Christ as personal Saviour and Lord in their daily lives. The Word was given to them as a lamp unto their feet and a light to their path (Ps. 119:105). Here God gave principles that apply to every circumstance in life.

To say the least, Mennonites find it rather impractical to be guided ethically only through the literal application of the Scriptures. Ethics always involve some secular rationalizing and are acceptable as long as they are honest in motive even when not expressed in a biblical manner. It is the literalness that causes the trouble. "Ethics is," says T. V. Smith,

> the secular and critical manner of taking account of the rationalizing process in conduct. Its temper is nonmystical, and its orientation is social rather than theological. Not that religious influence has not tried to furnish a theological foundation for ethics or more frequently still, tried to provide sanctions to budge conduct toward moral perfection. Rather, in spite of efforts and claims, the history of this relation since Socrates has been the story of the gradual moralization not only of religious machinery but of the gods themselves.[6]

SCRIPTURAL ACTION

Mennonites have always tried to make the actions of Jesus and the Apostolic Church the basis for their actions. Hoekstra (1822-1898), their theologian and philosopher, points out that they in their characteristic simplicity desired, whether right or wrong, to follow Jesus Christ's teaching and aimed to model their actions, as much as the Lord gave them grace, after those of the earliest Christian church.[7] The Sermon on the Mount furnished their doctrine on non-resistance, litigation, swearing of oaths and secret societies, living a separated life and a full

---

5 Kenneth Scott, Latourette, *A History of Christianity* (New York: Harper & Brothers, c.1953), p. 778.
6 R. V. Smith, "Ethics," *Encyclopaedia of the Social Sciences*, edited by Dewin R. A. Seligman and Alvin Johnson (New York: The Macmillan Company, 1938), V, 602-06.
7 S. Hoekstra, *Beginselen en Leer der Oude Doopsgezinden* (Amsterdam: P. N. Van Kampen, 1863), p. 110 and Dietrich Philips *EoH*, p. 17. Here exactly the same as in Hoekstra.

reliance upon the sustaining grace of God. Hatch agrees with them when he says that the theological conceptions in this Sermon "belong to the ethical rather than the speculative side of theology; metaphysics are wholly absent."[8] They say when one accepts the Bible in simple faith he will follow the ethical standards of the New Testament and express love to all men. Such reading of the Bible does not result in a Medieval type of speculation but in a simple following of divinely directed conduct. As early as the Disputations between Zwingli and the Anabaptists (the 1520's), those of like faith sat together to find further guidance and encouragement from its pages.[9] The Anabaptists or Mennonites (*Taufgesinnten oder Mennoniten*) says Anna Brons, endeavored even more than Luther and Zwingli to "re-echo the content of the Sermon on the Mount and the practical and ethical portions of the Epistles written to the common people."[10]

The Sermon on the Mount expresses the Master's words in action. What Tillich tried to do with the Christian faith in "theory" the Mennonites aim to express in deed. Tillich begins every chapter in his *Systematic Theology* "with a statement of the universal human needs, questions and problems to which Christian faith gives the answer."[11] In doing this he correlates man to man through a "natural theology" or a "know thyself" concept of the natural man. The Mennonites are painfully aware of the fact that such self-understanding differs from that of a Christian. "The judgment of God," says Elert for them, "as we find it in the law and gospel, is the point of reference for Christian ethics. . . . Ethics differs from other branches of theology in the fact that its sight is focused upon

---

8 Edwin Hatch, *The Influence of Greek Ideas on Christianity* (First edition; Harper Torchbooks; New York: Harper & Brothers Publishing, 1957), p. 1.
9 George Tumbult, *Die Wiedertäufer oder Monographen zur Weltgeschichte* (In Verbindung mit Anderen herausgegeben von Ed. Heyck; Heipzig: Verlag von Velhagen & Klasing, 1899), VII, 24.
10 Anna Brons, *Ursprung, Entwickelung und Schicksale der alt-evangelischen Taufgesinnten oder Mennoniten in kurzen Zügen übersichtlich dargestellt* (Dritte Auflage, neu bearbeitet von E.M. ten Cate Apeldoorn (Holland); Amsterdam: van Vaerlestraa Verlag von Johannes Müller, Boekhandel, c.1912), p. 9.
11 Walter Marschall Horton, *Christian Theology: An Ecumenical Approach* (Revised and enlarged edition; New York: Harper and Brothers Publishers, 1958), p. XIX.

man; it raises the question of what man is under divine judgment."[12]

ACTION AND ETHICS

Menno Simons with his pronounced *theo-socio* views packages the Scriptures, the New Testament Church's fundamentals, doctrine and practise, into one ethical capsule. He accepts Tillich's correlation but uses Elert's application. "Therefore," he says,

> with a humble heart and in the fear of God, examine by Christ's own Spirit and Word as much as in you is. Compare it with the doctrine and lives of the apostles; with the piety, love, customs, deeds, misery, cross and sufferings of the primitive church; and I hope by the grace of God that you may see plainly that our doctrine is the infallible doctrine and position of Scripture.[13]

Balthasar Hubmaier (1480-1528), a "spiritual and resistant" Anabaptist, even says that *"jeder Christ soll aus der Heiligen Schrift zu urtheilen im Stande sein"*[14] (every Christian should be able to judge from the Scriptures). The Dutch Anabaptists (later Mennonites) agreed with Hubmaier in the Spirit's assistance of understanding the Word's ethical implications. They said, *"God Geest gaat gepaard met de werking die God's woord op ons oefent"* (God's Spirit and Word work together within us). This cooperation of the Word and the Spirit made the Mennonites much more stable than the earlier Anabaptists to whom Hubmaier belonged. "Because our performances are indefinite, undefined and limited to the verbalization of the Scriptures," they said, "there is a good deal of inhibition and doubt. This makes it necessary to define our actions and set them forth according to the Scriptures."[15] Menno saw the danger at the time he took the leadership and exhorted his followers to chastise their hearts to the Spirit and Word of God and walk worthy of the Gospel.

---

12 Werner Elert, *The Christian Ethos*, translated by Carl J. Schindler (Philadelphia: Muhlenberg Press, 1949), p. 17.
13 Menno Simons, "Foundation of Christian Doctrine, 1539," *CWMS*, p. 192.
14 Johann Loserth, *Doctor Balthasar Hubmaier und die Anfänge der Wiedertaufe in Mähren* (Herausgegeben von der historish-Section der k. k. mähr. Gesellschaft zur Beförderung der Landwirtschaft, der Natur-und Landeskunde; Brön: Verlag der hist.-statist. Section, Druck von Rudolf N. Rohrer, 1893), p. 37.
15 Hoekstra, *op. cit.*, p. 113.

Menno's advice here to apply the Scriptures in such positive fashion was unique for his age. This active and positive scriptural emphasis caused the Roman Catholics to want to exterminate him and his followers. In his positive approach he stressed a direct relationship to God and personal responsibility in deeds of faith. "I desire," he writes,

> according to my humble talents to teach a Gospel that builds up, and not one that breaks down; one that gives off a pleasant odor, and not a stench, and I do not intend to trouble the work of God with something for which I have no certain Scriptural grounds. I can neither teach nor live by the faith of others. I must live by my own faith as the Spirit of the Lord has taught me through His Word.[16]

The divisions amongst the Anabaptists made it very difficult for Menno to lift those rules for conduct from the Scriptures that would apply in all circumstances. Every faction interpreted Scripture in its own way and placed an almost total emphasis upon a certain small portion; in much the same way that Peter Waldo came to his momentous decision in favor of poverty. Two general types of Anabaptists came to be recognized, the quietists and the revolutionists. The latter were "resistants" and like all fanatics, advocated the abolition of all existing authority in church and state. These read extremely far-fetched ideas for their conduct out of the Bible.

From observation one must conclude that in the Amish and other Mennonite-related Anabaptist branches, some of their ethics that are still lifted out of the Bible appear totally removed from their intended purpose. The Cross, it seems, receives more emphasis than the One on the cross. In recent days the Mennonite Professor B. H. Unruh, Karlsruhe, felt the need to reiterate: "the cardinal matter is not a cross but This Cross; not the cross but the One on the Cross; not one crucified but This One Crucified."[17] It has always been a problem for the Mennonites to do justice to both the ethical and the redeem-

---

16 Menno Simons, "Letters and Other Writings," *CWMS*, pp. 1051-52.

17 Benjamin H. Unruh, "Die Botschaft des Evangeliums in unserer Zeit," in *Botschaft und Nachfolge*. Bericht und Vorträge der mennonitischen Studententagung auf dem Thomashof 1947 zusammengestellt von Theo. Glück (Herausgegeben von der Konferenz der süddeutschen Mennoniten, Karlsruhe: Evangelische Sotiments-und Verlagsbuchhandlung Flügel & Co. Nachfolger, 1947), p. 23.

ing features of the Scriptures.¹⁸ Menno sensed the stupendous ethical problems he was facing but did not relent in his aggressive spirit to overcome them. Every contrary spirit to Scripture, he says, should be measured and demolished. In this concern to stay with the true spirit of Scripture, Hoekstra said they wanted only *"den Geest, die ons uit de leer en het leven van Jesus en de Apostelen tegenademt"* (the spirit that breathes towards us from the teaching and life of Jesus and the Apostles). This spirit was their total objective and needed no further embellishments by way of ritual. The place of worship positively needed no more than four bare, white walls and a roof.

ETHICS AND OBEDIENCE

The earliest Mennonites were never satisfied with the "study" of Scripture alone. Scripture had to be lived and obeyed. Its pages spoke of a faith for which they were daily called to give their lives. Many times their only reward was to have the inner assurance that they had been obedient to God. The fanatical Anabaptists had material and social gain in view but not the *oude Doopsgezinden* (Mennonites).

No obedience, however, was permitted to make allowance for rationalization. When sorely tried, only the Word was to determine actions. Mind and intellect, especially in the sense that Erasmus often employed them, were ruled out. Their ethics were determined by a total *Nachfolge* of the Scriptures. "I desire," said Matthia Cervas von Rottennem to his newly converted Anabaptist readers, "that you would know and feel from the Word of God which is the truth. It is neither the intellect nor the mind that is pertinent in the knowledge of the Scriptures."¹⁹ It is maintained that for such positive attitude to the Word of God, especially the New Testament, Protestantism must thank these witnesses to the Holy Spirit in their negative position to the Church of Rome. Here was an emphasis not of the letter but of the "spirit and the truth." It

---

18 J. Craandijk, *Iets uit de Geschiedenis der Nederlandsche Doopsgezinden* (Arnhem: Karel F. Misset, 1889), p. 19.
19 Matthiä Cervas von Rottennem, in *Güldene Acpffel in Silbern Schalen, Oder schöne und nützliche Worte und Warheiten zur Gottseligkeit* (Vorne im Buch ist mit der Hand geschrieben 'Wurde geschrieben 1527 zum zweiten male wurde es im Jahre 1702 gedruckt, n.p.').

led to a most unique amalgamation of the literal and the spiritual.

Menno in his letter to Callius Faber, who had bitterly attacked the Anabaptists in 1552, clearly stated the Mennonite position regarding the operation of the Holy Spirit through the Word of God. "The doctrine and ordinance of the Holy Ghost," he answered Faber, "is God's express Word and ordinance. . . . We point to the crucified Christ Jesus, to His Spirit, Word, ordinances and to the doctrine and usage of his holy apostles."[20]

In the eyes of the Mennonites only those were sincere believers who obeyed the Scriptures literally. Just who the sincere ones were was at times most difficult to determine, for right choices and opinions constantly vary. This has gotten the Mennonites always into trouble. Since cultures come and go it is often impossible to tell offhand what their morality should be. Even if we have no trouble in stating that murder, lying and theft are wrong, and kindness, truthfulness and honesty are right, the permanent standard still lies outside of the individual. For the Mennonite this superior, spiritual guide is the Scriptures where alone are found the ethical principles that are absolutely valid. To be a member of the New Testament Church is imperative for correct deportment.

Obedience and Church Membership

Membership in a Mennonite church has two prerequisites. The first, the candidate must have a scriptural, "actual personal conversion and regeneration" experience.[21] The other is a subscription to the church covenant of the church to be joined. These covenants differ somewhat from church to church and conference to conference but basically the obedience to the Scriptures and rules of the church are the same. After membership the ethics for the individual member are then prescribed by the church. The covenants of conservative branches describe the requirements in great detail. Less orthodox churches demand, more or less, only the regeneration experience, the observance of a few peace principles and the Lord's Supper. Some groups have obviously streamlined their re-

---

20 Menno Simons, "Reply to Callius Faber, 1554," *CWMS*, pp. 675-77.
21 Bender, "Church," *ME, op. cit.*, pp. 595, 596.

quirements as a reaction to the many rules and restrictions of the conservative branches.

For the Mennonites, whenever the regenerated band together there is a "redeemed community." Where such a band agrees on following Mennonite principles there is a Mennonite church. Such a church requires both regeneration through the new birth (John 3) and *"Nachfolge"* (obedience) regardless of the cost. Such in Menno Simon's evaluation is a "pure church." Today his followers base their ethics on these ideals and follow them with varying degree. Peter Friesen thinks Menno in spite of his somewhat speculative Christology[22] consistently strove for the attainment of a "pure church." His ideals have always seemed too high for some named after him. Real regeneration of all applicants for membership is exceedingly difficult to determine and for this reason children have been baptized at a traditionally set early age[23] to circumvent it. This is still the practise in places and most likely for the same reason. Baptism in such cases is not upon a confession of faith and therefore no different than infant baptism. For the early fathers this was an important matter. Other Mennonite churches try to adhere rigidly to basic Mennonite principles and doctrine.

CHURCH MEMBERSHIP AND SEPARATENESS

Early in the nineteenth century the Mennonites in Russia and America lived much by themselves. In Russia more than in other countries the idea sprang up that the Mennonites were a race (*Volk*) [24] as well as a church. In connection with this appeared a certain type of Mennonite culture, which, when it found it impractical to go back to the New Testament Church culture, reverted at least to a previous culture. The Amish, Hutterites and most conservative Mennonites do this to be removed from the "world." They want to be one with the true church of God that has been from the beginning. They say, "this requires that we flee false worship and separate from those who worship idols."

---

22 Peter M. Friesen, *Die Alt-Evangelische Mennonitische Bruederschaft in Russland (1789-1910) im Rahmen der mennonitischen Gesammtgeschichte* (Halbstadt, Taurien, Russland: Verlagsgesellschaft "Raduga," 1911), p. 35.

23 Cornelius Krahn, *Menno Simons*, Ein Beitrag zur Geschichte und Theologie der Taufgesinnten (Karlsruhe: Druck und Verlag: Heinrich Schneider, 1936), p. 103.

24 G. G. Kornelsen, K. J. B. Reimer, J. G. Toews, *et al.*, *Das 60-jährige Jubiläum, 1874-1934* (Steinbach, Manitoba, Warte-Verlag, 1934), p. 8.

The Scripture and Mennonite Ethics 43

In earlier years this withdrawal was from the Roman Catholic church with its ceremonialism, pilgrimages, adoration of relics and saints, and infant baptism. To them their church was a fellowship of saints, a brotherhood of redeemed sinners. It was a complete withdrawal from those in state affairs and hierarchical church business. Baptism meant much more than mere church membership. It was an external rite, symbolizing the washing away of sin. In their concept of ethics "baptismal regeneration" was totally unacceptable. Church membership was bona fide only when the "world" was shunned.

Today this withdrawal is from a local population and its churches in the same manner as the Apostolic Church withdrew from the Jews and pagans. It is an avoidance of conforming to the organized religion of the "world" and the usual church business. They say that what cannot be categorized as belonging to the Apostolic Church belongs to the "world" and must be shunned. All the redeemed are brethren and everyone is his brother's keeper. The church must practice love and not only speak in the idealistic language of sociologists and liberal theologians. Christianity has no validity if not dominated by piety and simple Christian motives as were found in the earliest New Testament churches.

Samuel Geiser told the Swiss Mennonite Conference in 1931 just why this going back to the Apostolic Church is so important to the Mennonite Church today. There the Old-Evangelical Anabaptist Congregations (Mennonites) find in the original and yet unadulterated form what their souls desire. There is the original report and obedience of Christ's words, spirit and example. When the "world" opposes them and seeks their destruction, they speak in consort with the first church, "Now unto him who is able to do exceeding abundantly above all that we ask or think, according to the power that worketh in us, unto him be glory in the church by Christ Jesus throughout all ages, world without end. Amen." Once more Christ's word, spirit and example become extremely real. The formal ritual of the church where the same words are spoken fall far short of the satisfaction experienced when these words are appropriated by the individual with childlike simplicity and piety. In such atmosphere the Mennonites find full relaxation and an absolute foundation in the deeds of Christ for their faith. The enthusiasm in this original brotherhood clearly defines morality and basic characteristics of the unity in the spirit and love as found in the first Corinthian Church.²⁵ Nothing less than the spirit prevailing in the Apostolic Church sufficed in their trials, later World Wars and revolutions. Paul's Epistle to the Ephesians, practically interpreted by the Apostolic Church, indeed played a major role in the dispersion of the Mennonites to all continents.

This re-emphasis of *"Urchristentum"* (original Christianity) had a strong appeal in its early stages. It was a going back to first principles, Christ's own Spirit, example and word. Everyone who accepted them for his daily life, became a believer and possessor of his own instead of being dependent upon an hierarchy. He came to his legacy by way of his own faith and hope. The formula by which it was obtained was simple enough so that every peasant could easily grasp it. Its principles of love and fellowship were so simply and realistically presented that little persuasion was needed to obtain members.²⁶ No wonder the followers of this new sect increased with unheard of rapidity.

SEPARATENESS AND FELLOWSHIP

This renewed practice of *Nächstenliebe* (love for the fellowman) evoked a new appraisal of the value of the individual. A high esteem of their neighbors has always been a very vital factor in the religion of the *Doopers* (Mennonites). It was significant to them that Scripture teaches that our first duty is to love ourselves. They were unequivocally taught to work out their own salvation with fear and trembling and then love their neighbors as themselves. On the basis of I John 4:20, "If we say we love God and hate our fellowman we are liars," Menno taught that no one is a Christian without love. As a former Roman Catholic priest he learned that the will to love is the foundation of all morality and "requires that the creature conform his will to the will of the Creator."²⁷

While he was still a priest, the Word of God convinced Menno of the truth and became the sole norm for his ethics. Elert ex-

---

25 Samuel Geiser, *Die Taufgesinnten-Gemeinden* (Herausgegeben im Auftrag der Konferenz der Altevangelischen Taufgesinnten-Gemeinden [Mennoniten] der Schweiz Karlsruhe [Baden] Karlstrasse 26: Druck und Verlag: Heinrich Schneider, 1931), pp. 15, 17.
26 Tumbült, *op. cit.*, p. 22.
27 John C. Noonan, *Ethics* (Chicago: Loyola University Press, 1957), p. 145.

plains that such "oughtness is not learnt apart from religion."[28] For Menno there had to be a turning away from his evil nature to a divine nature. Others who had the same experience associated with him to form a spiritual fellowship which those outside described as "radical and different." Their sharing of goods and confession to each other instead of to a priest was an original and living experience, for many difficult to understand. Disownment and martyrdom for members of the fellowship were common. In spite of all severities against them they pressed on because their Master went this way before and they had to follow. They felt the "oughtness" like Kant[29] but what he sought they found. "Little children," writes Menno,

> be courageous in Christ and despair not, for so long as we sincerely have God in our minds, seek, fear, love, honor, and serve Him with an upright pure zeal, walk in the truth, neither world nor flesh, nor tyranny, nor devil, nor sin, nor hell nor death shall hinder us, but the victory which comes with a firm faith in the blood of Christ will through the grace of God be on our side and this through the Spirit of Christ which abides in us.[30]

Through their conversion experience God gave them this feeling of oughtness for a purpose. They were to love in a cruel age as Christ had loved.

Mennonites are often accused of being too subjective. Perhaps the opposite is closer to the truth. Menno, Denck and other early Anabaptist leaders sought to objectify man more than others. They were much ahead of their day when they spoke of individual rights, separating state and church and tolerating each other in peaceful co-existence. Man was the object of love and respect, and this they learned not through human philosophy but from Christ in the Bible. But Christ did much more than merely teach it. He was in them and gave them the perfection acceptable to God. What the monk tried to be subjectively the Mennonites found objectively. Where the recluse stopped the Mennonite began. Virtue was not determined by what Christ did in them but what He did through them. What our moderns preach today the Mennonites taught

---

28 Elert, *op. cit.*, p. 3.
29 Immanuel Kant, *Kritik der reinen Vernunft* (Text der Ausgabe 1781 mit Beifügung sämmtlicher Abweichungen der Ausgabe 1787, herausgegeben von Karl Kehrbach, Zweite verbesserte Auflage; Leipzig: Druck und Verlag von Philipp Reclam jun., 1878), pp. 49, 657.
30 Menno Simons, "Letters and Other Writings," *op. cit.*, p. 1048.

centuries ago with the result that the "moderns" crucified them for it. To Mennonites only those were Christians who in some sense "were like Christ. For as He offered Himself up to the Father," writes Denck, "so they are ready to offer themselves. . . . They seek exactly the perfection which Christ never lost."

What the Mennonites found biblically was the *apriori* Kant and others tried to find philosophically. Kant tried to find it in his practical reason but instead of objectifying the Christ within, like Denck, he objectified himself through intense subjectification. The Mennonites on the other hand know that they are followers of Christ when they give themselves objectively to love, non-resistance and sharing with others. Instead of trying to satisfy this urge to morality philosophically like Kant, they turned to Christ in spirit and very simple faith and presented themselves as His workmanship. In this presentation and obedience lies their ethics.

Fellowship and the Worth of Man

Mennonite ethics lie not in "das wirkliche Wesen"[31] (the real essence) of the abstract but in Biblicism and man. They are not found in the individualism of idealistic philosophy but in the universalism of revelation. Salvation and Biblicism are the common bond. Instead of reaching up alone they reach for their fellow believer's hand. During their first years there was no other direction to take but up. It was like climbing the intellectual peaks of Kant, Hegel, Fichte and Schleiermacher, with this difference that results came not by way of what they were themselves but what Christ was in and through them.

Menno and his followers sought reality in the worth of man. Here they differed from the whole Renaissance movement which lifted out the thought of man. Here is a reason why they produced no outstanding learned leaders. In contrast, they idealized the "regenerated ones," who, according to Menno,

> use the true Supper, for they proclaim the Lord's death until He comes, I Cor. 11. Their pleasure is in the church of the righteous; their works are nothing but brotherly love, one heart, one soul, one spirit; yes, one undivided body, fruitful, serving, and fellowshipping in Christ Jesus which is symbolized by the outward cup and the outward bread. I Cor. 10. . . . They seek true teachers

---

[31] Kant, "Kritik der reinen Vernunft," *op. cit.*, p. 50.

who are unblamable both in doctrine and life; the true religion as taught and expressed in Christ's Word, namely, the dying unto the flesh (Rom. 12; Gal. 5); the service of the afflicted (Matt. 15) . . . to keep themselves unblemished and unspotted from the world.[32]

What the materialists find in matter, Menno and his followers found in the church. This had to be so as long as they were killed for their faith and their possessions given to those who killed them. Nothing independent of the Scriptures was really any good to them. They would have agreed with Forell when he says, "each alternative, whether naturalism or relativism independent of the Scriptures cannot be called good merely because man thinks so."[33]

Where the naturalist's "ethical standard is that whatever man thinks is good," the Mennonites say that whatever man thinks is carnal and bad. To them the natural man is carnal and does as he pleases. All carnality has to yield to a life in the spirit of Christ and pleasing to God. When struggles ensue, as they often do, Christ enables them to victory, for even Paul says, "I can do all things through Christ who strengtheneth me." In their older hymnbooks are many prayer songs asking Christ to help in the struggles all Christians must face. They recognize their weakness and Christ's almighty power. They look upon their deeds in the flesh as objectionable to the Lord. Such a stand is usually too drastic to be appreciated and comprehended by non-Mennonites.

Baptism to the Mennonites is the external evidence that the candidate has decided to live for Christ and follow Him obediently at all cost. It signifies that he has received Christ as His Redeemer from the old Adam and the "washing away of his sin."

Hoekstra thinks this idea of washing away sin and sins in adult baptism and of signalling the decision to follow Christ in obedience in the future, originated with the Mennonites. The reason for adult baptism before them was not the same. For the Mennonites it did what Christian realism did when it "declared its certainty on the basis of a moral and spiritual trans-

---

32 Menno Simons, "Admonition on Church Discipline," *CWMS, op. cit.,* p. 411.
33 George W. Forell, *Ethics of Decision* (Philadelphia: The Muhlenberg Press, c.1955), p. XVII.

formation of the individual."³⁴ "The rise of the Mennonite Brethren in Russia (1860ff.) can be viewed as an attempt to restore the lost original ideal of the church of converted believers."³⁵ To guard against baptizing "unbelievers" they demanded a public testimony from their candidates that their sins had been forgiven and that they desired to be baptized upon this confession. Then, too, they adopted baptizing by immersion, meaning that pouring was not enough for baptism.³⁶ When Luther argues against Emser of Leipzig about the "true Church" he seems to have the same belief that the true church is formed by baptism and confession.³⁷ Hoekstra has no doubt that Mennonites, Lutherans, and Reformed have this in common.³⁸

THE WORTH OF MAN AND DEFINITION

The Mennonites have a deep sense of self-consciousness. Like Kant, they arrive at this through a wide synthesis of the impressions their environment makes upon them. The two, however, differ greatly when it comes to the final solution of such synthesis.³⁹

The *Weltanschauung* of the Mennonites — whatever degree that may be — makes them what they are. Christ and the world both want to possess them and their actions must determine whose they will be. Their world consciousness is extremely sensitive. A most radical example is the Amish belief that even telephones belong to the "world." Several Mennonite churches still prohibit radios for the same reason and their attitude to clothes is known to all. Their relationship to the "world" is uppermost in their social and religious life and on how they will manage to keep out of the snares of the "world" depends their final destiny.

Since the Anabaptists and Mennonites were only a small minority they felt closer to the *Urgemeinde*⁴⁰ (New Testament

---

34 Warren C. Young, *A Christian Approach to Philosophy* (Wheaton, Illinois: Van Kampen Press, 1954), p. 220.
35 Bender, "Church," *ME, op. cit.,* V.I, 596.
36 Mennonite Brethren Church, *Fundamentals of Faith* (Third edition; Hillsboro, Kansas: Mennonite Publishing House, 1954), p. 45.
37 Martin Luther, *Works of Martin Luther* (The Philadelphia Edition; Philadelphia: Muhlenberg Press, 1930), III, 395-401.
38 Hoekstra, *op. cit.,* p. 3.
39 Kant, *op. cit.,* p. 661.
40 Franklin, Hamlin Littell, *The Anabaptist View of the Church* (Second edition, revised and enlarged; Boston: Starr King Press, 1958), p. 45.

The Scripture and Mennonite Ethics 49

Church community) than to the hostile church of their day. The society in which they had their first years was dominated by intolerance and cruelty, which was the exact opposite of their religious fundamentals. In their "fleeing the world" and "drawing nearer to God" the ethics of the Apostolic Church became real again. Their behavior was like that of the early Christians. Zwingli with his intolerance accelerated their recession to the earlier ethical standards as delineated in the Bible. It was a conduct much higher than Rome and even the Reformers offered.

On the other hand there was great difficulty understanding Mennonite behavior with its crass isolationism and radical independent views. They refused to conform to the social practices of the day, and in their estimation their doctrine of duty in respect to themselves and the rights of others was more real and true to the biblical definition than the traditions of Rome. Their opponents denied that they had any rules of conduct. It was said that they followed merely their own stubbornness when they repudiated all established ecclesiastical and hierarchical conveniences.

Even today Mennonite ethics are questioned with their emphasis on non-conformity and being so obviously "different." According to definition, ethics constitute the "science which treats of the nature and grounds of moral obligation." When this is applied to Mennonite behavior we must conclude that they are, because of their biblicism, more ethical than those with less literal biblical stress, for there are no lesser "grounds" than the Bible for their ethics. History knows of no book that has wielded greater authority. No other book has greater "moral obligation" to its credit and never has greater oughtness been felt than has resulted from its reading. Man never truly learned the doctrine of man's duty in respect to himself and the rights of others until the Bible taught him. It seems that the Mennonites advanced faster ethically than the rest of christendom when they made it their serious business to get to basic social fundamentals of no lesser authority than did the Apostolic Church.

Biblicistic ethics are still the norm of all Mennonite conduct. They have become a part of their life. Their highest obligation has been the restoration of love and worth to all men. This is fundamental, and since its relation is direct to God it becomes a most solemn restitution.⁴¹ In their view a reformation was not enough. It had to be a restitution with a much more demanding totality. Indeed they were the "radicals" of the entire Reformation.

DEFINITION AND THE TRUE CHURCH

The Mennonites looked upon the "restitution" of the church as an essential part of history and formed a voluntary organization to bring it about. Their aim was not to introduce something new but to restore something original. Luther, Zwingli, Calvin and Butzer had elements of restitution in their reform measures, but the Anabaptists had a much different and more radical view of "apostolicity" itself. "For them the question was loyalty," says Litell,

> not so much to a tradition of developed rites and others, to apostolic succession, as it was to "apostolicity" measured in terms of identification with New Testament ordinances. They believed that the devoted Christian could find guide lines in the Bible for the organization of his church life just as plainly as he could find the basic theological content of his faith.⁴²

John Horsch believes the "decline of the Christian religion" dates back to the time of Constantine. With his conversion to Christianity the church was furnished a new basis upon which to pivot its organization, ethics and morals. Churchianity took the place of the former apostolic faith and practice, setting up its own standards for clergy and laity on an unequal basis, making a priestly order necessary for the definition of ethical individual acts. The spirit of brotherhood and ministry was absorbed by a clerical professionalism displacing an inductive ethic with dogma and human tradition. The church as a whole was taken from its humble apostolic position and placed upon a political pedestal displaying an ethics all its own. Ethically, soon the evidence appeared that this was not a rise of the church as was jubilantly believed, but a fall.

Not only the Anabaptists dwelt on a definition of the Fall of the Church. "When the Church was persecuted by the Empire," said the Free Churches, "she was pure in motive and morals; but under the fashion of Constantine it became the

---

41 Dietrich Philips, *EoH*, pp. 299-332.
42 Littell, *op. cit.*, p. 80.

fashion for the Roman nobility and obsequious pagans to enter the church."[43] To do this the conditions of membership had to be changed and infant baptism began to play a dominant part. This meant "that the church could no longer claim to be a body of believers," and the word "sacrament," in earlier times used in the oath of soldiers attesting their allegiance to the Emperor, was taken into the church and applied to those loyal to the church and state. Those set apart for special religious purposes became "saints." The former bishop of Rome became the prince among the bishops and made and unmade doctrine. Sects with perverted services and churches with idolatrous ceremonies appeared under the guise of the holy gospel and faith. One of these sects was the Münsterites, whom the Joachimites, a Catholic order, had endowed with a great deal of apocalyptic literature which confused them.[44]

But this spirit of agitation was not confined to the sects. In their return to the Early Church the Anabaptists also became stirred by prevailing eschatological expectations as preached by the Joachimites. What poured oil on the fire was a keen sense "that the end and final reckoning was close at hand, and conjoined with this a vigorous missionary outlook which embraced the whole world in its sweep."[45]

The Münsterites got their immediate impetus from Bernt Rothman (c.1494-1535). In how far they expressed Mennonite ethics is a question but they, like the Mennonites, were of Anabaptistic stock. Both cherished the restitution of the church. The "restitution" was to Rothman what the Anabaptists and Mennonites stressed ethically. His main point was the restitution of the purity of the church. "The falling away from Christ and the Gospel," he says, is caused by the rationalism, intellectual acquirements and pleasures of the world. Mankind seeks its own pleasures rather than obedience to Christ. We cannot depend on the Reformers for our ethics for they also have been deceived. Now God has given the restitution to those who promise full obedience and are not dominated by Satan. The right

---

43 Henry Townsend, *The Claims of the Free Churches* (London: Hodder & Stoughton, 1949), p. 45.
44 Albert Henry Newman, *A Manual of Church History* (Revised and enlarged, twenty-fourth printing; Philadelphia: The American Bap. Publ. Society, c.1953), II, 552.
45 Littell, *op. cit.*, p. 53.

church is a congregation comprised of small and great who are stablished upon the Lord Jesus Christ through confession of faith. They are those who follow alone the teachings of Christ and are seriously concerned about doing His will completely. Such a congregation truly belongs to the church of Christ, which has been hidden for four hundred years by the Pope. "Now," continues Rothman, "I and my followers have taken it upon ourselves to make known the kingdom of the Lord and the fulness of the Scriptures. The sword of righteousness is to be used in doing this."[46] With the last statement Rothman forsook the "Schleitheim Confession of Faith" (Evangelical Anabaptists), and contributed to the "Hutterite" movement.[47]

The Mennonites and Anabaptists turned against the past centuries of Christian history with much greater abandon than the churches of the Reformers, for whom baptism and admission into the church preceded conversion and who asserted that the churches remain within the major political units and fulfil their function. Luther and Zwingli established and supported churches through the laws of the state and promoted their claims along the former principles of *cujus regio ejus religio* (the ruler of the region is the ruler of religion). Such the Mennonites said was a sharp deviation from the principles of the Scriptures and outside the realism of their ethics.

S. De Waard makes an important point when he asks, "*Wat baat het, of er al voor gewetensvrijheid wordt gestreden, en dat geweten zelf blijft immer even stug en onaandoenlijk*" (What is the point of fighting for freedom of conscience when that conscience itself remains stiff and apathetic)? He answers his own question when he says, "Know the life and ethics of the New Testament Church and govern yourself accordingly. . . ." "In the fellowship of the saints," he goes on, "rules the same spirit. They all say without exception, 'Abba Father.' It is on this high ethical level that their hearts unite and aim to be of service to each other."[48]

The Mennonites teach that the Scriptures fully describe the rights of men but are not permitted to claim them for themselves. They maintain that the knowledge of these rights is

---

46 Appendix II.
47 Appendix I, a.
48 De Waard, "Het Ontstaan Onzer Broederschap," *GBcDV*, No. 3, p. 1.

based on the experience of receiving Christian love through obedience to the New Testament. They say only those know how to love who have experienced the love of Christ in their own lives. It is a *"gelukkig worden door gelukking te maken"* (making others happy produces happiness within). The true nature of Mennonite ethics, in the words of De Waard, is, *"al het mijne is het uwe"* (that which is mine is also yours). It flourishes in an atmosphere of non-resistance and ripens and mellows in a spirit of assistance.

The Anabaptists, and later the Mennonites, were concerned about the question of mutual relations and actions of the human will towards each other and God. For their criterion they went back to the New Testament and the first Christian Church and found its "expression anew in various reformatory movements.[49] Switzerland was the *bakermat* (*Wiege*, cradle) of their early churches. Conrad Grebel and his close Christian friends were the *aanvangers*[50] (beginners).

49 Amalie Keller, "Scholar With a Mission," Mennonite Life, VIII (Oct. 1953), 192.
50 Hoekstra, *op. cit.*, p. 12.

CHAPTER II

MENNONITE ADOPTION OF ETHICS

LATENT ANABAPTISM

Prior to the Reformation we find considerable evidence of later Anabaptist thinking.[1] Deknatel maintains that there were many Anabaptists before Menno Simons' time.[2] The main point of all their thinking revolved about adult baptism. "At all times," says Friedmann, "have been . . . groups, which, out of a strict obedience to the Bible have refused to let their children be baptized, without otherwise having any connection with the Anabaptists."[3] When they first drew their ethical lines they found "their own image and ecclesiastical blueprints in the Bible and the martyr church of antiquity."[4]

Just how far the pre-Reformation Anabaptist thinking went seems to have been a question during the middle of the seventeenth century. Thielman J. van Braght says that one "may easily meet with opposition for it is not admitted that the Anabaptists or those who maintain such a confession as they have, to have existed in every century from the days of Christ." When Braght says this he seems to think not only of the Anabaptist's religion but their entire conduct and religious life. He objects to the use of the name "Anabaptists" because it only speaks of baptism when their whole being should be included. The Dutch Mennonites later expressed the same idea when they said that the name should designate the *"uitwendige . . . gron-*

---

1 G. Keizer, "De geestelijke ontwapening der Christenheid in haar geschiedenis geschetst," in *Geestlelijk Weerloos of Weerbaar?* (Samengesteld Door J. H. De Goede, Jr.; Amsterdam: Uitgevers-Mij Holland, n.d.), p. 51.

2 Peter M. Friesen, *Die Alt-Evangelische Mennonitische Brüderschaft in Russland (1789-1910) im Rahmen der mennonitischen Gesammtgeschichte* (Halbstadt, Taurien, Russland: Verlagsgesellschaft "Raduga," 1911), p. 11.

3 Robert Friedmann, *Mennonite Piety, Through the Centuries, Its Genius and Its Literature* (Goshen College, Goshen, Indiana: The Mennonite Hist. Society, 1949), p. 14.

4 George Hunston Williams, *Spiritual and Anabaptist Writers*, Vol. XXV of *Library of Christian Classics* (Philadelphia: The Westminster Press, 1957), XXV, 22.

den" (outward marks and behavior) as well as inner convictions.[5]

Outward expression of inward convictions, continues Hoekstra, is always in evidence even when the true and complete meaning of doctrine is not fully conceived. The social-religious behavior for the Anabaptists persisted as the truth and manifested itself as a permanent *grondkarakter* (basic character) of which the Reformation was the major eruption. Here they banded together to prove "*dat zij kinderen van een en dezelfden geest zijn*" (that they were children of the same spirit).

"In the fourth and following centuries," says H. S. Bender, "Anabaptism referred to the rebaptism of those who had been baptized by heretics, or of those who had been baptized by bishops who had temporarily and partially recanted under persecution." There was no repudiation of "infant baptism" but the bishop's authority. What happened later through Anabaptist practice was something different. *The Encyclopaedia Britannica* believes that there is a genetic connection between the earlier adult-baptizing sects and the Anabaptists even if the historical connection is lacking.

"Today," points out Littell on the assertions of Fritz Blanke, "we are inclined to interpret Anabaptism at least as a third type" of church "quite distinct from both Roman Catholic and Protestant territorial churches."[6] "From all sides we are coming to recognize in the Radical Reformation," reminds Williams,

> a major expression of the religious movement of the sixteenth century. It is one that is as distinctive as Lutheranism, Calvinism, and Anglicanism, and is perhaps comparably significant in the rise of modern Christianity.[7]

Muralt, not a Mennonite, differs with them about the Waldenses, their immediate predecessors. Neither does he accept the statement that the *Täufer* (baptizers) and others stem directly from pre-Reformation movements. He asserts that they are similar and that there are parallel movements but not that

---

5 Hoekstra, *Beginselen en Leer der Oude Doopsgezinden*, vergeleken met die van de overige Protestanten (Amsterdam, P. N. Van Kampen, 1863), p. 3.

6 Franklin, Hamlin Littell, *The Anabaptist View of the Church* (Second edition, revised and enlarged; Boston: Starr King Press, 1958), p. 1.

7 George H. Williams and Angel M. Mergal, *Spiritual and Anabaptist Writers*, Vol. XXV of *Library of Christian Classics* (Philadelphia: The Westminster Press, 1957), p. 19.

Note: After this abbreviated "*SAW*."

Anabaptism genetically sprang from them. "In spite of," he points out, "many similarities in the sectarian movements of the Middle Ages and the Anabaptists of the Reformation" there are still very definite differences. "The Waldenses," for instance,

> clung to the Catholic priesthood and the efficacy of the sacraments for salvation where the Anabaptists of the sixteenth century were directly opposed to this teaching and adopted a type of worship which expressed much more their own conviction. . . .[8]

The Bishop of the Mennoniten-Gemeinde, Elbing Ellerwald, at the four-hundredth observance of the beginning of the Mennonites asserted: "From the very beginning of Christianity there have been protestants against an hierarchical and popish organization of the church." Händiges adds that there always were voices that looked for reform of the Roman Church from top to bottom. The severity of Rome attests to this; she was always alert to take very cruel steps to choke such demands through subordination, opposition, absorption or martyrdom. The festering sores of the church, however, upon which such heroes as Peter Waldo, John Wycliff, Huss and Savonarola placed their fingers had not healed with their execution.[9] The reason for such inhibiting measures was not doctrine but ethics. As long as those who disagreed remained quiet not much happened. Many grew skeptical about the baptism, efficacies, pilgrimages and relics of the church but refrained from making it known. The Anabaptists and Mennonites baptized again, in processions carried Bibles instead of relics and disdained all special efficacy of priestly functions. They accepted the Scriptures in simple faith and adopted them for their way of life.

PATENT ANABAPTISM

When the "fulness of time had come" for Anabaptism it expressed itself in various forms. As in every reformatory movement, there were serious errors and fantastic dreams; but when

---

8 Leonhard von Muralt, *Glaube und Lehre der Schweizerischen Wiedertäufer in der Reformationszeit* (Zürich: Kommissionsverlag Beer & Co., 1938), p. 4.
9 Emil Händiges, *Seid Eurer Väter Wert!* Ein Gedenkblatt zum 400-jährigen Jubiläum der Taufgesinnten oder Mennoniten. Am 25. Januar 1925 (Herausgegeben von der Konferenz d. Südd. Mennoniten e.B., Ludwigshafen a. Rhein; Karlsruhe i.B.: Buch- und Kunstdruckerei Heinrich Schneider, 1925), p. 5.

the "slag" was drained off, the clear Anabaptist constituents coursed through history. Soon it was clearly recognized that there had always been Anabaptists, who had not been fanatics nor revolutionaries. Oehninger points out that Sebastian Franck, a historian of the time, tells us "that they took their stand because of their faith, love and obedience to the cross. They were wrongly accused of revolutionary motives and most cruelly persecuted."[10] De Bussy, a hundred years ago, added weight to Franck's words when he said the Anabaptists aimed to do nothing that was not moved by love, faith, obedience to the cross and rested upon an ethical foundation. For support he refers to Luther when he states that it is only "through faith and love that good works may have any merit."[11]

Still more recent and much more definite on this point is Kenneth Latourette. "Anabaptists were manifestations," he says

> of a continuing strain in Christianity which had been present from the very beginning and which before and since the Reformation had expressed itself in many forms. It was seen in the Christians of the first century who, impressed by the wickedness of the world, sought so far as possible to withdraw from it and live in it as distinct communities but not to be of it.... There is that in the Christian Gospel which stirs the consciences of men to be ill content with anything short of full conformity with the ethical standards set forth in the teachings of Jesus and which awakens the hope and the faith that, seemingly impossible of attainment though they are, progress towards them can be made and that they must be sought in communities of those who have committed themselves fully to the Christian ideal.[12]

"This original manifestation was accomplished by these honest radicals who overcame all opposition and bore a stamp of a strong and highly gifted spirit."[13]

H. Richard Niebuhr believes that the peasants of Germany had honestly and naively "believed that Luther's appeal to the New Testament was an appeal not to Pauline theology alone

---

10 Friedrich Oehninger, *Geschichte des Christentums in seinem Gang durch die Jahrhunderte* (Elftes bis zwanzigstes Tausend: Konstanz: Verlag von Carl Hirsch, 1897), p. 336.
11 J. L. C. de Bussy, *Ethisch Idealisme* (Amsterdam: J. H. de Bussy, 1875), pp. 178, 191.
12 Kenneth Scott Latourette, *A History of Christianity* (New York: Harper & Brothers, c.1953), p. 786.
13 Hoekstra, *op. cit.*, pp. 24-25.

but to be the ethics of the Sermon on the Mount as well." There was an overall lack of understanding of what freedom and justice really meant and involved. Christianity sensed that it meant more than "suffering only complete goodness and justice," or a blind following of visionary and revolutionary leaders. Menno Simons from the very beginning of his separation from Rome tried to build a church that based its actions upon motives of unadulterated love. There was serious confusion about the true meaning of Anabaptism, for its most violent contenders did not even discry infant baptism and fully accepted it.

In every social upheaval is an exuberance of surplus enthusiasm that leads to much rash action. In those days, the scanty knowledge of the Scriptures and social interaction led to sad results. Mennonites have never deviated from what they knew, but in applying what they knew they have. Their leaders at the time failed because of self-interest and an inadequate understanding of changing conditions. Communism in our day has several similar experiences. Those who looked only upon the shortcomings of their self-appointed leaders said, "deliver here, save here, help here, have mercy upon the poor people. Stab, hit, kill here, whoever can; and though you die in this, happy are you, for a more blessed death you can never find. . . ."[14]

PATENT ADJUSTMENTS

Every social adjustment with its apparently inevitable and undependable leadership also has sanity. For us, perhaps no phase of history shows this clearer than the American Revolution. Menno Simons' intense convictions of peace and the church came to the surface a few years later. Even as early as 1529 Georg Blaurock, cheerfully sacrificed everything "for the brotherhood he helped to found and his Lord and Saviour." What the Anabaptists got during these bad years by way of ethics was their own. Never did they hesitate though to adopt from any source for their conduct what had proven to be scripturally ethical.

The statement of Blaurock's accusation stated that he had left the priesthood, the papacy, considered infant baptism nothing and taught another, repudiated the Mass and discredited the confessional as it was ordained by the clergy, and taught

---

14 Richard H. Niebuhr, *The Social Sources of Denominationalism* (Living Age Books; New York; Meridian Books, 1957), pp. 34-36.

that one must not call upon and worship the Mother of Christ.[15] He and his brethren did not look upon themselves as those that correct or witness against monastic and clerical corruption; what they wanted was an entirely new pattern.[16] For them Luther did not go far enough when he did not ask for a simple obedience to the New Testament. They were extremely honest and went as far as they had clarity. No one before had been executed for defying the church in response to the Scriptures in this way. From their first days they paid the full price for doing all that the Scriptures required of them. Paying still is a part of their way of life.

With Blaurock's execution the issues became more clearly defined; all that was required for their implementation was a few more years of sound leadership. This Rome tried to prevent at all cost. Their opposition kept the waters muddy "for better fishing." Ten years later Menno Simons reluctantly accepted the leadership and forged his new way of life. How difficult this was we see when he says,

> Behold, dear brethren, against these doctrines, sacraments, and life imperial decrees mean nothing, nor papal bulls, nor councils of the learned ones, no long usage, no human philosophy, no Origen, Augustine, Luther, Bucer, imprisonment, banishment, or murder. For it is the eternal, imperishable Word of God; it is, I repeat, the eternal Word of God, and will remain that forever. *Etiamsi rumoantur ilia codro.*[17]

Menno had nothing left but the Word in which he found what he needed to know for his actions and practices. He saw the need of a biblical ethic based on the Word rather than on religion. The persecuted felt that the love expressed in the Scriptures should not bear down with such hatred upon those who merely differed in faith. It was difficult to understand why men like Marpeck (1495-1556), much needed for his engineering skill, should be killed just because he was an Anabaptist preacher.

---

15 Christian Neff, and Christian Hege, editors, *Mennonitisches Lexikon* (Frankfurt a.M. und Weierhof (Pfalz), 1913ff.) and Christian Neff, "Georg (Cajacob) Bauirock," *ME*, I, 359. Note: *Mennonitisches Lexicon* is from now on abbreviated *ML*.
16 Littell, *op. cit.*, p. 4.
17 Menno Simons, "Why I Do Not Cease Teaching and Writing," *CWMS*, p. 306.

In the Direction of Humanism

It cannot be said that the Anabaptists and Mennonites stubbornly refused all appeals to logical thinking and to refrain from stupidly following the Bible. They looked around for guidance, took what they could use with their convictions, but aimed at all times to be faithful to their Lord and His Word. With the rest of Christendom they looked to the Renaissance and Humanism to supply their needs and readily adopted what religion had to offer that was not contrary to Scripture. Erasmus played quite a part in bringing about Anabaptism in the form that it appeared. At least the Humanists were thinking and agreed to look to the past for more dependable ethical relations. It was of special importance that he prepared them with his Bible for the *militia Christi* . . . *Tatchristentum* (Christianity in action), *Pazifismus* . . . (and) *der Grundgehalt einer älteren Frömmigkeitsbewegung* . . ." (pacifism and the basis for an older type of pietism). Eramus in presenting Humanistic teaching was a good deal responsible for the later appearance of Mennonite ethics. He and Menno Simons were Dutch neighbors and had been heirs to much the same training and independent Dutch spirit. What Menno had gained of culture and ethical orientation he relayed to his brethren. "With Simons began," says Niebuhr,

> the inevitable tendency accompanying the rise of a religious group in fortune and culture — the tendency toward a relaxation of the ethical demand and toward formalization of the cult. From violent revolution the path of development led through stubborn non-resistance and unyielding assertion by non-assertion of the principles of equality and love to an accommodating quietism. The Anabaptists, however, were too broken by the Protestant Inquisition to become a strong church, affiliated with wealth and prestige.[18]

This relay from antiquity to Humanism and to Anabaptism was a far-reaching process. The Renaissance directed all of Europe, including the Mennonites and Anabaptists, to origins. For them it meant an almost fanatical cleaving to the New Testament Church and its possible restitution.

The Mennonite champion for the restitution of the Church was Dietrich Philips, who said that Christ was the great restitutor

---

18 R. Richard Niebuhr, *op. cit.*, pp. 38-39.

for He restored the creation of heaven and earth: the church now is like a pregnant woman who is to bring forth again which was begotten of Him.[19] For Ulrich Stadler (d.1540), one of the most powerful personalities of early Anabaptism, the most complete restitution was the highest part and degree of divine abandon and voluntary surrender to the Lord.[20] Franck asks, "Why should God wish to restore the outworn sacraments?"[21] To him God's restitution applied to the whole church. In this regard Franck was most sympathetic with the Evangelical Anabaptists but their exclusiveness distressed him and he deplored their feverish attempts to recover the wornout sacraments and other practices from the infancy of Christianity.[22] Why the Mennonites would adopt an ethics dating back to the original church, was beyond his grasp and that of many in our day.

The Mennonites believed that after a long period of dispersion and decay the true church would be gathered again. This would be brought about through non-resistance, non-swearing of oaths, and a simple form of mutual aid based on equality. The Communists in East Germany today make special effort to publish in great detail accounts of these first conflicts of the so-called Anabaptists, who, they say, were the sixteenth and seventeenth centuries' champions of their cause.

No one was born into the Mennonite Church. Membership was voluntary and granted upon a confession of faith and baptism. The election and ordination of ministers was carried out on a Scriptural church level and ignored any special academic or religious preparation. A minister was fashioned by the Holy Spirit through the study of the Scriptures. Organized religion for them had hopelessly disqualified itself through the vindictive persecution of simple and sincere Christians instead of committing itself unreservedly to divine guidance. When Anabaptism for a time during the sixteenth century all but disappeared, Obbe Philips and others found Old Catholicism more attractive and defected. What hopes they had entertained for a resurgence of Christian power and influence for social betterment, freedom of conscience and equality, were dashed to pieces.[23]

19 Dietrich Philips, *EoH*, pp. 330-31.
20 Ulrich Stadler, "Cherished Instructions on Sin, Excommunication, and the Community of Goods, *SAW*, p. 284.
21 Sebastian Franck, "A Letter to John Campanus, *SAW*, p. 154.
22 *SAW*, "Introduction," pp. 145.
23 Littell, *op. cit.*, p. 106.

CHAPTER III

SHAPING OF MENNONITE ETHICS

The first years of Anabaptism showed great activity in mining the raw material for its ethics. It sank its shafts deeply into the New Testament Church and continued to follow its many seams always looking for new material. Like all ore, this material required careful and repeated testing and refining. In shaping their ethics, the Mennonites approached their material from different angles and under various conditions. They are still engaged, in the light of new materials, studies, and violent social upheavals, in creating an ethics that harmonizes Scripture and the life of Christ's Church that is in the world but not of the world. The first avenue of approach to their problem was through the Fathers.

FATHERS

Menno Simons was most likely committed by his parents to the Franciscan Monastery at Bolsward. Here he studied the Fathers who later became an important factor in his doctrine and ethics. Perhaps the ones to influence him most were Tertullian, Cyprian, and Eusebius, the historian.

It was from the Fathers that Menno received his desire to investigate the validity of adult baptism.[1] In Eusebius' (c. 260-c.340) *Church History* he found that "infant baptism was not apostolic." In his discussion of baptism he refers to Tertullian, Alexander (bishop of Alexandria), Athanasius, and Cyprian, with whom he differs.

From Origen, perhaps because of his speculative tendencies, Menno did not get much more than a great respect for his originality and extended knowledge.[2] One can readily see how this man's original thinking would inspire a man like Menno, who himself always plowed a new furrow. With Jerome, the author of the Vulgate (d.420), he shared his bitterness when

---

1 Menno Simons, "Foundation of Christian Doctrine," *CWMS*, p. 137.
2 Menno Simons, "Meditation on the Twenty-fifth Psalm," *CWMS*, p. 86.

he remarked, "the truth is bitter . . . and they who preach it are full of bitterness."³ Menno was deeply touched when he read that Tertullian said the Lord's Supper is a "brotherly supper" in which the Son of God is close and a brother sufferer. Tertullian's simple and direct manner with his brethren led Menno to abstain from worldly pleasures and remain on the level of his peasant parishioners. Fundamental to Menno's emphasis of man's peaceful co-existence was Christ's humanity. Every member of his church was to be "perfect as Christ is perfect." As for Sheldon in our own day, the question, "What would Jesus do?" demanded of him an unequivocal commitment. Tertullian wrote that God was truly crucified, truly dead — not that God was dead but that which died was the human substances of Christ.⁴ From this Menno evolved his "following Jesus," which in the form of *Nachfolge* (obedience) became the core of Mennonite ethics.

Later in Menno's life Tertullian stirred up a deep pathos and longing for love, patience and humility. Both men were total Christians and looked upon the Gospel as being primarily an assured hope and holy law of the Judge who can cast into hell. To them it was an inflexible rule of faith and discipline, and like Paul, they counted the whole world but dung compared to the Gospel. These men were so close in their sentiments and understanding of the Scriptures that even in the matter of dress and amusements, in spite of being more than a thousand years apart, they had much in common.

PERSECUTION

Menno and the Mennonites were inspired by Tertullian to stand firmly in persecution. Their old adage "the blood of the martyrs is the seed of the church," goes back to him. Continuing in this the Swiss Brethren slowly reached the point where they were content to be called *die Stillen im Lande* (the quiet in the land).⁵ Their repeated emigrations in later years was a direct result of this. At one time even Menno wrote that the faithful men and servants of God filled with the Holy Spirit have fled. Later he says that so the blind, ungrateful

---

3 Menno Simons, "Brief and Clear Confession," *CWMS*, p. 454.
4 Reinhold Seeberg, *History of Doctrines*, Vol. I, translated by Charles E. Hay (Grand Rapids, Michigan: Baker Book House, 1954), p. 127.
5 John Christian Wenger, *Glimpses of Mennonite History and Doctrine* (Third edition; Scottdale, Pa.: Herald Press, 1949), p. 186.

world has always treated those who sought and feared God with all their hearts, with all their souls, and all their powers, as Cyprian in his *Apology,* Tertullian and other historians testify.[6]

Eusebius' numerous accounts of martyrdom were a moral support to the Mennonites in their misery. Zacharias Walther, (1736) the last minister in Hungary, in his 225-page book has numerous quotations from Eusebius and a strikingly large number of songs set to Luther's chorales. The quotations are likely references to his collection of martyrdoms of the earlier period.[7] On the first page he wrote "the Lord will dwell in your tabernacles, Oh God, help us in our plight and have mercy upon us."[8] Braght in the *Martyr's Mirror* does the same. They believed only a few *(Klaines heuften)* since Nicea (325) had remained. To them the world had a heart of stone and didn't believe until faith literally was thrust upon it.[9] "We prefer to suffer for righteousness sake," says Philips, "and enter into eternal bliss rather than being put with the world together into eternal perdition."

The Mennonites had this spiritual fleeing from the pains of persecution in common with such mystics as Eckhart and Tauler.[10] When Menno teaches that being carnally minded is death, there is a certain *Entwertung* (self-depreciation) before ethics are genuine. The practice of such denial had its roots in the East; from there it coursed through Augustine, the Scholastic mystics, and by way of the pre-Reformers came to the Anabaptists. Erich Seeberg has a very fitting observation of it when he says that it

> is that which is beyond all selfishness and imaginable piety. It is found in Eckhart, Ockam and Luther. Life consisted of submerging one's own will completely in God's will, wanting that which He wanted to be a tool in His hands at all times even when His way led down into the depths of hell.[11]

---

6 Menno Simons, "Reply to False Accusation," *CWMS*, p. 573.
7 Ervin Preuschen, "Eusebius of Caesarea," *The Schaff-Herzog Encyclopedia of Religious Knowledge* (Grand Rapids, Michigan: Baker Book House, 1952), IV, iv-120.
8 *Appendix* II, d.
9 *Appendix* II, e.
10 Erich D. Seeberg, *Luthers Theologie in Ihren Grundzügen* (Zweite Auflage; Stuttgart: W. Kohlhammer Verlag, 1950), p. 26.
11 Seeberg, *op. cit.*, p. 31.

The Halfway-Anabaptists also mention this ethic in their prayer-book entitled *Ernsthafte Christenpflicht* (True Christian Duties) and in their other book, *Probierstein des Täufertums* (The Touchstone of Anabaptism). Braght in his *Martyr's Mirror* says, "Come now, ye earthly minded and ungodly, and learn here to become heavenly and godly-minded; ye impenitent, learn here to repent, and believe in Jesus Christ." Wenger in our own day says that personal suffering is to be preferred to retaliation. Seeberg again translates such belief into ethical terms when he says,

> true ethics bring no joy for they are pleasureless. We are most wise when we do that to which we are most disinclined. When we do that which we like and also that which we do not like we are most ethical when we do that which we do not like to do. Being ethical depends on becoming and this in turn depends on the extent to which we have placed ourselves unreservedly at the disposal of that which tends to make us ethical.[12]

According to Seeberg overcoming evil with patience results in becoming ethical. Mennonites always preach that permanent satisfaction and joy come out of persecution and never from pleasure. Did not Paul write to Timothy, "Yea, and all that will live godly in Christ Jesus shall (*müssen*) suffer persecution?" Since persecution is the most painful way of overcoming it is most ethical. The outward is secondary, the real causes of evil are hidden. Being ethical depends on becoming and which in turn begins with the inner man. The external only assists the inner man in becoming more ethical when it buffets him. God chastises those He loves.[13]

The Mennonites accused the church of having become unethical for it was a church only outwardly. It no longer endured hardships for Christ's sake. After his conversion nothing saddened Menno more than that he had lived in sinful pleasures as a priest.[14] Being ethical, in Wycliff's words, is not satisfied by a mere outward correction but by the removal of the hidden causes.[15] Luther differed with Occam and agreed with Menno and Huss when he said, "the Church has fallen into

---

12 *Appendix* II, f.
13 Seeburg, *op. cit., passim.*
14 Benito Mussolini, *John Huss*, translated by Clifford Parker (New York: Albert & Charles Boni, 1929), p. 36.
15 Lars P. Qualben, *A History of the Christian Church* (revised and enlarged; New York: Thomas Nelson and Sons, 1942), p. 193.

apostasy, she has destroyed or spoiled her sacred orders, and these, according to their original forms as preserved in the Word of God, have to be reformed.[16]

The trowel with which the Mennonites have shaped the substance of their ethics is "blessed are ye, when men shall revile you, and persecute you, and shall say all manner of evil against you falsely, for my sake" (Matt. 5:11). Today they say every true Christian will sooner or later meet with persecution if he will give Christ undivided loyalty. Christians have forsaken the biblical standards of ethics when they no longer accept bitterness rather than being disobedient to Christ.

NON-RESISTANCE

It is exceptionally difficult for the average person to apply the ethics of non-resistance. Normally it is so much easier to fight for rights and life than to stand idly by and make no effort in their defense. The Mennonites studied the question widely before shaping and accepting it as a part of their permanent formula of behavior.

The fundamental authority for their stand of non-resistance, of course, was the Bible. Here they found non-resistance taught in six principal areas:

  i — Prophecies concerning Christ's peaceable reign. Isa. 2:4; 9:6, 7; 52:7.
  ii — Jesus' own teaching. — Matt. 5:38-48; 26:51, 52; Luke 9:56; John 18:36.
  iii — Teaching of the Apostles. — Rom. 12:17-21; II Cor. 10:3, 4; I Pet. 2:19-24; 3:8, 9.
  iv — The end of the law. — Luke 16:16; John 1:17; Rom. 10:4.
  v — Examples of Christ and the Early Church. — Matt. 26:52, 53; I Pet. 2:1-24; Acts 7:54-60.
  vi — The positive side. — Matt. 5:44; 22:39, 40; Rom. 12: 20, 21; 13:7-10; Eph. 6:10-18.[17]

Early in the history of the Christian Church they found that Laentantius in reference to the Sixth Commandment said, "It is always sin (*nefas*) to kill a man; God willed that he shall be

---

16 Seeberg, *op. cit.*, p. 39.
17 John Horst, editor, W. C. Herschberger, Joseph N. Nissley, member of a Committee appointed by the Southwestern Pennsylvania Mennonite Conference. *Instructions to Beginners in Christian Life* (Fourth Printing; Scottdale, Pa.: Mennonite Publishing House, 1947), pp. 68-69.

an inviolable being." From this, adds Heering, "arises that idea of humanity which means so much to a Christian humanist like Erasmus."[18] Herschberger in defense of non-resistance says that when God forbids us to kill, he not only prohibits open violence but warns against the commission of those things which are esteemed lawful among men, for God has given a revealed and specific moral law for the Christian who is not ruled by the passions of the natural man. Where the natural law tells us to kill, the higher law tells us not to do so. The result of this is that he who takes the life of a human violates the will of God. In the society of the righteous, war and every other resistance to evil has no place. Romans 13 does not apply to this state but to the administration of civil government exterior to the society of the Christians. Rulers deter evil in their society but cannot do so in the Christian society because there is no evil. There God directly deals with evil which is infinitely more exacting than that of any man-made government. God has provided civil government to keep evil removed from moral society so that it can function. It was for this reason that Jesus practically ignored the state and dealt directly with the judgments of God.[19] The Mennonites always quote, "My kingdom is not of this world." Their quick deduction is: if it were, we would be required to fight for this kingdom like the Moslems do for theirs.

There are many other incidents in the early stages of the Christian Church that the Mennonites find in support of their non-resistant stand. Eusebius gives an account of a Roman officer of high rank, who, when he became a Christian, refused to serve in the military and got his discharge. Others with him who did not get their discharge paid for their non-resistant views with their lives. One such specific case was Maximilian in 295 A.D., who, when he refused induction and the military uniform, said, "I cannot serve as a soldier; I cannot do evil; I am a Christian." To the question whether it is lawful to make an occupation of the sword, Tertullian answered that there must be either an immediate abandonment of military service

---

18 G. J. Heering, *The Fall of Christianity*, translated from the Dutch by J. W. Thompson, first American edition 1943 (New York: Fellowship Publications, 1943), p. 61.
19 Guy Franklin Herschberger, *War, Peace, and Nonresistance* (Scottdale, Pa.: Herald Press, 1953), pp. 67-70.

which has been the course with many or the individual must suffer martyrdom. According to the *Martyrs' Mirror* Tertullian greatly encouraged the Mennonites in their non-resistant stand.[20] Cyprian, who stood in high regard with Menno Simons, also wrote that

> the whole earth is drenched in adversaries' blood, and if a murder is committed privately it is a crime, but if it happens with state authority, courage is the name for it. Christians are not allowed to kill, but they must be ready to be put to death themselves. . . . It is not permitted the guiltless to put even the guilty to death.[21]

John Huss, one of the foremost pre-Reformers, pointed back in the matter of non-resistance to Origen and Neoplatonism,[22] like Menno did later.[23] He spoke well for the Mennonites when he said,

> I know that through this precious suffering I shall gain for my body the crown of martyrdom, I shall conquer the anger of my enemies, I shall set a good example, and perchance, by my patience I shall save the soul of my enemy, that my impatience or my resistance might have caused to be lost.[24]

Menno voices the same note of non-resistance and faithfulness when he admonishes his followers to "strive faithfully and earnestly after the Kingdom of God."

Today the Mennonites believe this Kingdom of God is a way of life that is entered when unreserved obedience is pledged to its Word. War "is the opposite of all that Christ taught, and therefore is sin." They say that most churches agree with them but do nothing about renouncing their participation in active warfare and blasting "sinners to their doom." To them it is gratifying that lately, not through the Word as they fondly hoped, but through the horrible prospects of total atomic warfare, some Christian denominations have begun to see this inconsistency.

Mennonites have arrived at an ethic of indifference when they are called conscientious objectors, pacifists, or draft dodgers,

---

20 Braght, *op. cit.*, p. 1080.
21 Herschberger, *op. cit.*, p. 68.
22 Seeberg, *History of Doctrines, op. cit.*, p. 146.
23 Menno Simons, *CWMS, op. cit.*, pp. 86, 137, 276, 305, and other places.
24 Mussolini, *op. cit.*, p. 47.

subversives or "huns." Their objections are grounded in the fundamental teachings of the Bible and not in popular notions of world betterment. They have no interest in joining the government, and compelling people to follow the teachings of Christ. Scripture teaches them to pray for those in authority and be law-abiding citizens at all times.

To the question "what would happen if everyone took Jesus' way seriously?" they, like all others, say they don't know. They believe though, that the power of God would be released in a way never known before. To them Jesus' teaching is not that kind of evangelism, conversion or believing in Jesus Christ, as is practiced so often today, but an obedience to the Word of God in the power of love. In this they are often misunderstood. The more they try to live like Christ the more they are misinterpreted and criticized. Their weapons are no more made by hands than were those of thousands of martyrs before them. Without these martyrs and the missionaries that gave their lives for the Gospel in undeveloped foreign lands, there would be no Christian Church today. Jesus prayed not for the church that has developed into a world-wide business but for the church of love in the hearts of man. They positively cannot participate in killing for that involves the destruction of the invisible church. Jesus prayed not for the outward church but for the church of love in the hearts of man. They are extremely thankful that they can live under governments that recognize their way of life which is based on love.[25]

ROMAN CATHOLICS AND ORDERS

Catholic religious orders played an important role in the shaping of Mennonite ethics. "The Brethren of the Common Life" occupy a prominent place among the pioneers of the Dutch Reformation. They were semi-monastic, and, generally speaking, loyal to Rome. But even among them ran a rill of heresy. . . . They furnished their quota of martyrs.[26] What appealed to the Mennonites was their stress upon practical Christianity coupled with mystical piety. In Germany the

---

[25] John H. Hostetler, *An Invitation to Faith* (Scottdale, Pa.: Herald Press, Second Printing, 1958), pp. 31-33.
[26] Henry Dosker, *The Dutch Anabaptists* (Philadelphia: Judson Press, 1921), p. 10.

Renaissance had much more of a religious revival of learning than in Italy, because of the Brethren.[27] Besides these, the Medieval sects influenced Protestantism indirectly.

The large number of citations from Erasmus found in Menno's writings indicate that he was well acquainted with him.[28] In the schools of the Brethren Erasmus had laid the foundation for his later marvelous success as a Humanist. As such he had great influence when he said, "What availeth it to reason high, secret mysteries of the Trinity if a man lacks meekness, whereby he pleaseth the Trinity?" Here he had learned the denial of one's will and the submission to the will of God, and living a holy and peaceful life.[29]

The majority of the early Mennonite leaders were former Catholic priests or had Catholic training and had seen first-hand the inside life of the church. One such example is William Reublin, a priest of St. Alban Catholic Church in Basel, whose services were attended by great crowds. It is said that he interpreted the Scriptures so well that the like had never been heard before. In a religious procession of June 13, 1522, instead of bearing some "holy" relics, he carried an open Bible, saying, "This is the true, sacred thing; the other is only dead men's bones." Menno himself in his treatment of the Twenty-fifth Psalm confesses how he as a Catholic priest committed gross sins that were deeply rooted in his pleasure-loving life.

Forsaking the world with its pleasures was for Menno an either or decision. He had "to overcome or be overcome." In his followers this zeal at times seems to have degenerated into stubbornness and senseless disputations and quibbling.[30] Obbe Philips in his "Confession"[31] says that right from the beginning "false commissions, prophecies, visions, dreams, revelations and unspeakable spiritual pride . . . stole in among the brethren." In his later days these disintegrating tendencies seem to have impeded Menno's success greatly.

Anabaptist roots in the church of Rome had a long period of sprouting. They always started with the Word and those

---

27 J. W. C. Wand, *A History of the Modern Church*, reprinted (London: Methuen & Co., 1957), p. 3.
28 K. Vos and N. van der Zipp, "Erasmus, Desiderius," *ME*, II, 239.
29 Matthew Spinka, editor, *Advocates of Reform*, Vol. XIV, of *Library of Christian Classics* (Philadelphia: The Westminster Press, 1953), p. 14.
30 *Appendix* II, g.
31 *Appendix* II, h.

who handled it, the priests in the monasteries. Wace thinks that even "'Luther could not have been the Reformer that he was if he had not been a monk.'" In the Bern area in 1527 numerous Anabaptists seemingly made a sudden appearance. Here, the Franciscan, Sebastian Meyer, had since 1510 expounded St. Paul's epistles to his brethren in the monastery and Confession classes of the Roman Church to the lay people. In both cases the Gospel proved to be furthered more than the pope. The listeners carefully screened that which was of man from that which was of God. The big business in relics and deception with the supposed skull of St. Anna opened the eyes of many Dominican monks with the result that a large number became opponents to the ethics of Rome.[32] Virgins and young women were seduced and obligatory celibacy among the priests resulted in public and permanent concubinage upon prior payment of a stipulated tax to the bishops.[33] Severe counter measures to such practices and the question of shunning drove Menno later to an impractical and untenable position in his striving for a pure church.

ROMAN CATHOLICS AND ESCHATOLOGY

The Church of Rome also affected Mennonite ethics eschatologically. We find the same agitated expectancy in the Anabaptist "Restitution" that was brought about by the Joachimites earlier. Like Joachim, who became an abbot of a Cistercian monastery in 1178, many Anabaptists had most fantastic and apocalyptic views of the Scriptures. Joachim in his expositions was not deterred by the popes nor the Emperor and from him come many of the later chiliastic systems.[34]

Rome claimed that the pope and the bishops alone were qualified by special divine inspiration to select and ordain ministers. The Anabaptists and kindred fanatical and eschatological sects believed that the Holy Spirit called and qualified men directly for the ministry independent of the hierarchy. Here two extremes met. Both claimed that the Holy Spirit through them

[32] Friedrich Nippold, "Beiträge vermehrt und herausgegeben," *Berner Beiträge zur Geschichte der Schweizerischen Reformationskirchen* (Bern: Druck und Verlag von K. J. Wyss, 1884), p. 12, 10.
[33] Mussolini, *op. cit.*, p. 7.
[34] Albert Henry Newman, *A Manual of Church History*, (Revised and enlarged, twenty-fourth printing; Philadelphia: The American Baptist Publication Society, 1958), I, 553.

called and qualified their clergy. Both believed that they continued to express the Incarnation and, as a community, to be the bearers of the objective ethos.[35] Both were striving to express the Christian ethic in their own terms with the result that Rome, because of its rigid demand for uniformity in belief and worship, developed an overt church life and ritual.

Horton points out that the ethics of adherence is not a certain clergy or an hierarchical structure but a "reality to which we all adhere," which in some sense is "the church."[36] About what this reality is Horton is much more indefinite than the Mennonites who unequivocally make their entry into the Kingdom through experience of the soul by way of repentance and acknowledgment of the Lord Jesus Christ as Lord of their daily lives. They look upon the church as a body of soul-cleansed disciples of Christ, united by faith to Him as Saviour and Lord, regenerated by the Holy Spirit, sharing a fellowship of mutual love and brotherhood with one another, witnessing individually and corporately for Christ in the world,[37] and anxiously waiting for His return for His own.

ROMAN CATHOLICS AND WITHDRAWAL

Latourette mentions another Catholic influence on Mennonite ethics when he says that "the Anabaptists were akin to the monks in seeking perfection in communities separate from the world, but, unlike the monks, they married."[38] Conrad Grebel reveals this kind of thinking when he considers taking up the monastic life as an escape from the tragedies of life. The only reason why he did not do it was the low estimation he had as a Humanist of "the ignorant and bigoted monks and priests of the time."[39]

Perhaps the most outstanding example of withdrawal and separateness today are the Mennonite-related Hutterites. We find that among their early members were several highly edu-

---

35 Joachim Wach, *Sociology of Religion* (Phoenix Books; Chicago: The University of Chicago Press, 1944), p. 19.
36 Walter Marschall Horton, *Christian Theology: An Ecumenical Approach* (Revised and enlarged edition; New York: Harper & Brothers Publishers, 1948), p. 208.
37 H. S. Bender, "Church," *ME*, I, 594.
38 Kenneth Scott, Latourette, *A History of Christianity* (New York: Harper & Brothers, c.1953), p. 779.
39 Edward Yoder, "Conrad Grebel As a Humanist," *MQR*, III (April, 1929, 141).

cated, converted priests and pastors. Hans Schlaffer had been a priest in Upper Austria since 1511. His emphasis in his preaching on the unadulterated gospel made it imperative for him to leave the church in 1526.[40] Another very active monk among them was Jörg Blaurock from Chur. He and Jacob Hutter had a high degree of spiritual consciousness and urge toward sinless living. Their ethic of withdrawal was "to leave the world with all its godlessness and believe in the almighty God." The same ethic is evident in the life of Leonhard Schiemer, an outstanding Anabaptist preacher. His parents sent him to different schools to prepare for the priesthood. When he saw the priests' worldly living he withdrew to become a Franciscan monk. Disappointed again he left the monastery. He now met Anabaptists and joined them and became their minister in Austria, Salzburg, Bavaria and Tirol. By this time there was no further escape for him; he had withdrawn to the place where he believed to stand on scriptural ground.[41] He was beheaded in Rotenburg in 1528. These priests and monks also brought along from Rome a high regard for the Church. In their clerical training they learned to lean on other brethren within the church organization.

Like Menno, who did not found a church, Hutter did not originate the "Bruderhof." The idea of the "congregation of the holy" existed in Moravia before his appearance in 1529. There had been movements towards communal living and nonresistance earlier.[42] Those were features of high appeal to a Franciscan monk. Both Menno and Hutter organized a church of those who had left the Catholic church and wandered about a prey of organized groups.

ROMAN CATHOLICS AND DECISION

The matter of conscience regarding religious decisions also had its roots in Catholic soil. The "liberty of conscience" slo-

40 Julius von Pflug-Hartung, *Im Morgenrot der Reformation*, herausgegeben in verbindung mit Hoh. Haller, Georg von Below, Walter Friedensburg, Jakob Wille, Walter Köhler und Otto Harnack (Stuttgart: Wilhelm Herget Verlag, n.d.), p. 83.
41 *Appendix* II, i.
42 Jacob Hutter speaks of "die Gemeinde der Heiligen" in the sense that Luther did speak of the "Gemeinde," viz., *ecclesia* not "Kirche." Bender, "Church" *CWMS, op. cit.*, p. 594. Also Julius von Pflug-Hartung, op. cit., p. 149. Also see Appendix II, i.

gan had tolled its message for years from the belfries of stout independent hearts. Typical was John Huss who said at the time of his trial, "Those bishops urge me to abdicate my position but I do not wish to do it; it would be to lie in the face of God, it would be to wound my conscience and divine truth."[43] When his persecutors attempted to harmonize his teachings with the pope's he refused to yield on the grounds that they were contrary to the doctrine of Christ and His apostles. For him the only cue for decision was Scripture.

The followers of Huss, and the Anabaptists later, agreed that the Scriptures should be the only basis upon which they should be required to make their decisions. Neither should they be asked to swear oaths or participate in worldly affairs and warfare. Peter Cheltchizki, the leader of the later Hussites known as the Bohemian and Moravian Brethren, even wrote a notable book in 1440 on the "Principles of Non-resistance."[44]

Pertaining to the Scriptures being the only norm for conduct some Anabaptists differed. They spoke much of an "inner light" that enabled them to interpret Scripture. "The Word of God," said Hans Denck, "is already with you before you seek it." Menno, through his training as a Catholic priest, relied much more on the Scriptures and accepted them as they were written. Instead of the "inner light" he depended more on original languages and etymology. All his life he could not forget how the Scriptures that he read as a priest in the Catholic church had convicted him of his sins and how he finally decided on their basis to be publicly baptized as an adult and join the despised Anabaptists. His experience was similar to Luther's and as far as Scripture being the sole norm, the *sola scriptura* of his actions, he agreed with him.

In the matter of Scripture interpretation, Menno had Huss's idea of "liberty of conscience." He could not repudiate his right to read and interpret Scripture which the Catholic church had invested in him at the time of his installation as a village priest and especially as head priest later at Witmarsum. In his decisions he fell back to Wycliff, Huss, the Swiss Brethren and other outstanding Anabaptists: "I . . . shall seek nothing . . . but the unadulterated Word of our Lord Jesus Christ and that according to Scripture." To him and others who endured

---

43 Mussolini, *op. cit.*, pp. 53, 93.
44 Horsch, *op. cit.*, p. 17.

torment for conscience' sake it was "not ethical autonomy but obedience to the Word of God speaking in a man's heart."[45] Rome made no allowance for conscience and Scripture, Scripture and obedience were identical. At first it was not the aim of the Evangelicals to disobey the Church but to obey God. When they decided to obey God rather than men Rome burned them alive or destroyed them in some other way like vermin and confiscated their properties usually for the benefit of the Church.

Other Anabaptists, especially Hans Denck, reacted much stronger to the traditional shackles of Rome in the interpretation of Scripture and depended greatly on that "inner light." Denck, a very active and influential Moravian Anabaptist during the 1520's, in the matter of conscience swung with others so far to the left that they again arrived at medieval mysticism. "In his concern for 'the deepening of his own spirituality' he was influenced by Thomas Müntzer's mysticism,"[46] which, when fortified by the earlier "freedom of conscience" independent of the Word, gave rise to sheer license for rebellion.

The Catholic Church was also an influence on the Anabaptists in their obtaining members. Rome had a complete social system of salvation and personal confession for its members of which the Anabaptists had nothing. As for Rome, people had to become its members, where the Anabaptists' membership was on a totally voluntary basis. There was much of this kind of church membership that we have today when for good business reasons membership is obtained in the most influential church in the community. Socially the Catholic Church is an institution with firmly established resources of salvation. Believers are born into it or become members by rule and not necessarily through experience. The Anabaptists are a brotherhood into which one enters by confession and religious experience which is for its members the form of the common life.

What Rome has by way of sacraments and ritual the Anabaptist sought through Scripture, adult baptism, mutual aid, communion and footwashing. For the Mennonites it was a decision

---

[45] Hugh Ross Mackintosch, *Types of Modern Theology* (Reprinted; London: Nisbet and Co., Ltd. 1954), p. 319.
[46] Christian Neff and Walter Fellmann, "Denk (Denck), Hans," *ME*, II, 33.

based on the "inner man" rather than on the "outer man." Their symbols (signs) tell "of the unspeakable grace of God..., (the) practice of church discipline . . ., and the separation between spiritual and worldly living. . . ."[47] Their "symbols" point not to means of grace but to ethical exercise.

WALDENSES

Besides the Roman Catholic Church there were small groups who played an important part in shaping Mennonite ethics. Perhaps the best known and most influential were the Waldenses. Braght devotes fifty-nine pages to their story,[48] telling us how Rome tried to stamp out their disbelief in its teaching of infant baptism, transubstantiation, the mass, image worship and its secular power. These are the same points that the Anabaptists bled for later: it is for this reason that they have always felt close even if a direct descendance cannot be established.

It is the concern of every religious group that its ethics make sense and bear up under scrutiny. It is a moral support to Braght to find that such pillars in the Catholic Church as Chrysostom, Augustine, Gregory, Ambrose, Jerome, and most of the ancient outstanding churchmen believed much the same as the Waldenses and Anabaptists. "Though the papists esteem these men greatly with their mouths," he says, they

> would be nothing better than Roman heretics if they were still alive, and would teach these doctrines and would have to expect nothing but fire and sword.[49]

In spite of this rallying for "moral support" Menno did not seem to pay much attention to it. He always admonished his brethren to be strong and steadfast in the faith. According to him one must stand solidly on his own convictions and not look sideways. Luther and Menno had this courage in common. Neither did Georg Blaurock falter in taking responsibility. "I am responsible," he said, for our baptism and the way we observed the sharing of the Lord's bread."[50]

---

47 John Christian Wenger, *Introduction to Theology* (Second edition, revised; Scottdale, Pa.: Herald Press, 1956), p. 231.
48 Braght, *op. cit.*, pp. 266-325.
49 *Ibid.*, p. 161.
50 Georg Blaurock: "dat zij zichzelven de aanvangers van den doop noemen." And later: "ik ben een aanvanger van den doop en van het brood des Heeren met mijne uitverkoren broeders in Christus, Conrad Grebel." Hoekstra, *op. cit.*, p. 7.

On the other hand the Mennonites and Anabaptists had reason to resort to former voices, such as the Waldenses, for their support. The distance between them and the *Schwärmer* (fanatics) was not very great and their confession and ethics had a common source. Then, too, they were as a rule untrained people who refrained from literary activities and intricate arguments of defense. They knew that it was better for their cause to be linked up with the Waldenses than with such radicals as the Münsterites. Whatever their motive, it is difficult to think of any particular sect during the Middle Ages that could directly be connected with them later.

The Waldenses, Anabaptists and still later the Mennonites derived their principles of action from the Scriptures which they accepted as ethically correct, Mennonite or not. "The Mennonites," says T. M. Lindsay,

> have been identified with the earlier Anabaptists on the ground that they included among their numbers many of the fanatics of Münster. But the continuancy of a sect is to be traced in its principles, and not in its adherents, and it must be remembered that Menno and his followers expressly repudiated the distinct doctrines of the Münsterites.[51]

Beyond the historical the Waldenses and Anabaptists had ethically much in common. They shared in the "left wing" views of the Reformation pertaining to the Early Church and Its Fall, and were the first really to have such an interpretation of history.[52] It is agreed generally that there is a genetic if not a historical connection.[53]

Sound Scriptural and ethical actions cannot be stamped out by public burning and hanging. The truth can never be permanently squelched. Bonhoeffer in our day proves the veracity of this with his statement of the "divine mandate of the Church." He joins the ranks of the Waldenses, Anabaptists, and Mennonites at this place and says that the task of enabling the reality of Jesus Christ to become real in preaching and organization of the Church and the Christian life, must be indubiously put into action by the individual.[54] Keyser points

---

51 T. M. Lindsay, "Anabaptists," *EB*, I, 858.
52 Littell, *op. cit.*, p. 77.
53 Lindsay, *op. cit.*, p. 787.
54 Dietrich Bonhoeffer, *Ethics*, edited by Eberhard Bethge (New York: The Macmillan Company, 1955), p. 76.

out that there are many categorical imperatives besides Immanuel Kant's. We must be born again because we must.[55] This divine must makes life extremely intense. What this means Bonhoeffer makes unquestionably clear when he says

> that man must allow Jesus Christ to accomplish in him the reality of the incarnation of God and of the reconciliation of the world with God. In the forms of a theory of "estates" the doctrine of the divine mandates threatens to lead to a perilous disintegration of man and of reality; yet it is precisely this doctrine which serves to confront man with the one and entire reality which is manifested to us in Jesus Christ. Thus here again all the lines converge in the reality of the body of Jesus Christ, in which God and man become one.[56]

The Waldenses, much ahead of their day in the discernment of the Scriptures, endured terrible persecution. Later the Anabaptists and Mennonites also were almost exterminated. In our day Bonhoeffer and his clan have taken it upon themselves to make known the ethics of the Christ at the cost of the supreme sacrifice. All had the same evangelical spirit and urgency. Historically and morally they held to the same type of worship and ethical principles.[57] Their lives had to be a testimony of the principles of the Sermon on the Mount. It was an ethical concern rather than a theological controversy.[58] They laid stress upon justice and equality of all men — "thou shalt love thy neighbor as thyself." Not rituals or abstract theological disputes were determinative but a personal faith and an individual conviction. It was a pious spirit of brotherhood that expressed itself in everyday life.[59]

OTHER GROUPS

Besides the Waldenses there were a few other groups that affected the ethics of the Mennonites. As early as 1524 Zwingli connected the Swiss Brethren with the Donatists and refused to have anything to do with the Mennonites.

---

55 Leander S. Keyser, *The Philosophy of Christianity* (Burlington, Iowa: The Lutheran Literary Board, 1928), p. 212.
56 Bonhoeffer, *op. cit.*, p. 77.
57 Hoekstra, *op. cit.*, p. 5.
58 Albert Roland, "The Waldensians — Their Heroic Story," *Mennonite Life*, V (April, 1950), 17; Qualben, *op. cit.*, p. 182.
59 Roland, *op. cit.*, p. 17.

Cyprian was well-known to the Mennonites in connection with baptism. For a pure church, he said, there had to be a valid baptism even at the expense of rebaptism. The Donatists followed Cyprian's views. Menno Simons frequently referred to Cyprian in defense of rebaptism of those baptized in infancy. To the honest and law-abiding citizens who were drawn ignorantly into the Münster scandal he said that he and his group strenuously disapprove of the Donatists, Circumceilions and those of Münster and seek to follow only the Word of God.

Christian Neff, the European Mennonite historian, points out that the Albigenses are often erroneously listed with the Anabaptists. "This," he says, must be "negated" because of their "unscriptural" and "dualistic-Manichaean doctrine." They resembled the Waldenses and "allied religious movements in their moral earnestness and rejection of the priesthood, but held to other erroneous doctrines and practices."[60]

There is also the question whether the Cathars can be considered as having contributed to Anabaptist ethics. "Though both groups rejected infant baptism," says Horst Quiring, "their motives were far apart. The Anabaptists based their doctrine on the Bible, the Cathars on the . . . opposition of light and matter and a devaluation of everything earthly." In the matter of war, "the Anabaptists based their belief on Biblical prohibition,"
> whereas the Cathars' belief was based on their un-Biblical conception of sin as the inclination toward matter. The Anabaptists also were distinguished for their purity of conduct, as their preference for the Sermon on the Mount indicates, but they conceived moral living as a natural conduct of the regenerated man who follows in the steps of Christ. There are no external connecting lines between the Anabaptists and Cathars.[61]

SOCIAL CONDITIONS

A concluding word should be said about Mennonite ethics and their direct relation to the social, political and economic conditions of the sixteenth century. Even if the Anabaptists and Mennonites, like these other groups, came out of the Catholic Church, their ethics were their own. They had the conviction that Christianity had to "meet the religious needs of

---

60 Neff, "Albigenses," *op. cit.*, I, 34.
61 Horst Quiring, "Cathars," *ME*, I, 532.

peasants,"[62] and the downtrodden in terms of the Sermon on the Mount. Their whole movement remained that of the unlearned and peasants even if they had a few leaders who were university graduates. What they sought had to be obtained with great effort, cost and often radicalism. In their view the world did not believe *"biss in der glauben in die hendt würdt geben"*[63] (until this faith is forced upon them). Zwingli accused them of open rebellion and considered their belief a sin in the light of a divine sanction of private property implied in the Sixth Commandment. The leaders in the Protestant camp that led the poor "were fined, banished, and in some instances executed."[64]

[62] Richard H. Niebuhr, *The Social Sources of Denominationalism* (Living Age Books; New York: Meridian Books, 1957), p. 34.
[63] Schaffers, *op. cit.*, p. 105.
[64] Niebuhr, *op. cit.*, p. 37.

CHAPTER IV

THE PHILOSOPHY AND THEOLOGY OF MENNONITE ETHICS

THE BASIC CONCEPTS

The basic concepts of Mennonite ethics have been stated in different countries by three of their early leaders. In Switzerland Conrad Grebel (1498-1526), the first of the Anabaptists, wrote in 1524, "I believe the Word of God simply from grace, not from learning." In Holland Dietrich Philips (1504-1568) said a few years later, "The foremost fight is the wisdom that results from the fear of God and enables us to discern right from wrong." Almost a century ago Izaak Jan le Cosquino de Bussy (1846-1920) in Holland wrote, "There is a sense of moral purpose in the hearts of man that none can obliterate and without it one is a spiritless being."[1]

The Mennonites recognize that these three constituents of grace, fear of the Lord and moral purpose belong and operate together and furnish the material for their moral fibre. That these are of one essence and indivisible, says de Bussy, Kant failed to see. The question arises whether to speak of philosophy or theology in reference to their ethics. When the Bible is made the source book, conduct is not necessarily ethical but religious. Here lies the reason why the Mennonites never have stressed a written ethics. They have been "biblicists" and how ethical they were in the eyes of the public was a minor matter. De Bussy questions just how much ethics there are in such case. Towards God we have no duties, only obedience. It is only towards our fellowmen that we have duties and this because we are obedient to God.[2] The Anabaptists find it necessary that they continuously stress this *Nachfolge* (implicit obedience) to the Master.[3]

1 *Appendix* II, j.
2 "Velen zullen het evenwel met mij eens zijn, dat de mensch geen plichten jegens God hebben kan." De Bussy, *op. cit.*, pp. 47, 48.
3 *Appendix* II, k.

The purpose of this obedience is to glorify God in that we love our neighbors as ourselves. Without such conscious purpose man is no more than an animal. Taking such a position makes Mennonites a pronounced ethical people. When people search out an environment in which to fulfill the purpose of their existence they become ethical. By definition, "in the absence of social environment ethical feelings have no existence." When Mennonites withdraw from society they try to avoid ethical responsibility. They hope that the ethical implication of obedience will find justification in avoidance. At this stage, according to Schaff-Herzog, they and their like became philosophical because

> ethics is that branch of philosophy which treats of the theory and nature of moral obligation, and which determines the rule of right conduct, setting forth the moral relation of man to self and others and aiming to giving a philosophical and practical basis of discrimination between right and wrong.[4]

On the other hand, when Albert Schweitzer contends that the problem of ethics is "finding a foundation in thought for the fundamental principle of morality,"[5] the Mennonites maintain that this fundamental "principle of morality" is the shaping of character. Some Mennonites, the Amish and Hutterites, go so far that it must give evidence in appearance as well as in conduct. If it doesn't they say that a person belongs to the world, and to them the Bible says,

> love not the world, neither the things that are in the world. If any man love the world the love of the Father is not in him. For all that is in the world, the lust of the flesh, and the lust of the eyes, and the pride of life, is not of the Father, but is of the world. And the world passeth away, and the lust thereof; but he that doeth the will of God abideth forever.

Considering how the Mennonites experience their basic concepts of the grace and fear of God and the way that they express their moral purpose, one must conclude that both philosophy and theology do play a part in their ethics.

---

4 Henry S. Nash, "Ethics," in New Schaff-Herzog *Encyclopedia of Religious Knowledge*, edited by Samuel McAuley, Jackson Charles, Colebrook Sherman, George William Gilmore (Grand Rapids, Michigan: Baker Book House, 1950), IV, 185.

5 Albert Schweitzer, *An Anthology*, edited by Charles R. Joy (Boston: Beacon Press, 1947), p. 236.

The Norm of the Concepts

When considering the biblical norm of Mennonite ethics one cannot escape noticing that it has much in common with the philosophy of the Stoics. Some believe that Senaca, Epictetus, Marcus Aurelius and others had direct contact with Christian ethics through St. Paul. Hatch does not accept this, for even if such contacts existed, he says, we must accept that Stoic ethical "principles form an integral part of their whole philosophical system and that their system is in close logical and historical connection with that of their philosophical predecessors."

Just what did the Stoics do philosophically that makes one think of Mennonite ethics? During Stoic days paganism went through a reformation which proceeded from an ethics related to a philosophy of life that had to be preached and lived. They trained their will to be unthwarted in the application of good and evil and by rigorous discipline exercised their inclinations to be at all times in harmony with their environment. They moved in the crowd but heard not its noise and trained their souls not to swerve or retreat from that which "was their immediate duty." This, however, meant not that they were to be in harmony with their environment but rather that their environment was to be in harmony with them. Their position was that of only the few who reached their level. It was their aim to draw others by their preaching and living from a lower position unto themselves. This new level was so high that they at times were not understood and tolerated. They accepted this gladly for to them the world was "perverted and degenerate" in its outer and inner life and they felt that those who practiced philosophy should be marked so that they would be different from a perverted world. "They let their beards grow as a protest against the elaborate attention to the person which marked the fashionable society of the time." To signify their independence in thought and practice, they had to be different from the masses. One who was not different from the rest had to be put down as one of them even if he professed to be a philosopher. The usual dress of a philosopher was a coarse blanket as "a protest against the prevalent luxury in dress and as badge of his profession." Being differently garbed gave them influence and drew attention. By word and deportment they proved that they were not of the world.

This moral reformation affected the ethical teaching in that it raised philosophy to a religion, conceptions and emotions helping to make the transfer. It remained philosophy though because its religion was still that of nature and applicable to particular objects. The great concern was "good and evil." The good pertained to themselves and the evil in relationship to others, which entailed a constant "fitting into" the lives of others.

Perhaps the most outstanding person to teach this moral philosophy in terms of religion and from the standpoint of others was Epictetus. To him human life began with God and moral conduct was his creation. But just here was a great difference between Greek and Christian ethics. To Christianity ethics rested on a divine command where to Greek philosophy it was an "independent morality." The Christians in their ethics performed Christ's will where the Greeks obeyed the laws of nature. Where the first encountered sin the latter had only a shortcoming and a loss for which they had to suffer. Nevertheless, even if the Greeks operated on the natural level and the Christians on an above-natural level, Greek ethics carried over into Christianity. This had to be so because truth is the same in religion, philosophy and all other branches of knowledge.

Since Mennonite ethics aim to follow those of the New Testament Church, they draw close to the Greeks. What the Mennonites have by way of ethics came directly out of the Bible, but indirectly a large portion came out of Greek philosophy. They are philosophical even though they are deliberate in their attempts to be total "biblicists." A semi-philosophical way of life requiring greater moral perfection in conduct and appearance has always been at the heart of Mennonite ethics. There is considerable evidence of semi-Pelagianism and a lesser reliance on Christ's total efficacy for our transgressions. They share the Greek principles of their way of life, that of self and that of self in relation to others. The Greeks took their principles from the laws of nature and the Mennonites directly from God by means of the Sermon on the Mount. It is not a life of self-love but a love that expresses itself to one's neighbor. When it becomes impractical to spread this love in the world at large they withdraw to smaller communities where it is practical and remain in conflict with the outer world. Amish and Hutterite colonies are obvious examples.

Through this abstinence from social intercourse on the larger scale sprang up a party that was under "the yoke of the Lord" and tried to give a higher expression to Christianity. It was only a little distance to Neo-Platonism when the age was such that a revival in this area was needed. Every decadence was repaired with a renewed emphasis on perfection. Old Stoic emphases of rough blankets, places, long hair and rigorous self-discipline were re-enacted and resorted to for special sanctity. There was a constant seeking for a higher moral average. This was typical Stoic philosophy.

Greek philosophy linked with Paul's emphasis on the spirit of Christ appealing to the inner man gave rise to a new "spiritually-mindedness." Here the Mennonites, in their biblicism, left the Greeks and became "philosophers of St. Paul"; where they swung to the left, Ambrose of Milan had swung to the right. Where the former had an obedience through fellowship the latter had an inward holiness through meditation. Both had their roots in the early Greek emphasis on separation and discipline.[6]

From the beginning of the sixteenth century the Anabaptists once more challengingly employed a fusion of Greek philosophy and the practices of the Christian Church. The immediate basis of their ethics was Roman and Stoical, the proportion depending on their demands of practical living and preaching. Epictetus, Thomas a Kempis, the Brethren of the Common Life, Erasmus, Conrad Grebel, Menno Simons, the Philips brothers, and others met and gave the Mennonites their ethics. What Smith writes about the Amish is an example of the above and can be applied to all formative Anabaptist thinking.

> The whole movement was one toward a strict observance of the older customs, or at least a crystallization of the customs and practices then current, a sort of Chinese worship of the past, and of suspicion of all innovations in the affairs of everyday living as well as in forms of church worship; an ever present fear of the dangers of "worldliness." This spirit of conservatism did not grow mellow with age. The old was seldom discarded for the new in styles of dress as these changed during the centuries. And so hooks and eyes were retained instead of buttons; shoestrings instead of buckles; and belts instead of suspenders, long after these once common articles of wearing apparel had

---

[6] Edwin Hatch, *The Influence of Greek Ideas on Christianity* (Harper Torchbooks; New York: Harper & Brothers Publishers, 1957), pp. 139-53.

been discarded by the folks at large. Beards, too, and long hair once merely a common custom, acquired a religious significance, and became the object of constant solicitude on the part of the church fathers.[7]

At this stage ethics become religion and literal Biblical interpretation, persecution and martyrdom stamp it as a definite type. The same thing happened in colonial New England where we still have numerous references to the philosophy of the days "when the meeting-house of colonial New England stood for certain customs, principles and opinions which were believed to be as immutable as a divine decree."[8]

Mennonites have always believed that the finest thinking results from an intimacy with God through Jesus Christ. What they have contributed in thought and an unlearned philosophy has usually been the by-product of practice and obedience. "This wisdom which effects such power as yields such fruits," writes Menno in answer to the charges of John a Lasco,

> I consider to be the very finest that can be named, even if it is taught and recovered by an ignorant teamster and hod carrier; yes, it is the only oil of gladness for my perturbed heart, the only cure for my heavy care. This philosophy . . . I have not learned from any famous doctors nor in any institution of higher learning.[9]

Sebastian Franck adds, "This wisdom God gives to those that ask and are obedient." The Mennonites thought after the Gospel and responded in many instances in the way of the Stoics. They refused to argue philosophically in their disputations with other clerics. "Nothing is gained," says Elert, "by discussing with contemporary philosophers what we mean by morality, virtue, duty, ethical values. . . . Philosophy has mechanical determinism."[10] Sebastian Franck, who examined Anabaptism in its initial stages, said, "The Scriptures will take their rightful place when we ask God for wisdom to interpret them correctly."

---

7 C. Henry Smith, *The Story of the Mennonites* (Berne, Indiana: Mennonite Book Concern, 1941), p. 141.
8 William Root Bliss, *Side Glimpses From the Colonial Meeting-House* (Boston: Houghton Mifflin and Company, The Riverside Press, Cambridge, 1896), p. 2.
9 Menno Simons, "The Incarnation of Our Lord," 1554, *CWMS*, pp. 791-92.
10 Werner Elert, *The Christian Ethos*, translated by Carl J. Schindler (Philadelphia: Muhlenberg Press, 1949), pp. 8, 9.

The Purity of the Norm

The use of Scripture in preserving the purity of sound conduct has two outstanding ethical significances. The first is an investigation into the nature and constitution of human character. The other is concerned with the formulation and enunciation of rules for human conduct.[11]

The Mennonites assert that man in the development of sound character needs "more than philisophy. He must have the eternal verities of divine revelation."[12] With Keyser they say *"All moral good in the world comes from God and is so clearly taught in the Holy Scripture that it needs no further elaboration."*[13] In the latter they have been most careful to set aside world wisdom, philosophy, reason and opinion for "godly vision." Each church member must practice Christian conduct; relying on the grace of God only does not tell the whole story. "They saw too many people," says Hordern, "who used the doctors as an excuse for not living Christian lives." They said profession of the faithful became devoid of commitment and demanded that "the teachings of Jesus become the rules to be followed by those who join the church."[14]

At all times have the Mennonites tried to stay away from what Elert calls *"Vermischung"* and *"Vermittlung"* (mixing up and compromising) of ethical principles.[15] To avoid such they adopted an either-or philosophy and withdrew from society. It is not surprising to find Keyser's *Philosophy of Christianity* used widely in Mennonite schools when it teaches that "the Bible from the beginning to the end clearly draws distinguishing lines between good and evil."[16] They believed the Gnostics had polluted Christianity and "it was their task to get back to the teaching of the time before its adulteration. They began to link up their ideas with Christianity," points out Hordern, "but in doing so they changed Christianity to fit their ideas."[17]

11 *The Century Dictionary and Cyclopedia* prepared under the superintendency of William Dwight Whitney and Benjamin E. Smith (Revised and enlarged; New York: The Century Co., 1911), III, 2017.
12 Wenger, *Introduction to Theology*, p. v.
13 Leander S. Keyser, *The Philosophy of Christianity* (Burlington, Iowa: The Lutheran Literary Board, 1928), p. 190.
14 William Hordern, *A Layman's Guide to Protestant Theology* (New York: The Macmillan Company, 1957), p. 41.
15 Elert, *op. cit.*, p. 7.
16 Keyser, *op. cit.*, p. 185.
17 Horndern, *op. cit.*, p. 17.

Philosophy and the Horizontal Reach

In spite of caution, legalism and withdrawal, philosophers and theologians have affected Mennonite ethics. Scripture must be interpreted and ethical principles formulated. Failure to do this, says one of their early elders when he observed the conduct of his own flock, results in quibbling and intolerance, schismaticism and bigotry, vulnerability and strange religious expressions. There soon is a shift from faiths to beliefs, from spontaneousness to formalism, from a genuine restitution of the church to a limping and compromising churchianity.[18] Peter M. Friesen, another elder three centuries later, remarks that since the time of severe persecution too often Mennonites have been occupied with financial advancement, pride in economic progress, former piety and glorying in traditional faith and ethical principles. Only the naive reader will believe that all our fathers were saints.[19]

Mennonites have always found a great need for church discipline. Fundamental to all disciplinary demands is the belief in the free will of man. Socinian philosophy made direct contact with the Anabaptists and a number of Mennonites in Holland adopted it. They agreed that "the Christian life consists of the renunciation of the world, humility, and patient endurance . . . (and) obedience. Both rejected all authority of the Catholic Church and found its source in the Scriptures. . . . They rebelled against the prevailing views of human inability and total depravity. Socinianism did not a little to free religion from the bondage of dogma and to favor the unprejudiced study of Scripture."[20]

Even if the Socinians were not able to work out a union with the Mennonites they managed to bring about a serious split. Friesen thinks that this need not surprise us seeing that they always welcomed splitting and avoiding continued orthodoxy. One group, the Waterlanders, remained orthodox, followed Socinius, and somewhat the mystical rationalism of Hans Denck (1527). Influential Dutch *Doopsgezinden* now helped to prepare the way for the oncoming rationalistic religious movement that swept over Christendom. To the Mennonites this resulted in great loss of membership and in indifference. Ration-

---

18 Dietrich Philips, *EoH*, pp. 297-332.
19 *Appendix* II, 1.
20 Williston Walker, *A History of the Christian Church* (New York: Charles Scribner's Sons, 1945), p. 277.

alism did not affect the Mennonites in Russia, Switzerland and America as much as it did in Holland and immediate areas.

Mennonite ethics based on the Scriptures found champions once more in the preachers Hans de Ries (1773), Jacob Denner (1749), and Johannes Deknatel (1759). They were outstanding "believers," diligent and dependable teachers. Their stability in the faith, tolerance and brotherly love towards all Christians led the churches back to an ethic that they had given birth to two hundred years ago. Contention between the ultra Armenian position of free will and a final hope and a more "saved-by-grace" position prevailed. Menno had been a middle-of-the-road man and a follower of Luther. Spurgeon later was of this sound Mennonite tradition, especially in regard to oaths and war.[21]

This sound Mennonite tradition, in the words of Ritschl, had to have "practical consequences." The Schleitheim Confessions state that "baptism shall be given to all those who learned repentance (and) walk in the resurrection of Jesus Christ. . . . Only a metaphysical and theological discussion does not suffice." With the Sermon on the Mount they strike out horizontally towards their fellowman and by living together bring to fruition that which uplifts. Jesus showed man all he needed to know about God, says de Bussy. Human philosophy is all too prone to emphasize the difficulties, if not the impossibility, of God entering into relationship with man in history. De Bussy and Wenger set forth the philosophical position of the Mennonites over and against the philosophies of the professionals when they point out that they seek the reality of God not behind the metaphysical as the "absolute being of Greek philosophy, nor do they side with the pantheist and look for God as if He were a part of matter and dependent on matter, but in the high ethical ideals of Jesus Christ."[22] In the words of Mackintosh they attempt to spell out the infinite meaning of Jesus Christ in terms of a Christian-activated mutual aid program rather than a *Kulturprotestantismus* as envisioned by Ritschl.[23] "Christian love in action as an aspect of the Christian way of life,'" points out the Mennonite sociologist Winfield J. Fretz,

---

21 *Ibid.*, p. 30, 31.
22 Wenger, *op. cit.*, p. 45.
23 Hugh Ross Mackintosh, *Types of Modern Theology*, Schleiermacher to Barth (Reprinted; London: Nisbet and Co., Ltd., 1954), pp. 143-51.

is using the resources God has given us for His glory and the good of ourselves and our fellow men. It is a way of limiting selfish desires for the good of the larger group or the community of which we are members.[24]

The practice of love principles (gospel), Menno points out, is the "true evangelical faith" which "sees and considers only the doctrine, ceremonies, commands, prohibitions, and the perfect example of Christ and strives to perform thereto with all its power."

Moral consciousness depends on outside influence. When light from our fellowmen is thrown upon our character a morality (*zedelijkheid*) is awakened. When Jesus gives the divine command "be ye perfect,"[25] He alludes to the power that is available and that as soon as the inner man responds he becomes ethical. The course followed depends on the philosophy and theology a person may have acquired through observation or learning. Books may be used but sometimes the urge for hopeful progress operates rather independently.

Mennonite ethics at this point place more emphasis on doing than on learning. It is enough to know the Scriptures and the traditions of the groups; the blueprints of its structure are secondary. Justification and purification come by doing and living one's faith. "The just shall live by faith," says Menno,

> for the true evangelical faith, which makes the heart upright and pious before God, moves, changes, urges, and constrains a man so that he will always hate the evil and gladly do the things which are right and good.[26]

The reason for the Amish and Hutterites to leave the Mennonites was their still greater stress on "doing."

THE UPWARD REACH

Beyond making a personal application of Christ's finished work on the cross a Mennonite is mandated to take the cross of Christ also upon himself. This is part of man's ideal reach to God. Menno believes that the number so disposed would always remain comparatively small, "for the world does not relish the heavy cross and the narrow way." The ideal in any

---

24 Winfield J. Fretz, *Christian Mutual Aid* (Section for Mennonite Aid Publication Number 3; Akron, Pa.: The Mennonite Central Committee, 1947), pp. 8, 9.
25 *Appendix* II, m.
26 Menno Simons, "The True Christian Faith," *CWMS, op. cit.*, p. 337.

case can only be reached by a few. Greek idealism also had only a few qualified. "The virtue proper of this class," says Windelband, "is wisdom, insight into that which is for the advantage of the whole, and which is demanded by the ethical aim of the whole."[27] Our "ethic of love and nonresistance," reminds Wenger, "is sorely needed in a world of wars and rumors of war." The main motive for the realization of this ideal of perfection is love for everyone. The Mennonites take their place at one of the apexes of a triangle of which the other points are covered by God and his fellow man. "Against this whole method in the name of a more biblical and more religious type of theology," Luther protested.

Mennonite ethics draw near to Schleiermacher when he tries to make religion independent of philosophy and science and bases it on the individual's personal experience, in "a reality all its own." But with his proposition that religion is from the heart of the believer and not from the Bible they definitely disagree. Some of the early Anabaptists (*Schwärmer*) substituted also the "inner light" for the Scriptures but later Mennonites operate with the love that comes from the Word of the Father, the Son and the Holy Ghost. As a Christian he must make this love known to the world and be its light for "the world is reading our lives rather than the Bible, and unless our lives reflect the light of Jesus we will by our walk and conduct and influence lead people the wrong way. . . ."[28]

Perhaps the best way to understand the ideal upward reach of the Mennonites is by comparing their ethics with those of two of the best known idealists, Kant and Hegel. Hoekstra believes that a person is born with this urge to reach ever upward for greater perfection and nobility of character. When this perfection is directed towards God it expresses itself in a desire for greater holiness; when directed to a self-made god, including oneself, in greater efficiency in rationalizing. Whatever it may be the phenomenon is in the form of ethics.[29]

Both the Mennonites and Kant are very sensitive to the world. They both want to get away from it; the first find it wicked and cruel, the latter too mundane. The one has a personal power

---

27 Wilhelm Windelband, *A History of Philosophy* (First Harper Torchbook edition; N. York: Harper & Brothers, Publishers, 1958), p. 126.
28 John Horst, editor, *Instructions to Beginners in Christian Life* (Fourth edition; Scottdale, Pa.: Mennonite Publishing House, 1947), p. 86.
29 de Bussy, *op. cit.*, p. 33.

ruling the world, the other an impersonal power. Where the Scriptures rule the Mennonite, reason rules Kant. There is a divine must for the Mennonites and a categorical imperative for Kant. Both are subjected to their own powerful forces which make them highly independent. The Mennonites are motivated through obedience, Kant by a genius for abstract reasoning.

When Kant revered God "as a presupposition of the moral system he comes closer to Erasmus than to Luther."[30] The Mennonites come close to both[31] when they express confidence in one's own powers of moral self-discipline. Both are idealists in this respect and find grandeur in the moral imperative of the Old Testament. The Mennonites give glory to the Scriptures through the moral system as Kant conceived it. "We must," says Menno, "travel with the faith of Abraham in unknown lands. . . . This pious man dead to himself . . . honored his God and . . . walked according to His commandments."[32]

When Kant in his later life speaks of "merit" he reveals what he longs for but in his belief that man must have total freedom and his own divinity he does not accept the Mediatorship of Christ. And yet, the Anabaptists draw close to him when Hans Denck says,

> All Christians are in some sense like Christ, for as he offered himself up to the Father, so they are ready to offer themselves. Not, I say, that they are as perfect as Christ was, but rather that they seek exactly the perfection which Christ never lost.[33]

Christ here is not the Divine Mediator but the promoter of ethics. Only thirty-four years later Dietrich Philips was much more scriptural on this point. "No one can come to God except through the Son," he said. He continues, "We believe that Jesus Christ is the Divine Lamb of God which took our sins away and we are sprinkled with His blood."[34]

Another area where the Mennonites and Kant draw close is in the matter of war. Kant does not believe that war can be outlawed, for the nature of man is such that it "will never resolve to do what is required to bring about the result that leads to perpetual peace. . . . The individual . . . must supervene

---

30 Mackintosh, *op. cit.*, p. 24.
31 Menno Simons, "Admonition On Church Discipline," *CWMS*, pp. 407-19.
32 Menno Simons, "The True Christian Faith," *CWMS*, p. 352.
33 Hans Denck, "Whether God Is the Cause of Evil," *SAW*, p. 99.
34 Philips, *op. cit.*, *EoH*, p. 116.

... in the particular wills of all...."[35] Later he continues, "War is only a melancholy necessity of asserting right by force where, as in the state of nature, there is no common tribunal with the rightful power to adjudicate on causes of quarrel."[36]

The Mennonites also think that the nature of man is such that efforts for total peace by way of the natural man are futile. They say, man has always

> made provisions and signed agreements not to fight, but always fought again.... The failure is found in the people who made them. As long as the hearts of men and women are not changed, wars will continue to be fought.[37]

Hegel found in man through reason that which was divine. The Mennonites as idealists found the same but arrived at the divinity of man through the Word rather than reason. Really they found so much divine in man that the body was not worth keeping. To Hegel man's destiny finally came to a spiral.[38] The Mennonites, as did the Old Testament prophets, moved in a straight line towards hope. The former came from hope to despair and the latter from despair to hope.

The Ideal Upward and Forward Reach

Going a step further than the idealists we have those thinkers who once more strike out towards society from the upward idealist position. Here again we find that Mennonite ethics at times have the same tendency.

Troeltch assumes that "history is the fruitful mother soil in which we mortals stand rooted" and looks for "some central stretch of phenomena which unveils the meaning and secret of the whole." He looks to history to give him his answers. De Bussy answers him for the Mennonites, "He that will want to save his life will lose it"; the ultimate answers are not found in history but in the destiny of man. Here Schleiermacher differs in that he looks at the universe and contends that

> religion is essentially ethical because when one becomes aware of his dependence upon the universe he is immedi-

---

35 Immanuel Kant, translated by W. Hastie with an introduction by Edwin D. Mead, *Eternal Peace* (Boston: The World Peace Foundation, 1914), p. 104.
36 *Ibid.*, p. 74.
37 Howard Charles and Jessie W. Hoover, *Before You Decide* (Akron, Pa.: Mennonite Central Committee, 1948), p. 68).
38 Mackintosh, *op. cit.*, pp. 110, 114.

ately aware of his relationship with his fellow men who are likewise bound to the source of their being.[39] De Bussy asserts that both are ethical, for in man "the royal spirit lives that makes him a being of love."[40] Mennonites do not use creeds or ritual; religion and worship they say is within and morality is the soil to be worked. Their concern is love and peace towards all men. In so far as they aim to "reconcile the individual's existence with the social order" they are highly ethical.[41]

One often hears from Mennonites themselves that their ethics are not founded enough on the Scriptural basis for salvation. For this reason some groups do not commit themselves unequivocally to the principle of conscientious objection in time of war and rigid church discipline. They contend that compassion is natural to the moral person. It may be independent of any meeting with God in conversion.[42] The moral person is such through outside influence. Such a person may be "ethically moral" through honest self-examination. But all this does not say that he has reached the ethical stage that Christ works through His atonement. The moral person is still too much on his own. One here is reminded that Emil Brunner in his *The Mediator* does not discuss the "Mediator of the Scriptures" but the "mediation" of man. What Horton says seems rather fitting when he points out that Brunner admits that "hope in the limited sense, hope closely bound up with the present, is more obviously necessary to human life than hope in the ultimate sense, gathering up the whole of life. . . ."[43]

At this point there has always been a difference among Mennonites. Some follow Zwingli's "feelings" and others Luther's "recognition of our personal relation to God."[44] Luther's religious experience was much deeper than Zwingli's. The latter had a religious experience only after he was driven to his knees through sickness. This is very obvious in their later theology. The Mennonites do not express Christ's "real pres-

---

39 Mackintosh, *op. cit.*, pp. 47-59.
40 De Bussy, *op. cit.*, p. 7.
41 Reidar Thomte, *Kierkegaard's Philosophy of Religion* (Princeton, New Jersey: Princeton University Press, 1949), p. 40.
42 *Appendix*, II, n.
43 Horton, *op. cit.*, p. 245.
44 Henry Wace, *Principles of the Reformation* (New York: American Tract Society, n.d.), p. 203.

ence" in the Supper as Luther does but with the spirit in that "presence" they fully agree. For some ethics remain more "moral" than for others. The extent of the forward reach is proportional to the dimensions of the moral constituent.

THE ATONING REACH

Beyond the outward reach of Ritschl, the upward reach of the idealists, and the moral swing back to society we come to the ethics resulting from the Atonement as portrayed in the Scriptures. Their course is directly downward from God, through society and back to God. Ethical expression in this case is the result of what Christ has done to redeem man. God is the author and finisher. Linking this with the concepts of freedom and standards Elert points out that "not he who can do what he wants to do is free but he who wants to do what he ought to do."[45] True freedom reaches the subject from God through the Holy Ghost who is sent in the name of Jesus Christ. Those that are freed are indeed free to do what God directs them to do.

Over the question of freedom the sects broke with the other Reformation groups. Some of the Anabaptists carried the principle of freedom to unreasonable extremes. The basic principle was the acceptance of Christ as Saviour and Lord of their lives. Evidence of this acceptance was practice. The Sacraments played no part. They loved all men because God loved them first and now commanded love towards all. Their ethics were theological instead of philosophical. Only those who had received this theological ethical sense through the new birth and consequent church membership were included in their brotherhood. To their dismay they soon found how difficult it would be for them to maintain this position. Even before Menno died the groups were threatened with disintegration over the questions "Who are the saints?" and "Whom must we shun?"

Freedom is not freedom when not controlled by some standard. Undefined freedom in society clashes constantly with other "freedoms." At best we can resort only to the ideal standard that gives most good (freedom) to most people. We can go still further and agree with Elert that this totality of freedom must include the total man, or speak with Kant that it "depends

[45] Elert, *op. cit.*, p. 23.

on an analysis of the whole man."[46] To this the Mennonites say, "The place to which to go in order to determine which standard is nearest being scriptural is the Scriptures themselves." The born-again member is in a position to discern and obey the demands of the Scriptures upon his life. In his deep concern that this standard be truly scriptural the noted Mennonite preacher, Daniel Kauffman, points out that the

> advocates of the New Theology are making the same fight against the orthodox Christian faith that men like Paine, Owen, Hume, and Ingersoll made during the last century, only under a different guise. . . .[47]

When the Scriptures become the undivided standard for conduct, both philosophical and theological ethics appear. In these "the basic difference," says Elert,

> lies in the fact that theological ethics judge human quality exclusively by God's standards and looks at man as God sees him, while in content and method philosophical ethics is man's understanding of himself.[48]

Even when the Scriptures are the norm of Mennonite ethics we notice two different tendencies. There are those who lean towards John Locke when he says, "As long as the golden rule is available it is not of primary importance to write a speculative treatise upon ethics."[49] Others, and the majority, fully agree with Keyser when he says, "Christ saves men from the unethical unto the ethical, from sin unto righteousness."[50] De Bussy for the Mennonites goes deeper than Locke when he says that we of ourselves have only a relative and undependable moral. The terms "good" and "evil" are only used as society at the moment decrees. It is only something accepted and not one's own. On this level all people are inwardly still the same. A dependable ethic must follow a dependable norm, the Scriptures, because man is dependent upon God.[51] Never can he achieve moral

---

46 Immanuel Kant, *Kritik der reinen Vernunft*, text der Ausgabe 1781 mit Beifügung sämmtlicher Abweichungen der Ausgabe 1787) Zweite verbesserte Auflage, herausgegeben von Karl Kehrbach; Leipzig: Druck und Verlag von Philipp Reclam jun., 1878), p. 45.
47 Daniel Kauffman, *The Two Standards* (Scottdale, Pa.: Mennonite Publishing House, 1924, pp. 8, 15.
48 Elert, *op. cit.*, p. 7.
49 T. V. Smith, "Ethics," *Encyclopedia of the Social Sciences*, edited by Edwin R. A. Seligman and Alvin Johnson (New York: The Macmillan Company, 1938), pp. 602-06.
50 Keyser, *op. cit.*, p. 194.
51 De Bussy, *op. cit.*, p. 23.

victory by himself. By nature we are corrupt and a Higher Power must inhabit us, and we must speak with Aulèn: "God was in Christ, reconciling the world unto Himself, overcoming the forces that separate God and man by victory in a divine conflict with the evil forces of the world."[52]

The roots of such ethics lie in conversion and the joys and rewards of service in this life.[53] With the emphasis on love and service it is possible that the motive for service may be only on the human level. Man needs the application of the Golden Rule and it is only logical to use it to the satisfaction of conscience. In Mennonite groups where the "service consciousness" is very strongly developed there is considerable evidence of this. It is for this reason that the Mennonite Brethren Church directs its members to Christ in their Christian service. It says it is God's will for them, the Spirit urges them to do so, and it is their sacred obligation to show in this way their appreciation to God for what He has done for them. St. Paul teaches: "present your bodies a living sacrifice, holy acceptable unto God, which is your reasonable service."

THEOLOGICAL ETHICS

Luther lifted the theological and scriptural ethics out of the philosophical and traditional reservoir of the Roman Church. He saw the difference between philosophical and theological conduct clearer than anybody else, and spared no effort to reinstate the Christian into his natural environment. For him neither Locke nor Aristotle had the answer. Only in Christ and Scripture did he find the essence of his ethics.[54]

Theological ethics came into its own when Ernst Calixt made the Christian the subject of dogmatics. Luther spoke well of Aristotelian philosophy as presented by the Scholastics. What he objected to was that they spoke of it as a theological ethic. Aristotle was a pagan and as such he had nothing to teach to a Christian. The Greek philosophers spoke also about life but knew nothing about the life in Christ Jesus. This, according to Luther and Menno, came only through faith. "Luther writes," says Menno, "in a book on the education of man that that which

---

52 Harold H. Lentz, *Reformation Crossroads*, A comparison of the Theology of Luther and Melanchthon (Minneapolis, Minn.: Augsburg Publishing House, 1958), p. 10.
53 John Horst, editor, *op. cit.*, p. 105.
54 *Appendix* II, o.

is not commanded of God in religious matters of faith is by that token forbidden. Let it be glossed over ever so much. Here Luther and Melanchthon have correctly expressed themselves according to the Scriptures."[55]

The ethics in Luther's day had become a philosophical ethics bent on satisfying pagan philosophy and the scholastics. Luther in his *On the Freedom of the Christian Man*[56] taught Menno that it was not the law, nor Aristotle dressed in modern garb by the Church, but grace as spelled out by the gospel that opened the door to an entirely new ethics. Both found freedom when the emphasis was shifted from the law to the person. Christ set them free, not the law nor philosophy. This profound salvation from deeds could only be grasped with utmost simplicity. The poles were God and man, not truths for ethics' sake. The new relationship applied ethical principles in the form of God's grace for man's sake. Where Aristotle's ethical principles were only for those who could comprehend, theological ethics spoke to everyone that came to Christ. The new relationship was based on love, that of the scholastics on a natural relationship with God. Theological ethics required that there be a knowledge of God before they could operate.[57]

Anabaptists' ethics were derived directly from this knowledge of God and rooted in a person who was none other than the Lord Jesus Christ. Their ethical manner became even more direct in that it originated with His person who imparted justification and blessedness to everyone that believed. Good works no longer were prerequisite to salvation, the only stipulation was an obedience resulting from simple faith. The deeds of Jesus, and not philosophy, offered complete knowledge for conduct. Those prescribing conduct philosophically, said Sattler, even if they call themselves evangelicals, only misguide others. Circumcision must be of the heart that is born again;[58] and this has a burning desire to do that which is good, moral and its sacred duty. Here theological ethics directs the Mennonites to Jesus Christ where the law of the Spirit makes them free from the law of sin and death and enables them to perform deeds that are motivated by the spirit of love. The goal of these deeds is defi-

---

[55] Menno Simons, "Confession of the Distressed Christians," *CWMS*, p. 514.
[56] Menno Simons, *CWMS*, p. 6.
[57] Luthardt, *op. cit.*, p. 18.
[58] *Appendix* II.

nite, their principles defined and objective,[59] and their ethics proceed from a Person, through a person, to a person.

Mennonite ethics are primarily theological. Menno's religious thinking revolved around a pure church doing the will of the Father. He wanted no more formal philosophy than was required to keep his entire structure of ethics erect. The basis of this ethics was leaving the "old person" and taking on the "new person." As a new person he was dominated by new Christian ethics, new works, a new Master and a new gospel. As a priest at Pingjum he served the old master, the Catholic Church, the old world and its vices, the old ethic of the professional cleric. In later life he often lamented that it had taken him past the age of forty to learn this simple lesson. As a priest in the Catholic Church he says, "I did not order my life in accordance with my knowledge, but led an impure, carnal, fruitless life in youthful lusts, seeking nothing but earthly gain, ease, the favor of man and a great name. . . ."[60]

Like Luther, Menno received his "new man" through the faith that justified him before God.[61] All the church's philosophy and tradition could not resist the power of the Holy Spirit who opened up the Scriptures to him, gave him favor, grace, light and power to enter into that fuller life of service for the Lord. Even when he was still a priest in the Roman Church he preached this new ethic openly from the pulpit. After his conversion he resolved to right the old idolatry and perverted worship in the eyes of the Lord, who had given him grace to become a new person and see the new life with a true humbleness. His preaching produced a people that was concerned about the love of men, the fear of the Lord, the welfare and salvation of others, and the shunning of evil. The Bible now made its impact where formerly an outward ethic had tried to control in Aristotelian fashion. They were gripped by an inward consciousness of grace and wisdom that Christ imparts to all His own. Their new ethic aimed at a life of peace, which had died out to the old godless ways, submitted in full obedience to the Word and will of God, lived after the spirit which

---

[59] Warren C. Young, *A Christian Approach to Philosophy* (Wheaton, Ill.: Van Kampen Press, 1954), p. 220.
[60] John Horsch, *Menno Simons* (Scottdale, Pa.: Mennonite Publishing House, 1916), p. 24.
[61] *Appendix* II, q.

meant to be free from hell, sin, enemies, death and the devil, and to put on the Son of God and thus obtain eternal life.

With this inner consciousness of obedience arises the question of Christian liberty. Luther through his faith in *sola scriptura, sola gracia,* and *sola fide* in the finished work of the atonement of Christ became a free and justified person before God. No papal traditions had any more hold on him and he taught only what the Scriptures said. No one could curtail the liberties of the Scriptures.[62] For Menno being free still meant being under the law of the gospel. The liberty in Christ Jesus required an obedience of high ethical standards. The pressing question was *"Nachfolge"* and the application of the commandments of the Sermon on the Mount. This resulted in a constant ambivalence between reason and obedience. A living faith within contended with a compromise prompted from without. Even when the traces that hitched the Mennonites to the law were unhitched the bits with which Christ controlled them were still in their mouths. We have become free in the highest sense through Christ, through God and His Word, says Friedmann,

> but at the same time also we are truly bound in contrast to that freedom which the irreligious man means when he speaks of his "autonomy" and glories in his rationality, and to whom therefore there is scarcely a word so painful as the word "obedience." Indeed we are free and unfree at the same time. God is in us and at the same time outside of us; we are apostles as well as instruments, co-workers as well as servants of God, and both always at the same time. Here lie paradoxes for the intellectual thinker which are not to be dissolved.[63]

62 *Appendix* II, r.
63 Robert Friedmann, "Reason and Obedience: An Old Anabaptist Letter of Peter Walpot (1571) and Its Meaning," *MQR*, (Jan. 1945), XIX, 27.

CHAPTER V

HUMANISM AND MENNONITE ETHICS

DEFINITIONS

Humanism is defined as a "general disposition of mind belonging to man as such."[1] Händiges, a Mennonite, says that it is a movement "since the middle of the fifteenth century" that places man's natural and intellectual development in the foreground."[2] Edward Yoder in "Conrad Grebel a Humanist" says "humanism in a broad sense signifies the cultivation of the human spirit for its own sake."[3] To this adds Händiges, "Man sought to be free from all hierarchical and scholastic restraints (and) build a new culture and *Weltanschauung* on the foundation of the purely human."

PREPARATION

The "Dutch Reformation did not spring full-grown into the arena," says Dosker. There were many pre-Reformation tendencies that heralded the inevitable coming adjustments.[4] Just what course they would take no one knew. A constant probing and seeking for that which rightfully belonged to every individual had gone on for a long time. The skirmish during the earlier part of the sixteenth century had so thoroughly sprouted and taken root that all attempts to uproot or cut it down failed. Perhaps no branch of thought and conviction displayed this more than that of the Anabaptists. The chapter of the history of the church in Holland, where the Anabaptists were most influential and numerous, is almost too sad to read. In

1 *The Century Dictionary and Cyclopedia* prepared under the superintendency of William Dwight Whitney and Benjamin E. Smith (Revised and enlarged; New York: The Century Co., 1911), V, 2913.
2 Emil Händiges, "Humanism," *The Mennonite Encyclopedia*, edited by Harold S. Bender and C. Henry Smith (Scottdale, Pa.: Menonite Publishing House, c.1956), II, 841.
3 Edward Yoder, "Conrad Grebel A Humanist," *Mennonite Quarterly Review* (April, 29), III, 132.
4 Henry Elias Dosker, *The Dutch Anabaptists* (Philadelphia: The Judson Press, 1921), p. 8.

spite of this, the dawn had come and the day could not be far behind.

"Heresy was in the air everywhere. Scholars began to devote their new zeal to "the works of classical antiquity." Even such orthodox places of learning as Louvain had their early uneasy days. At this school, famed for its orthodoxy,

> and later on one of the fulcrums of the Inquisition, from which Erasmus was compelled to flee, through a feeling of growing uneasiness, the professors, at this earlier date were not altogether free from the suspicion of heresy.[5]

Working in these deeper convictions "Humanism was preparatory to Anabaptism."[6] According to Littell it is difficult to prove direct "classical influence upon the radicals"; nevertheless, there are marked parallels between classical primitivism and Anabaptistic thought. "We may," he further points out,

> remember the Anabaptists' debt to Erasmus, Zwingli, Oecolampadius, and especially Sebastian Franck. And, although the best-educated leadership was martyred during the first years the early leaders — Grebel, Hübmaier, Denck, Hetzer — were men of marked accomplishment in the university world, a world inspired by the new Humanistic studies.[7]

COMPARISONS

When beginning to compare we are in danger of being carried too far in the direction from Anabaptism towards Humanism. Vos draws our attention to a great difference when he says, "The Anabaptists were far more Biblical-evangelical than humanistic."[8] Littell also points out that they "rarely cited any book but the Bible." This difference in Dr. Bender's opinion is great enough to reject "the theory that the Anabaptists were children of Humanism."[9] On the other hand, Christian Neff and Vos believe that German Anabaptism "shows no small degree of influence by Erasmus," and Anabaptist writers "often quote him in their writings and speak of him in terms of great apprecia-

---

5 Dosker, op. cit., p. 9.
6 Robert Kreider, "Anabaptist and Humanism," Mennonite Quarterly Review (April, 1952), XXI, 123.
7 Franklin, Hamlin Littell, The Anabaptist View of the Church, (Second edition, revised and enlarged; Boston: Starr King Press, 1958), p. 61.
8 K. Vos and V. van der Zipp, "Desiderius Erasmus," The Mennonite Encyclopedia edited by H. S. Bender, C. Henry Smith (Scottdale, Pennsylvania: Mennonite Publishing House, 1956), p. 240.
9 Kreider, op. cit.

Humanism and Mennonite Ethics 103

tion."[10] Later in our observance[11] how this humanistic spirit cut across all denominational and political divisions, we must conclude that Humanism had a far-reaching influence on Anabaptism. Walther Köhler in his description of the execution of Michel Servet[12] makes us feel that Calvin's defiance of this spirit was in vain. In its independence it ignored the border of Calvin's theocratic state's laws. It is not surprising to find this quietistic branch of Anabaptism take such firm root in the independently spirited Netherlands.[13] Here Humanism at first proved to be the very medium required to turn speculation and dogma into "pious ignorance." Ecclesiasticism, on which all were to depend for enlightenment, was forsaken and a simple ethic from the Synoptics took its place. Humanism sponsored a "human" ethic, not an ecclesiastical one. Secondary sources which the church offered were no longer good enough. Luther saw this much clearer than Calvin who substituted the state for the Church to subject the individual's faith. In true humanistic manner Luther and Menno contended that the Scriptures contained the truth, even a hidden truth.[14] For Luther pure doctrine of faith did not depend on burning alive those who read the truth in original materials but on *sola fide*. All Humanists felt like Luther but he expressed it better than anyone else.

When Sebastian Franck says that Luther later changed in his attitude towards the Anabaptists that is true. But his reason was not his humanistic relationship to the Anabaptists but their rebellious attitude to the state and others. Menno Simons agreed with Luther but instead of attacking others he ethically attacked himself and his flock. "Is it not grievous error," he writes,

> that you suffer yourselves to be so woefully seduced by such worthless persons, and so sadly misled from one unclean sect to another?[15]

10 Vos, *op. cit.*, p. 239.
11 *Infra*.
12 Walter Köhler, *Reformation und Ketzerprozess*, Sammlung Gemeinverständlicher Vorträge und Schriften aus dem Gebiet der Theologie und Religionsgeschichte No. 22 (Tübingen und Leipzig: Verlag von J. C. B. Mohr [Paul Siebeck], 1901), p. 1.
13 August Karl Meisinger, *Erasmus von Rotterdam* (2. Auflage, Veröffentlichungen des Instituts für Reformationsforschung R. V. München Nr. 1; Berlin: Albert Mauck Co., 1948), p. 343.
14 Köhler, *op. cit.*, p. 13 and Littell, *op. cit.*, pp. 15, 51, 53.
15 Menno Simons, "Foundation of Christian Doctrine," CWMS, p. 215.

It is obviously incorrect to condemn all Anabaptists and Mennonites for the sins of the Münsterites and others, who, on top of being non-resistant, were downright rebels. Later it was proven that Luther had reasons to take a stand against them. When the Anabaptists learned to live their religion without detriment to others, and non-Anabaptists learned that there was much truth in Anabaptism, burning at the stake was no longer necessary.

It is important to note that Humanism came into open conflict "with the former world of culture" and not with religion. Luther was occupied primarily with "the faith in the Word," and remained spiritually aloof from Humanism. His watchword was "from Aristotle back to Paul and Augustine." He was primarily concerned with the Scriptures and the gospel of justification by faith and left the organization of his message of law and gospel to Philip Melanchthon. His new theology was the result of reforming the traditional message of the Church. The message of the Anabaptists and Humanists was the result of reinstituting the first principles of the Church. The first served the purpose of the Reformation, the second the fashioning of a new ethic denuded of tradition and conformity. It accepted the Word only as a direct promoter of faith in Christ Jesus and obedience to do all that it demanded.

Proof of the fulfillment of these demands were repentance and obedience. The Anabaptists were more imbued with the culture and practice of religious principles than with the establishment and attestation of such principles. They considered man "the measure of the universe and the architect of his own fortunes,"[16] for God, and not man, was the architect of faith and fate. Men were equal before God and needed none to interpret Scripture and religion. They went back to the Scriptures and to some extent to the Fathers, and lifted out directly what to them was the true way of life. All that was required of them was obedience to these truths directly from God.

Through a clearer awareness of self and personal responsibility in matters of faith, the people awoke from serfdom and proceeded to maturity.[17] In this aroused spirit of investigation and proclamation Menno went far beyond Erasmus. He did not only accept that which came out of the enlightenment of the

---

16 Kreider, *op. cit.*
17 Händiges, *op. cit.*, pp. 841, 842.

Renaissance but he also had the courage and self-reliance to disagree openly when his convictions differed. Humanism taught him to search for himself whether the Scriptures made allowance for infant baptism. This independence and intuitiveness became one of his very pronounced characteristics. He told his followers to "put their trust in Christ and His Word and in the practices of the Apostles. Where Humanism had been characterized by an increased interest in Greek and classical models, Menno admonished "by the grace of God to refrain from all false doctrine" and penetrate the truth. Niebuhr points out that rationalism in Humanism tended to influence the modification of doctrine[18] which men like Menno resisted right from the beginning. We have no evidence that Humanism sponsored the simple Gospel for salvation; it did, however, prepare the way. Where it was concerned with the enlightenment of the spirit through art and culture, the Anabaptists believed that this enlightenment came by knowledge of the Bible and by the grace of God. Their higher spiritual life was not conditioned by art, knowledge and culture alone but also by faith which said, "But his spirit beareth witness with our spirit that we are the children of God."

Where Humanism had great confidence in rational ability and historical consciousness Anabaptism "was primitivistic and eschatological. Its norm was the past and the hope for the future was the Restitution of the Early Church." In this church every member was a worthy, believing individual. Those who proved undependable were not considered members but "Judases." Everyone worthy of membership heard the voice calling to obedience, believed, accepted and rightly fulfilled the work of the Lord.[19] Humanism inspired the Anabaptists but did not have any power of its own to transform; what was needed had to be much deeper and potent. The required inward renewal, religious transformation and spiritual revival experience, depended on a Higher Power.[20] To them evidence of such were religious toleration and examplary moral living.

Erasmus had advocated "that the common man should drink

18 Richard Niebuhr, *The Social Sources of Denominationalism* (Living Age Books; New York: Meridian Books, 1957), pp. 99-102.
19 John Horsch, *Mennonites in Europe* (Second edition, slightly revised; Scottdale, Pa.; Mennonite Publishing House, 1950), p. 339.
20 Händiges, *op. cit.*

at the fountain of life"[21] The Anabaptist fathers wanted to satisfy their desire to know, the same as the Humanists. When the Swiss Brethren arrived on the scene in 1524 Bible instruction assemblies sprang up everywhere. Simple readers and interpreters like Andreas Castelberger had tremendous influence; they taught that everyone could understand and live by their teachings. The humanistic thirst to know cut across all confessional and political lines. But where Humanism wanted a purer Latin the Anabaptists wanted a return to the purer life of the Early Church and a revitalization of that which later Latin influence had corrupted.

"Humanism was in part an attitude to life, aspiring to fulfillment rather than renunciation."[22] The Anabaptists in their aim to get "back to the sources" and leaving behind all self-appointed authorities became so sensitive that they were even concerned with the mode of baptism practiced in the Early Church. Their spirit gave them no permission to deviate in any way from the unquestionable practices in the initial stages of Christianity. After the Swiss Brethren had disputed at length with Zwingli they came together once more to strengthen each other in the Word and determine how to remain faithful to their convictions irrespective of what would happen to them. The truth they wanted was not that of the Greeks but that of the Apostles. This became the basic ethics of their decisions. "To the Humanists nothing was alien," says Bainton; "all learning, all systems, and even all religions should be studied and sympathetically understood."[23]

Conrad Grebel (1498-1526) by training was a Humanist and by conviction an Anabaptist. Theology for him became an ethics and conversion an open door into Christ's laboratory where to experiment with these ethics. His assurance of success was his conversion and implicit obedience to his Master. The tests he had to pass were submitted by none other than Him who said, "come unto me all ye that labor." In spirit this was total Humanism. He and the brethren wrote their dissertation only from original sources.

[21] Harold S. Bender, *Conrad Grebel c.1498-1526 the Founder of the Swiss Brethren Sometimes Called Anabaptists* (Scottdale, Pa.: Herald Press, 1950), p. 90.
[22] Roland H. Bainton, "*The Travail of Religious Liberty*, Nine Biographical Studies (Philadelphia: The Westminster Press, 1951), p. 56.
[23] *Ibid.*, p. 56.

Felix Manz had learned to master Hebrew and Greek and the Bible was absorbed by him in true humanistic style. Hubmaier too, thoroughly prepared in the Latin schools of Augsburg and speaking as a true Humanist, said,

> I listened to my teacher and how zealously I took down his lectures — an industrious reader, an untiring listener, and a busy teacher of the other hearers. So I won the master's degree with the highest praise.... What progress I made is attested by my learned lecturer, my sermons before the people and my scholastic exercises.[24]

Like the other Anabaptist leaders he made constant reference to the Fathers and Erasmus. He agreed with Menno in that he used the materials at hand as a Humanist, but in the application of these materials he was an Anabaptist. Never could he nor his brethren be induced, like Erasmus for instance, to compromise and be more "human" than "honest" to avoid conflicts. They wanted to be ultra honest at all times; mistakes they made in their weaker moments they corrected with extreme severity to themselves.

Hans Denck seems to have been the super Humanist in his approach to the question of the "freedom of the will" and unconditional liberty of faith and conscience, and his principle of tolerance. In Basel he got into close touch with Oecolampadius and applied himself to the study of the classical languages, especially Hebrew, and he belonged to a circle of students who associated with Erasmus. His sensitive and contemplative manner had definite humanistic tendencies. As a true Humanist he translated, together with Hetzer, the Old Testament Prophets and published them at Worms in 1527. In the ethics of his productions he was far above the Humanists of his day, but in what he produced he ranks as one of them. His philosophical approach to the problem of evil is Humanistic, but what he writes is mystical and Anabaptistic. With his "free inquiry, particularly with regard to the historical documents of the Church and the Christian religion itself" he belonged to the other Anabaptist brethren.

Under the spirit of "free inquiry" the Anabaptists focused their attention on baptism which led Menno by way of the Christian Fathers back to the Apostolic Church; and after he had established what the pre-Humanists said, he quoted Eras-

---

24 Händiges, "Humanism," *op. cit.*, II, 842.

mus and others of his day. Mennonite ethics have always aimed to go back to first principles in their attempt to put their extremely high ideals into practice. Many times when opposition would get too fierce they fled to new areas and tried it all over again. Even today society seems to have only a partial solution for what they stand for. They are dismissed as "queer" and not sufficiently "advanced."

The cardinal principle of Mennonite ethics is based on love, tolerance and voluntarism as these were practiced in the earliest stages of Christianity. Dorothy Thompson, after staying in Mennonite homes for a while, wrote: "It is perfectly true — observable in everyday life — that whatever is done for love is well performed, and that the element of love makes the performance voluntary, pleasurable and free."[25] This voluntarism was part of the Erasmian tradition even if he arrived at it rationally where the Mennonites came to it spiritually. Nevertheless, Erasmus stirred them to action when he said: "The sum of our religion is peace and unanimity and these can scarcely stand unless we define them as little as possible and in many things leave each one free to follow his own judgment."[26]

ERASMUS

Erasmus also entered into the mystical tradition of the Anabaptists. In perfect Anabaptist language he asserted that a Christian must show with his conduct rather than his tongue that he is a follower of Christ. "What does it matter," he says, "if there be no blasphemy of the tongue if the whole life breathes blasphemy against God? If the Beatitudes which bless the meek and the persecuted are called a lie? What blasphemy could be more detestable?"

For Erasmus the welfare of the state and society lay in the morality and intellectual enlightenment of every citizen.[27] Controversies of his day appeared of small consequence to him because they pertained merely to the external, not affecting the spiritual. It was supreme blasphemy to him "to turn the spir-

---

25 Dorothy Thompson, "Queer People," reprint from the January issue of *Ladies' Home Journal* (Philadelphia, Pennsylvania: The Curtis Publishing Company, Independence Square, 1952), pp. 1, 2.
26 Bainton, *op. cit.*, p. 58.
27 "Voor Erasmus was al het heil van staat en maatschappij altijds slechts een kwestie geweest van persoonlijke moraal en intellectuele verlichting"; J. Huizinga, *Verzamelde Werken, Biografie* (Haarlem: H. D. Tjeenk Willink & Zoon N. V., 1950), VI, 146.

itual into the carnal, to burn men simply for observing kosher laws." In his eyes it was monstrous and ineffective perversion of religion for it was only the right spirit that mattered. This convergence of Humanism and Mysticism was the source of later liberal Catholicism and Protestantism and even became a part of the Anabaptist ethic to the consternation of Menno and Luther.[28] Here again, says Mussolini, appeared the spirit of Huss, who "not only preached (but) also practiced, and like Francis of Assisi, wed *coram populo* and Dame Poverty."[29] Word and spirit were placed together and each driven into the extreme.[30] It was only natural for Anabaptist baptismal candidates to ask for baptism on the basis of their own investigation, understanding and acceptance. The Anabaptists sensed correctly that Humanism in its origin was not an academic movement but one that rooted deep in a spirit that the Middle Ages had left uncultivated. It now nourished not only intellectual exercises but also furnished the conditions required to germinate the seed that promised to bring forth rich spiritual and cultural fruits, so far unknown and unexpected.[31]

Rufus M. Jones interprets Anabaptism in terms of mysticism. Wenger says that the Anabaptists vigorously objected to the mysticism of their day on the grounds that they were Biblicists and literalists. When one observes how Humanism and Mysticism work together in "diverting attention from dogma to experience,"[32] giving a new feeling of life to religion and in bringing forth new piety, *devotio moderna*,[33] allowance must be made for Humanism to have operated in the mysticism of the Anabaptists.

In their desire for freedom of conscience and interpretation of the Scriptures, the Anabaptists went beyond the thinking of their day. They found God not only in the established churches and within ecclesiastically recognized forms but wherever two or three were gathered in His name. Those who no longer recognized the established church as the mediator between be-

---

28 Bainton, *op. cit.*, p. 59.
29 Benito Mussolini, *John Huss*, translated by Clifford Parker (New York: Albert & Charles Boni, 1929), p. 75.
30 S. Hoekstra, *Beginselen en Leer der Oude Doopsgezinden*, vergeleken met die van de overige Protestanten (Amsterdam: P. N. Van Kampen, 1863), p. 97.
31 *Appendix*, II, s.
32 Wenger, *op. cit.*, p. 9.
33 Bainton, *op. cit.*, p. 20.

lievers and the grace of God were called heretics. As the spirit of Humanism spread their number increased everywhere. Even the great Vadian of Vienna University, Conrad Grebel's brother-in-law, said that Aristotle was no god and there was no reason why he should be slavishly and religiously followed. The time had come for the spirit of emancipation to disseminate the impelling desire to be different from the Latin cleric.[34] Many wanted a practical education in which many Anabaptists already excelled. One such outstanding example was Pilgrim Marpeck (1495-1556), an engineer much in demand for his skill and an Anabaptist preacher.

Erasmus had direct influence upon the Anabaptists through the *"Nachfolge Christi"* he himself had learned at Deventer and later handed down to them.[35] He had appreciated the honest and unpretentious atmosphere of Deventer and found its life of peace and obedience quite attractive. But even though the kernel of this kind of life was sweet to him, the shell of self around it which would have to be broken he found too hard. He preferred to avoid all conflicts at the expense of an unreserved obedience and honesty which alone can furnish a total and abiding peace. He, for instance, did not care what happened to Luther or how many were martyred for their faith. All he wanted was to be left alone and permitted to continue his own independent humanistic thinking, utterance and idealism.[36] "He was primarily too intellectual," says Walker,

> to have sympathy with the Lutheran revelation. . . . To him Christianity was but the fullest expression through Christ. Primarily the Sermon on the Mount was the universal and essentially ethical religion. . . . He had little feeling for the sacramental . . . elements in religion. A universal ethical theism, having its highest illustration in Christ, was his idea.[37]

Even if the Anabaptists and Lutherans were not in the same boat with him, the same winds blew into their sails.

Erasmus nourished his idea of a "universal ethical theism"

---

[34] Verner Näf, "Vadian und seine Stadt St. Gallen," *Humanist in Wien* (St. Gallen: Buchdruckerei, H. Tschudy & Co., c. 1944), *passim*.
[35] Kreider, *op. cit.*, p. 123.
[36] G. Sihler, "Humanism," *New Schaff-Herzog Encyclopedia*, editors Samuel Macauley Jackson, Lefferts A. Loetscher (Grand Rapids: Baker Book House, 1950), p. 402.
[37] Williston Walker, *A History of the Christian Church* (N. Y. Charles Scribner's Sons, 1945), p. 330.

by reviving "a knowledge of Christian sources."[38] But just this revival gave him the same concern that the Anabaptists always voiced. He wrote to Fabricius at Basel, "My chief fear is that with the revival of Greek literature there may be a revival of paganism. There are Christians who are Christians in name but are Gentiles at heart."[39] Apparently there was reason for the Swiss Brethren to stress greater obedience and earnestness than Zwingli and Luther had manifested.

Erasmus' direct influence is evidenced in two other ways. There are large numbers of Erasmian citations found in Menno's writings.[40] He wrote about "the very wise and learned Erasmus of Rotterdam, a man who has read and understood all the worthwhile writers of the world." This acquaintance is also evident in the writings of Adam Pastor and Dietrich Philips who may have been less influenced. There are also examples of sixteenth century Dutch Anabaptists who believe in the freedom of the will as defended by Erasmus against Luther.[41] "On baptism and communion, the Trinity and the freedom of the will" writes Neff,

> Erasmus offered so much that was in accord with Anabaptist teaching, that he was suspected not only of promoting their cause, but even of being one of them (Rembert, 26). In designating the Bible as the sole source of Christian truth, in promoting the use of the Bible in the vernacular, in stressing that "Christianity is essentially a life of discipleship of Christ" he expressed common Anabaptist demands.[42]

This "Imitation of Christ," however, was to Eramus not so much a response to divine grace as man's rational capacity. He thought a person should be called a Christian when his outward conduct displayed such qualities. Menno maintained no one is a Christian without an inward evangelical faith, love and irreproachable life. Erasmus never stresses grace but points rather to a perfectibility achieved through effort and the right exercise of the freedom of the will.[43] Nowhere does he refer to a mediated Christian conduct but only to one based totally

---

38 *Ibid.*
39 Sihler, *op. cit.*, p. 402.
40 Menno Simons, *CWMS, op. cit.*, pp. 138, 248, 270, 520, 695, 802, 803, 822, 862, etc.
41 Vos, *op. cit.*, p. 239.
42 Christian Neff and H. S. Bender, "Desiderius Erasmus," *ME.* II, 239.
43 Kreider, *op. cit.*, p. 124.

on self-effort.⁴⁴ Menno also leaned towards semi-pelagianism, even though he taught that Christ's redemption of man through mediation was absolutely imperative.

According to Preserved Smith, Erasmus was "the champion of undogmatic Christianity," neglecting doctrine and ceremony, and placing "the emphasis on the ethical and the reasonable."⁴⁵ Menno follows again but demands the abolition of all extra-Biblical ceremonies and institutions and that theology and doctrine never be discussed as a separate system but always in relation to holiness and obedience.⁴⁶ Erasmus cultivated a detachment from the institutional phases of Christianity, favoring a more agreeable psychological and religious environment. As for Menno, the Bible was the only factor of importance for the Christian faith.⁴⁷

In spite of these similarities the reasons for separating from the world were different for Menno than for Erasmus. The Humanists went their separate ways for the sake of satisfying their craving to establish man's worth for man's sake. The Anabaptists separated from the world so as to be fully at the disposal of God for God's sake. For Menno "Christianity was more than faith only; it was faith and works: the resolute abandonment . . . of all carnal strife and war and all the sin of the worldly social order."⁴⁸ The Brethren of the Common Life were held in great esteem by Menno as well as by Erasmus.⁴⁹ Menno spoke their language when he turned to the Lord and gave the world a farewell, for which he was mocked and sorely defamed.⁵⁰ When Erasmus reconciled the claims "of piety with those of reason" Menno said,

> we prefer to endure misery, poverty, tribulation, hunger, thirst, heat, cold, bonds, and death in our mortal bodies, and continue in the Word of the Lord, rather than to lead secure, easy lives with the world, and for the sake of a short, transitory life ruin our souls.⁵¹

---

44 Leonhard von Muralt, *Glaube und Lehre der Schweizerischen Wiedertäufer in der Reformationszeit* (Zürich: Kommisionsverlag Beer & Co., 1938), p. 6.
45 Preserved Smith, *Erasmus: A Study of His Life, Ideals and Place in History* (New York: Harper and Brothers, Publishers, 1923), p. xi.
46 John C. Wenger, "Notes," *CWMS, op. cit.*, p. xi.
47 Muralt, *op. cit.*, p. 6.
48 Bender, "A Brief Biography of Menno Simons," *CWMS, op. cit.*, p. 4.
49 *Appendix* II, t.
50 *Appendix* II, u.
51 Menno Simons, "Foundation of Christian Doctrine," *CWMS, op. cit.*, p. 177.

Menno expressed his ethics in Humanistic terms but instead of being rationally obedient he was spiritually obedient. His ethics, unlike those of Erasmus, were not a "discountenancing obscuranticism with a cherished morality"[52] but, since "the church was the representative agent of Christ on earth, he, as its member, was to keep it holy and pure in life and doctrine, and was to give a faithful witness of Christ until He came."

HUMANISTIC TEACHING

Beyond the direct Erasmian influence on the Anabaptists was the Humanistic teaching of peace and the freedom of the will. To the Anabaptists and Mennonites persecution and martyrdom were very real. They understood only too well what Erasmus meant when he said the "Church was founded in blood."[53] The Humanists had revived the Stoic idea of the inner kingship of God and man (Acts 17:28).[54] This kingship in the case of the Anabaptists was brought about by conversion and obedience which was so real to them that all that this world had to offer did not compare with all the riches awaiting them in heaven after this woeful life. One of their outstanding Scripture verses is "What shall a man be profited if he shall gain the whole world and forfeit his own soul (Matt. 16:26)?" Menno knew Seneca,[55] who, when he saw the gladiatorial sports said, "*Homo sacra res homini*"[56] (sacred man degraded into a tool of slavery). Through such evaluation of man the Humanists rekindled an interest in primitive Christianity and its negative attitude to war. "The rulers of this day," wrote Erasmus,

> govern all by the sword and whereas war is so savage a thing that it rather befits beasts than man, so outrageous that the very Poets feigned it came from the Furies, so pestilent that it corrupts all man's manners, so injust that it is best executed by the worst of men, so wicked that it has no agreement with Christ; and yet, omitting all the other, they make this their only business. Zeal, Piety, and Valour have invented a new way by which a man may

52 Preserved Smith, *op. cit.*, p. xi.
53 Desiderius Erasmus, *The Praise of Folly*, with a short life of the author by Hendrik van Loon of Rotterdam (New York: Walter J. Black, 1942), p. 220.
54 O. J. Heering, *The Fall of Christianity*, translated from the Dutch by J. W. Thompson (First American edition; New York: Fellowship Publications, 1945), pp. 61, 62.
55 Menno Simons, "Reply to False Accusations," *CWMS, op. cit.*, p. 562.
56 Heering, *op. cit.*

kill his brother without the least breach of that charity which, by the command of Christ, one Christian owes another.⁵⁷

This writing had a great influence on the Dutch Remonstrants and the Mennonites. Even today do their libraries give prominence to Erasmus' peace literature. Such sponsors of peace as Ludocius Vives and Sebastian Franck, who felt that the ethic of pacifism and the Primitive Church, belonged together, remained solitary figures. To Erasmus, on the other hand, Humanism and a certain pacifism were inseparable.

Ludocius Vives' (1492-1540) basic "motivation was the restoration and maintenance of Christian unity. Since he did not believe . . . in the possibility of world peace" in human terms, "he worked for inner peace in the individual and looked forward to real peace in eternity." A war of peace "battling against all alarms, revolution and senselessness with thorough demonstration," says Erasmus as the more devoted to Humanism, "does not belong to the Kingdom of Christ but is nothing else than a devilish, bestial, unchristian, and inhuman thing. . . ."⁵⁸

The question of free will was revived in the sixteenth century when the Protestant Reformers espoused the Augustinian viewpoint in the controversy of Pelagius. "Erasmus, Sebastian Franck, the Anabaptists and certain other dissenters generally rejected the Augustinian position" and often went to the "opposite extreme of asserting complete human freedom." These men asserted that man's ability to will was from God but what he willed was his own. They "held that within certain limits God had granted free will and that each person could at least either accept or reject divine grace offered to all.⁵⁹ The Anabaptists held various opinions as to the precise degree of freedom enjoyed by men. They were not in total agreement with Erasmus, and yet, he offered so much in accord with their teaching that he was suspected of being one of them.

The Dutch Anabaptists, in the great majority of cases, were believers in the freedom of the will as defended by Erasmus against Luther.⁶⁰ They asserted that our wills are depraved by the fall and in need of salvation through grace and faith, not

---

57 Erasmus, "The Price of Folly," *op. cit.*
58 H. S. Bender, "The Pacifism of the Sixteenth Century Anabaptism," *Mennonite Quarterly Review*, XXX (January, 1956), p. 5.
59 E. J. Wray, "Free Will," *ME, op. cit.* I, 387.
60 Vos, "Desiderius Erasmus," *ME, op. cit.*, I, 239.

through merit and good works. Menno, Philips, Marlpeck and many others took their stand with Melanchthon and Erasmus against Luther's "stiffest possible assertions of determinism and predestination".[61] Those who act only as their reason dictates never do anything wrong and therefore never have occasion to repent. This was unacceptable to the Anabaptists for, they said, the fall of man had not affected man's will but had perverted it in such a way that he did not want to accept salvation by grace but through his own reasoning. Where Humanism demanded freedom of investigation and the exercise of the will, Anabaptism said, for the very reason that man is on his own, his will is bound to violate the rules of conduct as laid down by Scripture and he must repent. No works, merit, or reasoning of his own are enough to right wrongs; they have to be forgiven by the grace of God. This happens when man's will is congruent with God's will. Humanism taught the Anabaptists that since man has a free will he will commit wrong acts. How right or wrong these were, Scripture defined. It was Humanism that made them Biblical Evangelicals.[62]

Several leading Anabaptists were scholars who had gone beyond the thinking of their age. Grebel, Hubmaier, Obbe Phillips, Hans Denck, and others had been students and independent thinkers and accepted what Humanism had inherited from the Renaissance. This inheritance directed outward thinking into space and an inward thinking into the soul. The outward resulted in momentous discoveries about the laws of the universe, and the sciences drove men to discover and explore hitherto unknown lands and seas. The inward thinking entered the soul of man and moved him, south of the Alps, to produce the finest in the arts and north of the Alps the finest in religion and literature.[63] This independent thinking accepted no borders and often resulted in sectarianism. In spite of the fiercest opposition from the Catholic Church, it served in a measure to check dogmatic intolerance within Catholicism and proved a powerful solvent when transmitted to the Reformation.[64]

When the Anabaptists had the choice of following the independents or Humanists they chose the latter. This involved

---

61 Walker, *op. cit.*, p. 353.
62 Neff, "Desiderius Erasmus," *op. cit.*, p. 240.
63 Julius von Pflug-Hartung, *Im Morgenrot der Reformation*, Herausgegeben in verbindung mit Joh. Haller, *et al.* (Stuttgart: Wilhelm Herget Verlag, n.d.), p. iv.
64 Bainton, *op. cit.*, p. 20.

the direct use of the New Testament, to follow the practices of the Primitive Church, and accept the Bible as full authority. "I by the grace of God," said Menno, "seek and shall seek nothing upon earth but the unadulterated Word of our Lord Jesus Christ and that according to Scripture." The old allegorical interpretation of Scripture was left behind. In no uncertain terms does Menno voice his opposition to chiliastic speculations. He calls them "dreams . . . fantasies, enthusiasms, rhetorical figures, and . . . magic illusions ahead of the wisdom of the Holy Spirit."[65] He accepted Luther's formula of justification by faith with the insistence that this faith be evidenced by *Bussfertigkeit* (a repentant attitude) and newness of character. This had kinship with Erasmus' *devotio moderna in his Philosophia Christi* where the Church is a brotherhood composed of voluntary members, who, through faith, are devoted to the love ethic and mutual aid. The Hutterites went so far in this that they arrived at Christian Communism. Anabaptism in its ethical emphasis was related to the Erasmian tradition of a moral reformation, but where the latter was a philosophical concept the first was a living faith prompted by an earnest intention to actualize the will of God. At no time do we find the commitment in the Humanists that there was in the Anabaptists. Even if Erasmus had a well-thought-through peace plan he was not and never became a non-resistant. The Anabaptist's acceptance of original sin, free will, individual responsibility and voluntarism was never predicated on man's independent and inherent moral authority; it was grace. For the Anabaptists ethics were Christocentric and for the Humanists anthropocentric.

At no time did the Anabaptist fathers admit that religious faith was subject to external restraint and coercion. Where the Franciscans and Jesuits accepted unreserved obedience to the founders of their orders and to the pope, the Anabaptists pledged the same to God and the Holy Spirit. Freedom of conscience accruing from unrestricted investigation was their most highly prized heritage of the Renaissance. When Joachim Vadianus followed Zwingli in accepting predestination and thus curtailing the free will, he was chided by his humanistically trained brother-in-law and earliest Anabaptist, Conrad Grebel, "Why do you exercise only the power and arm of the flesh, using the

Scriptures against us instead of free will?"⁶⁶ The Swiss Brethren, refusing to be shackled by Zwingli and others, were truer to the principles of Humanism than even the great Vadianus.

The early Anabaptists sought to reflect their faith in a universal church setting. Historically they saw the church demonstrating God's marvellous grace and providence. They wrote their experiences in true Humanistic fashion in diaries and other records. It is noteworthy that Humanism and Anabaptism sprang up in the same places. This indicated that methods and attitudes were the same even when the specific ideas and doctrines were not. Humanism nurtured Anabaptism; where the former apprehended truth intellectually, the latter used a Christian norm in promoting faith and minimizing reason. The proof of this was the dearth of missionary effort on the part of the Humanists while for the Anabaptists it was their foremost interest. This was a natural consequence. Anabaptism belonged to the common people. The Humanists had their eye upon man and the end of man was to know man. The Anabaptists had their eye upon God and the proof that they saw and knew God was that they loved man.⁶⁷

ANABAPTIST LEADERS

Besides the Erasmian effects on Mennonite ethics we have the humanistic spirit and training that their early leaders were exposed to. Perhaps most agree that Conrad Grebel, the founder of the Swiss Brethren, played a very great role in delineating all Anabaptist and Mennonite conduct to this day. For eight of his most impressionistic and important years, he was an out-and-out Humanist and part of that time a thorough Zwinglian. These formative years included the time he spent in Basel with Clarean, a Humanist director of his *bursa,* three years in Vienna with Vadian, two years of storm and stress in Paris under Clarean's influence, and two years, except for two months in Basel, in Zurich, where he was vitally associated with Zwingli.⁶⁸

"In his student days at Basel, Vienna and Paris, Grebel imbibed the Humanism which was popular in that day."⁶⁹ In Basel he received a "thorough discipline in Latin," in Paris

66 Kreider, *op. cit.,* p. 139.
67 Kreider, *op. cit.,* p. 139.
68 Bender, "Conrad Grebel . . . ." *op. cit.,* p. 65.
69 Kenneth, Scott Latourette, *A History of Christianity* (New York: Harper & Brothers, c.1953), p. 780.

in the Greek language and literature, and in Vienna a training in the Humanistic arts. The time he spent with Vadian was "most fruitful for his intellectual development.[70]

Back in Zurich, Grebel's friends and acquaintances included prominent scholars. On the basis of conscience and ethical principles he disapproved of his father's method of receiving pensions. His loyalty to his home and patriotism were typically humanistic. Like all Swiss Humanists he showed great interest in geography and pacifism. This shying from warfare may have been his opposition to the mercenary military practices of his time, but more likely it was the result of the study of the New Testament and the Fathers in their originals. Upon Grebel's return to Zurich in 1520 he read a pacifistic manuscript entitled, *Philirenum*, by Ryconius, which circled among his friends, and was given to him by Zwingli. He read it with great delight and expressed the hope that it might be published. The writing drew heavily from Erasmus' *Querela Pacis* and had great merit; but for some reasons the circle discouraged its publication.

Humanism came from Italy across the Alps to Basel, Vienna and Paris, where it lost much of its Italian paganizing tendencies. Here religious and ethical indifferentism gave way to pious and spiritual ways."[71] This does not mean that all the northern Humanists had an interest in religion as had Erasmus. Many of them were deeply attached to their homeland and people and lacked appreciation for the cosmopolitan. There non-Erasmians sponsored a provincial ethic not based on the universal message of Scripture. To these belonged Vadian and Clarean, Conrad Grebel's teachers, who taught their student to think after them.[72] This was Grebel's background when he and his friends formed the incisive Anabaptist movement.[73]

Grebel's position as a Humanist before his conversion differed with that of Erasmus only in direction — they remained on the same plane. After he had promised God that he would be obedient to his convictions he also chose another level than Erasmus held. Where Grebel aimed to revive, Erasmus wanted reform; where the one was a biblical Humanist the other was a

---

70 Bender, "Conrad Grebel. . . ." *op. cit.*, p. 66.
71 Edward Yoder, "Conrad Grebel as a Humanist," *op. cit.*, p. 139.
72 Bender, "Conrad Grebel. . . .," *op. cit.*, p. 69.
73 Balfort E. Bax, *Rise and Fall of the Anabaptists*, Part III of *The Social Side of the Reformation in Germany* (London: Swan Sonnenschein & Co., Ltd., 1903), p. 11.

religious Humanist. Grebel and his co-obstreperists and former Dominican priests, Blaurock and Manz, left the church where Erasmus didn't.

After his conversion Grebel became a biblical, humanistic enthusiast; a forerunner of the Mennonites who still are branded as "enthusiasts" (Schwärmer). He became "a man on fire for God" with an intense desire to know and do the will of God at any cost. "The Scriptures were to be the norm of his thinking, his rule of faith, and his guide in life."[74] His objective was to live the life of an entirely obedient Christian. Erasmus, on the other hand, saw in Christianity

> an undogmatic, simple, practical morality, which had found its fullest and most perfect expression in the early Christian Church of apostolic times with its spiritual unity based upon mutual love.... Through the "renaissance" of this Christianity he hoped for peace between nations as well as the exorcism of all dogmatic strife within the church.

The Erasmian Humanism had no "conversion motive" nor the revival experience resulting in a will to obey God. His aim was to acquire knowledge, religion and morality through an obedience to his own intellect. His chief interest was "the moral, religious, and ecclesiastical reform of the existing Christian society ..., the new learning ... (and) a more peaceful, sane, and Christian way of living."

Erasmus was a rather free spirit and patriotism did not mean much to him. He lived in different countries and was quite at home in all of them. The Anabaptists were humanistic peasants attached to the soil (Scholle). The former had a cosmopolitan and international outlook and "lived in the rarefied atmosphere of intellectual and moralistic theory without practical and personal commitment and sharing of local and cultural obligation, loyalty and patriotism." Grebel's Humanism called for a "solid character, moral earnestness, clean living and a strong personality. He was far removed from the paganism of the Italian Humanists and was traditionally sound and evangelical.

When looking at the Humanism as founded chiefly by Grebel we note three contributing factors. The first is his contact with Erasmian Humanism and its conception of Christianity

---

[74] Wenger, "Glimpses of Mennonite History and Doctrine," *op. cit.*, pp. 18, 19.

which was "primarily an ethical culture based upon simple, universal and religious ideas."[75] These ideas had their roots in the Sermon on the Mount that called for a universal brotherhood based on everyone's need of redemption, contrasting with a religion of dogmatic theology. Erasmus' cosmopolitan love and dogmatic theology constantly relied on definitions furnished by the mind.

Second, the Anabaptists depended on an ethics expressed dogmatically in the Scriptures. What they were they were; they could not change their views, because Scripture demanded faithfulness unto death. Erasmus depended on his mind and not on his soul and heart for the emotions that usually accompany religious experience and love. "The mind," he says, "ought to be fortified well in advance by prayer, the words of the wise, the teachings of Holy Scripture, the examples of pious men and especially of Christ." Nevertheless, when he pointed to the Scriptures and not to the church and tradition for the knowledge required for the Christian ethic he did the Anabaptist a great service. Scripture, prayer and piety instilled a "brotherly love" that the rational mind could not grasp. Erasmus stayed with Romans 7 and pointed the Anabaptists to Romans 8. When man relies on his own ability for his ethics he comes to the discouraging place where St. Paul found himself at the close of chapter 7. Even if the Anabaptists went beyond Erasmus, the spirit of the "fuller" Christian moved him to say that "brotherly charity has urged me that I at least promote and aid your pious proposal to the best of my ability."[76] It was through his influence that the Anabaptists became a "definite and permanent group,"[77] which had its roots not in rationalism, intellectualism, and Humanism but in implicit obedience to the Master.

Third, the Humanists as well as the Anabaptists withdrew at first from society for religious reasons. In time the Humanists again took their place in society but not all the Anabaptists, who still insist on being different from the world. They, like the Humanists, take their religious expression out of the monastery and put it on the street, into the family, behind the

---

75 Bender, "Conrad Grebel. . . .," *op. cit.*, pp. 68-74.
76 Matthew Spinka, editor, *Advocates of Reform*, Vol. xiv of *The Library of Christian Classics* (Philadelphia: The Westminster Press, 1953), pp. 294, 378.
77 Bender, "Conrad Grebel. . . .," *op. cit.*, p. 14, 213.

plough. It is still the practice of many Mennonite ministers to work alongside their parishioners.

Erasmus did not believe that a monastic life was more pious and holy than a secular life. "Monasticism is not godliness," he says, but "a kind of life, either useful or useless to anyone depending on one's habit of body and of temperament." After chiding the church for its misuse of monasticism, he, in Mennonite fashion, exhorts her to establish godliness everywhere, and not give the impression that there is no Christianity outside the cowl. He points her to gaze upon those things that give a true image of Christ.[78] Harold Bender believes that since Grebel's words are strongly colored with Pauline thoughts it is possible that he used the paraphrases of Erasmus' books on the New Testament.[79] Nevertheless, having been trained in the schools of the Brethren of the Common Life, he does not believe that removal from society in order to obtain a holier life is fruitless. "By these efforts," he goes on, "the generous natural qualities can be kindled to the love of divine Scripture."[80] Here Luther and Grebel said "no." To them the ethics of a Christian do not root in natural qualities, not in man, but in Christ. Grebel dwells on this in his epigrams (1524).[81]

Menno Simons' frequent quotes from Erasmus indicate that he also was influenced by him. It was through Reatus Rhenanus (1485-1547), the Humanist scholar and friend of Erasmus, that he got acquainted with Eusebius' Greek *Church History* and original material on baptism, which, together with the ideal of a pure church, was to him the cardinal factor of his doctrine. His material was of Humanist origin but the doctrine and ethics were his own. The Humanists were true to their name and hoped to achieve their goal by human means. The Anabaptists started with the Scriptures and the human heart, and then developed their own ethic revolving around adult baptism and a confession of a willingness to accept Christ as Lord of their daily lives.

The radical difference between Humanism and Anabaptism was that the former had a reformation on the level of man, the latter a rebirth from a level higher than man; the one had a this-worldly ethic, the other an other-worldly ethic.

---

78 Spinka, *op. cit.*, pp. 378-79.
79 Bender, "Conrad Grebel. . . .," *op. cit.*, p. 81.
80 Spinka, *op. cit.*, p. 379.
81 Philips, *op. cit., EoH*, p. 163.

MEDIATOR

In conclusion it is important to point out that the question of a mediator became an important issue for Humanists and Anabaptists alike. The former looked for "mediation" and the latter for a Mediator. The Humanists resorted to man's own capacities; the Anabaptists accepted nothing less than the Mediator of the Scriptures, which meant a denial of self to make room for the Mediator. For the Humanists mediation meant more of self and less of the beyond. A most typical example was Spinoza who sought this "self-salvation" in the self of nature. "Humanism is concerned," according to Händiges,

> with the creation of a new culture; Anabaptism with the realization of a new kingdom of God, including the relations of earthly life. To Humanism knowledge was an end in itself; to Anabaptism it was merely a tool of preparation. Humanism promotes the feeling of life and aesthetic enjoyment of life; Anabaptism demands self-denial and willingness to bear the cross to the point of martyrdom. In many of its representatives Humanism teaches that what pleases is permissible; Anabaptism requires fulfillment of the divine commands in the obedience of faith. Humanism pursues a philanthropic ideal and creates an elite of the spirit; Anabaptism seeks a reconciliation of difference in love to the brethren. Humanism is generally indifferent to the Christian ordinances; Anabaptism recognizes in the ordinances of Christ and the apostles a means for the realization of the New Testament Church.[82]

Anabaptism in the sixteenth century and later felt the responsibility of disseminating its message as a heavy burden. For the success of its promulgation Humanism must be given much credit. In every transition from the old to the new the medium is vital. For Anabaptism Humanism was this medium.

82 Händiges, op. cit., p. 243.

CHAPTER VI

MENNONITE ETHICS AND PIETISM

Mennonite Ethics and Seventeenth Century Pietism

The Anabaptists and Mennonites have always been known for their piety. Most of their first leaders were former Roman Catholic clerics who found piety natural as a result of their training in the church. Then, again, they went back to the Primitive Church for their ethics where they found many reasons and examples for its perpetuation. When it recurred after the Thirty Years War even, the Jesuits made their direct contribution. Jean de Labadie (1610-74) who, as a former member of the Jesuit order in France, found his way to the Mennonites at Altoona by way of the Huguenots, the "Precisianists" in Holland and the Lutherans in Germany. He found the true church represented in every church by those twice-born and separated from the world and Babylon, and regarded them as the one true Evangelical Church belonging to the millennial reign of Jesus Christ.[1]

Seventeenth century pietism had so much in common with earlier Anabaptist piety that many believed there existed a close historical kinship. It was asserted that even the Great Awakening during the eighteenth century in which Jonathan Edwards and George Whitefield were so outstanding, had its beginnings among the Mennonites. Max Goebel and Albrecht Ritschl, observing the tremendous impact pietism had on the Mennonites everywhere except in Holland, linked it closely with Anabaptism. Johannes Deknatel of Amsterdam was influenced by the Moravians and later brought pietism to the Mennonites on the Lower Rhine and in the Netherlands.

In spite of these and other similar contacts, Robert Friedmann concludes that the relationship of the two pietistic expressions is questionable because of their basic differences.

---

1 Ruth Rause and Stephen Charles Neill, editors, *A History of the Ecumenical Movement*, 1517-1948 (Philadelphia: The Westminster Press, 1954), p. 100.

Pieticism, he asserts, is a "heartfelt" religious phenomenon and seeks to bring men through an emotional religious experience to an inner peace and godliness. Mennonitism endeavours to achieve piety through the understanding of the Gospel, doctrine and Christian ethics.

These pietistic expressions were similar but in motives they often differed. According to Harold Bender the motives of the sixteenth-century Mennonite piety were a "complete discipleship of Christ, a voluntary Church of believers only, the sincere practice of Christian love and brotherhood, and the renunciation of all forms of force and violence including warfare."[2] In comparison, the seventeenth-century pietism was an "assertion of the primacy of the feeling in Christian experience, a vindication for the laity of an active share in the upbuilding of the Christian life, and the assertion of a strict ascetic attitude toward the world."[3]

The Thirty Years War almost extinguished Anabaptism in Württemberg and destroyed practically everything that can be used to establish the relationship of the earlier and later pietistic movements. That they belong together is strongly felt because of their great similarities even if concrete evidences and "sharp characterization" of the transition are lacking. In 1648 the "great Anabaptistic movement had been crushed" in Germany. Almost everything pertaining to understanding and living one's own religious heritage was gone. The recurrent waves of warfare almost totally destroyed evidences of earlier piety that may have become part of the constituents of the new. Only with the return of peace, Kolb believes, did pietism return in the form of a resurrection out of Anabaptist heritage; a leaven of the remaining Anabaptism began to be active again.[4] A case in point was that of the Jesuit Jean de Labadie.

Perhaps partially to blame for the little evident carryover from the early Anabaptist piety into later pietism are the Menno-

---

2 Robert Friedmann, *Mennonite Piety, Through the Centuries, Its Genius and Its Literature* (Goshen College, Goshen, Indiana: The Mennonite Historical Society, 1949), pp. vii, 3, 4.

3 Williston Walker, *A History of the Christian Church* (New York: Charles Scribner's Sons, 1945), p. 496.

4 F. Fritz, "Die Wiedertäufer und der württembergische Pietismus," *Blätter für württembergische Kirchengeschichte* (im Auftrag des Vereins für württembergische Kirchengeschichte herausgegeben von Julius Rauscher; Stuttgart: Druck und Verlag von Chr. Scheufele, Neue Folge. 43. Jahrgang 1939), Heft II, p. 83.

nites themselves. The Anabaptists were deeply hurt by Luther's furious attacks on all Anabaptists because of the Münster episodes and peasant revolts, which again in our day are held up by the East German Communists against Luther. They accused him of laying too much stress on doctrine and doing very little in practicing love and tolerance. When they said that he had only words and not deeds they failed to take into account that all preaching those days, including that of Zwingli, Calvin and Menno Simons, achieved not the desired results. They looked upon Luther's utterances as a blemish upon his scriptural messages and a reflection on the whole Reformation. In their eyes Luther was unethical and what piety there was was on their side. When pietism again makes its appearance, and this time first in the Lutheran and Evangelical churches, we have a reversal of the earlier Anabaptist concept.

The Anabaptists failed to make allowance for the prevailing piety that originated with Luther himself, who was a most religious and sincere truth-seeking priest while still in the Church of Rome. What he preached and fostered "was no abstract principle."[5] He most unquestionably repudiated the Roman Catholic double standard of morality and the whole corrupt practice of hierarchical immunity, and, like Menno and other former priests and monks, exposed them mercilessly. He deposited sharpness of characterization in every way, as did the Anabaptists a little later. No one to this day has approached the clarity with which Luther discussed "law and gospel." His utter dependence for salvation on God's Word and grace, through faith, was the greatest foundation-laying message for Christian ethics the world has ever heard.

In the expression of ethics Luther's foundation, no doubt, had to come first. After this foundation was laid, the Anabaptists could begin to erect their structure of ethics. There was the danger, however, that the Lutherans would stay with the foundation too long and the Anabaptists not long enough.

Just as the Lutheran, Evangelical and Anabaptist Reformers had much in common during the sixteenth century so had the earlier piety much in common with the latter. Where the influence of the one ended and the other began is difficult to say.

---

5 Harold C. Letts, editor, *The Lutheran Heritage of Christian Social Responsibility. A Symposium in Three Volumes* (Philadelphia: Muhlenberg Press, 1957), II, 36-43.

The influence was gradual. "Lutheran orthodoxy tried to keep its doctrine pure and Pietism reacted sharply against what it regarded as an ossified and polemical theology whose dry bones were unproductive of a genuine Christian life." The seventeenth century Pietism sensed its relationship to earlier Anabaptism.[6] Walker says that among the many sources of the later Pietism we must not forget Anabaptist influences, the Roman Catholic mystical piety and the example of the Reformed ecclesiastical life of Holland or England.

Friedmann, in reference to other ancestral sources of later Pietism, says the "grandchild of Anabaptism" was the revival of Anabaptist tendencies and therefore a weakened form of pietism. Where Bossart saw in it a form of sanctification, Wiswede looked upon it as a continuation of the spirituality of the Schwenkfelders, the Pietists before Pietism. Wernle went back to the Swiss Anabaptists since they gave rise to such groups in the Canton of Berne. Here the Amish later manifested an almost extreme pietistic ethic. Then, too, in a Swiss book of 1722 we find support for this idea for it makes no distinction between the so-called Anabaptists and Pietists, even though they differed in points of doctrine. Edward Becker draws attention to the fact that "a considerable number of villages which were well known as centers of Anabaptism later became centers of Pietism. Keller later links it up with the Waldenses.

On the other hand we have evidence that Pietism led back to Anabaptism. The Dunkers, for instance, in 1708 were led from Pietism to adult baptism, and the exiled Carinthian exiles[7] became adult baptizers when they came in contact with the Hutterites in Transylvania. The latest such movement is the "Hutterian Bruderhof" founded by Eberhard Arnold in Germany. Of still more recent activity in this area are the Hutterite colonies in England and Paraguay and their difficulties in Canada and the United States to exercise their legitimate share of civil rights. Everywhere it is their ethic of piety that is not comprehended.

After Menno (1561) Anabaptism and its piety declined. It reached its lowest point at the end of the Thirty Years War. Quiet groups, such as the Schwenkfelders and Anabaptists that had the good fortune to be able to continue in their own small

---

6 Friedmann, *op. cit.*, p. 4.
7 *Ibid.*, pp. 3, 7.

way, remained under its influence. Its spirit was destined to make its appearance once more in newer forms. The war had caused a great moral and material devastation. A desire for nobler spiritual living that sprang up refused to abide with dead formalism and ignorance. Positively it reached for active pietism for which it did not have to go back any further than the Reformation. Here was the kind of pietism that had its pendulum in the middle. The seventeenth century pietistic tendencies swung way out to the left and its counter-actions to the extreme opposite. Halle and Hamburg later represented both of these extremes.[8]

ANABAPTIST PIETY AND ETHICS

Sixteenth century Pietism took piety out of the monasteries and gave it back to everyone that believed. Luther started with the home and the individual. To him true piety was to believe in our salvation through faith and then strengthen it from time to time through the Sacraments. The Anabaptists applied piety to every believer. The thesis was demonstrated in obedience and adherence to the principles of the Primitive Church and Biblicism. Its establishment took place earlier in the Catholic Church and was perhaps more profound in the monasteries than even with the Anabaptists. Pietism at this time was a historical and Scriptural evaluation. The Catholic Church in the estimation of the Anabaptists was corrupt and the pietism it practiced was mere sham. Only fully obedient and baptized believers could be pietists. It was not a pietism for its own sake but rather a pietism that wrapped itself around the Word and the believer. The Anabaptists and Mennonites were Pietists because *"Nachfolge"* could not show itself otherwise. To them the pietism of the Catholics in secluded places was meaningless. The priests and their parishioners had to be pietists. To those of true Mennonite faith it is axiomatic that all church members are pious.

The Anabaptist ideal of pietism struck hard at the Catholic Church. When we read the records of the 1528 Synod of the Catholic Church in Zurich we see how corrupt the conditions in the Church of Rome were spiritually.[9] The Anabaptists were not deliberate pietists. They were different from the peo-

---

8 W. J. Mann, *Hallesche Nachrichten* (Allentown, Pennsylvania: Verlag von Brobst, Diehl & Co., 1886), I, 420-30.
9 *Appendix*, II, v.

ple in the Catholic Church just because they had the Scriptures, studied them, and tried to obey them at all times. Pietism came naturally; never did the mass, holy water, genuflexion, the sign of the cross, pilgrimages, praying after the rosary and revering people and places make them any more pious. Such ritualistic manipulation was to them only "a noisy gong or a clanging cymbal."

Pietism is the composition of overt pious acts, whereas piety is made up of the inner urges to act piously. The dominant Mennonite urge for piety was the example of the Primitive Church. Neither the Church of Rome nor any of its disengaging factions during the Reformation could possibly satisfy. The Renaissance had taught Mennonites well to go back to originals. In the Apostolic Church they found a simple brotherhood that had no need to be bolstered by religion. They even refused pretentious names; they preferred to be called *"Täuferische Brüder"* (brethren that baptize). They were sure that in God's sight they were all equal; they had no hierarchy in the church and since they separated church and state and belonged to God's Kingdom, they had no higher and lower social status. They made no demands other than to live for God in this world, not to hate but to love, not to harm but to assist, and never make demands for selfish reasons but share. They applied the pronoun "they" in Acts 2:42 directly to themselves and "continued steadfastly in the Apostles' doctrine and fellowship, and in breaking of bread, and in prayers, having favour with all people."

Such artlessness and abandon of ingenuous devices in the name of religion brought about unrehearsed socialistic tendencies. Their adumbration was the custom followed fifteen centuries earlier in the first Christian Church. They dispensed with taking of interest and making of profits, and adopted various modes of communal living. God created the earth for all and everyone had an equal right to possess it. No government had a right to disown or banish anyone and no religious group had a right to use force of any kind. It was a gross injustice to interfere with another's existence and well-being. Using force in any way was transgressing the laws of God by which men should live together. The difficulties and inconsistencies arising from the refusal to use restrictions were ignored.

The many problems that arose out of this type of society were answered with great diversity because of varying circumstances, times and interpretations of the Scriptures. Some made allowance for the use of some force, others insisted on the right to bury their dead wherever they saw fit. Marriage for them did not belong to the state but was a private concern. These are some views still prevalent amongst the Amish and similar groups. Homogeneity depended on the extent of literalness introduced into the interpretation of the Scriptures.

Robert Friedmann points out that we cannot understand Mennonite piety unless we make an analysis of their original "ideas."[10] We must accept that these were very virile and sound to attract the attention the Mennonites have had. Basically these ideas were pietistic because they sought to substitute the Christian emotional experience and the devotional for the intellectual. Since Mennonitism today in numerous cases makes considerable deviation from the original, and seventeenth century Pietism made such impact upon them we must go back to the thinking of their earliest leaders. Egli, almost a century ago, compiled from the *Zürich Staatsarchive*[11] the following list of original statements made by early Anabaptists:

— Lienhart Bleuler von Zollikon: "I am a servant of God and no longer my own. I am a soldier of Jesus Christ and must be true to Him until my last breath. What He commands I must do regardless of what may happen to my person."

— Rotsch Hottinger von Zollikon: "What God has planted in my heart no one can take away."

— Conrad Grebel: "You are not to consider the person that speaks and commands. You are to obey only God. You are to follow only the sayings coming from the mouth of God."

— Jakob Hottinger von Zollikon: "The Word of God is free. As soon as a government uses it to apply force it is no longer free. So no government can according to the Word of God use it to execute force."

— Hans Müller von Medikon: "Faith is a gift of God. God is gracious to give it to us. Not all people possess it. The mystery of God is hidden like a treasure in the field, which no one can find unless the Spirit of God show it to him. I pray you not to force my conscience but permit me to act according to my faith. I know only too well that faith cannot be picked up like a stone."

10 Friedmann, *op. cit.*, p. 19.
11 Emil Egli, *Die Züricher Wiedertäufer* zur Reformationszeit nach den Quellen des Staatsarchivs (Zürich: Druck und Verlag von Friedrich Schulthess, 1878), p. 75.

— Hans Bruppacher von Zumikon: "What we profess to be our faith we must prove with our deeds. Our promise to the Lord when we become Christians must be kept on its own merit. Oaths are not needed for a consistent walk before the Lord."

— Botsch Hottinger von Zollikon: "No adulterer, whoremonger, covetous person or profiteer knows the Word of God."

— Peter Fuchs von Bülach: "A preacher must preach without being remunerated."

— Caplan Hans von Laupen zu Bülach: "When preachers present themselves in pride and covetousness we cannot learn from them. They can only annoy us."

— The Anabaptists at Bülach: "No one should go into the temple (church buildings made by other church organizations, the chief being the Catholic Church) for it is made by sinful hands."

— Georg Blaurock: "Infant baptism is an invention of men and what comes by way of men is of the devil."

— Pfr. Ulrich (Zingg von Dürnten?): "There is no salvation in baptism."

— Conrad Grebel: "The best weapon against the pope is Anabaptism."

— Jakob Falk von Gossau: "God has spoken: beware of false prophets. The pope's priests are these prophets. . . ."

— Heine Frei, genannt Gigli: "Goods should be held in common ownership. . . ."

— Georg Blaurock: "All those who follow me in faith should pay and ask tithes and interest."

— Felix Manz: "Christians are non-resistant."

— Balthazar Hubmaier: "The best way to convince the state that our faith is real is to practice adult baptism."

— Michel Meier von Nerach: "My brother believes the earth is created for everyone so he has the moral right to bury his wife where he wants to."

Fritz believes that much of the later Mennonite piety has its genetics in these utterances. Later Mennonites were not so much responsible for present pietistic practices as these earlier ones. Intrinsically, however, the earlier and later piety were the same. Both had "Scriptures as their background," the same characteristics with tradition and philosophy playing their parts.[12] Even Barth seems to have imbibed the earlier spirit of Anabaptism when he says the church's "task consists of

---

12 Letts, *op. cit.*, p. 36.

preaching other-worldly Biblicism and an inactive quietism."[13] This agrees with the Mennonites today when they say that piety in the church can only be preserved through a "nonconformity to the world."[14] Their baptismal candidates are taught that their lives must not conform to this world but to the things of God.[15] Neither does their piety rely on theological treatises but on biblicism.

Hutterian Brethren literature that had circulated in large volume in the sixteenth century appeared again at the time of the literary production at Halle. "Interest in Anabaptism became lively" again through a spiritual kinship, a demonstration of true regeneration and quietism, and an invariable piety even in suffering and martyrdom. This quietism is a major element of Anabaptism in all lands. It started with the Swiss Brethren in the sixteenth century and coursed through the rest of Europe and the Americas. Today it completes the cycle by the reappearance of Mennonitism in European countries and in the teaching of Karl Barth in Zurich where Anabaptism began.

Our modern church life has also been reminded of Anabaptist piety by Dietrich Bonhoeffer. His witness for Christ has much of the quality of the earlier martyred pietists. When he said, "Piety cannot lead separate lives but has to be a witness to Jesus Christ before the world,"[16] he repeated the words written by the Anabaptists in 1526. "A Christian man," they said, "should not fear but should openly confess his faith. Christianity is neither an affair of dark alleys nor a smuggler's ware *(keine Winkelsache, keine Schmuggelware)*. Therefore, dear brethren, do not keep it to yourselves, but do as the dear Apostles did who publicly declared that one must obey God rather than man."[17] The urge to send out a large number of missionaries from Halle during the seventeenth and eighteenth centuries is of the same spirit.

All expressions of piety tend to be orthodox. The earlier

---

13 Otto Weber, *Karl Barth's Church Dogmatics*, translated by Arthur C. Cochrane (Philadelphia: The Westminster Press, 1953), p. 7.
14 Wenger, *op. cit.*, p. 114.
15 John Horst, editor, *Instructions to Beginners in Christian Life* (Fourth printing; Scottdale, Pa.: Mennonite Publishing House, 1947), p. 74.
16 Dietrich Bonhoeffer, *Ethics*, translated by Neville Horton Smith from the German, published by Munch Chr. Kaiser Verlag Munich, 1949 (N. Y.: The Macmillan Co., 1955), p. 69.
17 Friedmann, *op. cit.*, p. 27.

piety, a direct sequel of the Renaissance, reverted to the Primitive Church, the latter to the orthodoxy of the theology and doctrine of the sixteenth century.[18] The former stressed discipleship where the latter put more emphasis on theology and formulations. Where the earlier piety was urged to do what the Scriptures demanded, the latter felt subjected to its passions and experiences; where the first had direct objects, the second had direct subjects. Bender thinks that Anabaptist piety was more sharply focused and radical than the German Pietism.

In a larger sense, "Pietism is a quiet conventicle-Christianity,"[19] primarily concerned with the inner experience of salvation and only secondarily with the expression of love toward the brotherhood. Never is it radically engaged in a world transformation.[20] Here Humanism assisted Pietism; both were concerned about withdrawal to receive the full impact of religious knowledge. Calvin felt its influence when he remarked, "By piety, I mean reverence and love of God arising from a knowledge of his benefits. . . ."[21] Here the Anabaptists "lean again towards Kant when he accentuates the ethical dimensions of personality and religion (and) defines religion as the interpretation of all duties as divine commands."[22] Their piety, in its high regard of the worth of the individual, placed the dictates of conscience above everything else. The answers to these were their own and often in utter defiance of all conformity.

This implicit compliance to the demands of the Scriptures settled for nothing less than total and explicit obedience. They said with Kant that "everything in creation except personality can be used by man as a means to an end; but man himself, the rational creature is an end in himself. He is the subject of the moral law and is sacred by virtue of his individual freedom.[23] Mennonite piety has its seat in a total personality. No cost is too high to express total freedom in total obedience. Kant and the Mennonites of course differed in their estimation of that which is beyond the rational, but agreed philosophically about

---

18 Letts, *op. cit.*, p. 66.
19 Walker, *op. cit.*, p. 498.
20 Friedmann, *op. cit.*, p. 11.
21 John Calvin, *A Compend of the Institutes of Christian Religion*, edited by Hugh Thomson Kerr (Philadelphia: Presbyterian Board of Education, 1939), p. 5.
22 Wayne E. Oates, *The Religious Dimensions of Personality* (New York: Association Press, 1957), p. 45.
23 *Ibid.*, p. 23.

the total personality (man being his own and the highest symbol). Wenger asserts that we do not express fully the constitution of men when we speak about a "trichotomy" or even a "dichotomy." "Man," he says, "is a psychological" and a reconstituted "full personality."[24] This total personality engages a person's profession, confession and conduct. Proof of being a Christian lies in the attitude taken to others. Theological concepts are garbed in pietistic ethics which are quiet, consistent and religious expressions. A Leipzig professor in 1684 defined a "pietist" more in Anabaptist terms than in his own when he said, "What is a Pietist? He is one who hears the Word and lives a holy life in terms of what he has heard." Mennonite pietistic and religious expression insists on a *praxis pietatis* in a daily life which requires a total transformation of the being. His first reaction to the divine message is not to be a "pietist" but to be "pietistic." From the very beginning of Anabaptism there was evidence of "something pietistic"[25] about their religious expression in worship, daily living, doctrine and literature. Their concern was their religion and the spirit around it was pietism. Among extremely conservative branches of Mennonites, the Amish and the Hutterites, piety has developed into a form of Pietism. "The New Life (is) viewed as a subjective process, rather than Justification, which is the act of God."[26]

PIETISTIC INFLUENCE AND MENNONITE ETHICS

Seventeenth century Pietism includes a number of "mystics" and "rationalist-mystical societies . . . for the promotion of greater freedom and inwardness in religious thought." Men like Calixtus placed emphasis on religion rather than on doctrine. Jacob Spener gave rise to a preaching that would induce "a complete transformation of the whole being" through "a better knowledge of the Bible." To him Christianity was "far more a life than an intellectual knowledge, a piety as much as scholarship.[27] In spite of these paramount features of Pietism, the Anabaptists observed that through its introversion and for-

24 J. C. Wenger, *Introduction to Theology* (Second edition, revised; Scottdale, Pennsylvania: Herald Press, 1956), pp. 80-82.
25 Letts, *op. cit.*, p. 59.
26 Hugh Ross Mackintosh, *Types of Modern Theology*, Schleiermacher to Barth (reprinted; London: Nisbet and Co., Ltd., 1954), p. 11.
27 Newman, II, 527 and Walker, *op. cit.*, p. 497.

malism it led to rationalism, secularism and inner decay. To their dismay they found that it became dry and empty because it atrophied from pious faith (*herzgläubig*) to an organized faith (*rechtgläubig*).[28]

The middle-of-the-road Mennonites do not promote a pietism that depends on culture, but, with Spener, on one that is based on a conversion experience. They, like the English Puritans, agree with his "ascetic tendencies, including moderation in food, drink, dress, rejecting the theater, dances, cards, which contemporary Lutheranism regards as indifferent."[29]

It is believed that the Anabaptists exercised considerable influence on the Rheinland and Westfalen Pietists when the verility of their smoldering faith after the Thirty Years War resurrected and its embers fanned into fresh flames. When it returned it contributed directly to later radical Pietism and was responsible for Johann Kipping, a later Pietist, saying,

> the Apostles did not command nor practice infant baptism. Its beginning comes from the works of Antichrist and the pope. To this conviction I have come through an old Anabaptist book which I found about eight weeks ago in a peasant's room in the castle of Schaubeck.

Other examples of influence are such as the Konsistorium investigating Bauer, a peasant, for staying away from church and Communion, who gave his reason in typical Mennonite manner, when he said, "The New Testament tells us only about the baptism of people that have come to the age of accountability and confessed their faith in Christ."[30] The book Bauer used was most likely *Probier-Stein der wahren Christen-Tauff*, because it makes Bauer's statement in his exact words. How much Bauer and other Pietists came under direct Anabaptist influence remains a question. Most likely they only referred to previous dynamics of their "new beliefs," for later radical Pietism in Württemberg was of an eclectic character. Johann Georg Rosenbach wrote to Raab that he read all kinds of writings which gave him his Pietistic and Anabaptistic views.

When the Pietists say that they were influenced by the Anabaptists the opposite is also the case. The flow most likely was

---

[28] Peter M. Friesen, *Die Alt-Evangelische Mennonitische Bruederschaft in Russland (1789-1910) im Rahmen der mennonitischen Gesammtgeschichte* (Hapbstadt, Taurien, Russland: Verlagsgesellschaft "Raduga," 1911), p. 49.
[29] Walker, *op. cit.*
[30] Fritz, *op. cit.*, p. 92.

in both directions. If the Anabaptists influenced the Pietists to raise the age of baptism then the Pietists influenced the Mennonites to lower theirs. Peter Friesen comments,
> There was a direct Pietistic influence on the Mennonites. From them they obtained a better knowledge of the Scriptures, living Christianity and an understanding and appreciation of schools and missions. . . . The children were dedicated in the presence of the congregation and baptismal candidates were received at a very early age. . . .

Friedrich Wilhelm Lange (1841-1894), a former Lutheran, became a bishop in the Mennonite Church at Gnadenfeld, Russia. Also Pastor Wüst from the Württemberger Pietisten Church was very active in the Mennonite Church. Lange left the Mennonites in 1849 and again became a Lutheran teacher and assistant to the pastor in the Swedish colony at Schlangendorf, Russia.[31]

Georg Heinrich Burchard, cathedral-preacher in Schlesweg, wrote as early as 1674 that *Die Bourisnon* had accepted much from the teaching of David Joris, an Anabaptist who had separated from the others. Joris had fantastic ideas about his being a prophet of the third world age and the Holy Spirit. Baptism was to be administered only by those who had a reviving experience and were obedient to the Scriptures. Both deemed themselves as bringers of a new light and to know God's mysteries without reading books. They preached that Jesus would come again and triumph with all His followers. Joris also said that the kingdom of Christ is a visible one upon earth.[32] Before accepting, however, that Joris was an Anabaptist and later a Mennonite we must note what the Mennonite John Horsch says about him:
> David Joris, after his renunciation of Romanism was for a time a Lutheran, then a Melchiorite, and about 1535 became an Obbenite. . . . He advised his followers to profess the creed prescribed by the government of the state or country in which they happened to live, thus preventing persecution. He was a fierce opponent of the evangelical Anabaptists. His followers practiced infant baptism. . . .[33]

Chiliastic expectations were always a considerable factor in Pietism. There was constant and urgent admonition to be ready at all times for the Lord's appearing. Fritz does not know defi-

---
31 Friesen, *op. cit.*, p. 83.
32 Fritz, *op. cit.*, p. 92.
33 John Horsch, *Mennonites in Europe* (Second edition, slightly revised; Scottdale, Pennsylvania: Mennonite Publishing House, 1950), p. 221.

nitely whether Peterson's Chiliasm can be traced back to Anabaptist influences, as he found Chiliastic views still further back, even in Calvin. It is possible that he was influenced by Melchior Hofmann whom he met in Strassburg. Since the Millennium was still in the future, every social disturbance impregnated their superspiritual sensitivity,³⁴ and fanned latent potentials into a flame. During the French Revolution social disturbances and resistance became paramount. With the Anabaptists this had been an issue since the first quarter of the sixteenth century and with the Waldenses still earlier.

Mennonite and Pietistic expressions pertaining to military service were strong during the social upheavals toward the turn of the eighteenth century. The reasons given for non-resistance were those of the earliest Anabaptists. In 1794 Rapp and his friends wrote Herzog Ludwig Eugen that he and his people were not fit to be soldiers. They had been appointed by Christ to change hate into love. Losias Hengsteler in Brittheim also said that he did not doubt that there were many Christians in the army, however, he could not serve as a soldier because he found too much in connection with it that would mislead him. The army had many requirements that he could not submit to. On similar grounds the swearing of allegiance was refused. Menno Simons had previously written: "Daily are murdered before our eyes those who do no greater crime than to refuse to swear an oath but answer only in 'yes' and 'no' and are always truthful." Fritz says this kind of Pietism reminds us of the Anabaptists in that it seeks solutions by way of the "spiritual." They came very close to Hans Denck when they referred to Communion as an "inner supper." Rapp, the Pietist, spoke as an Anabaptist when he said:

> I recognize no religious confession other than that which is instituted by Christ Himself. This religion must be an obedient following in Christ's footsteps. Those who show this with their fruits I love, whether they be Jew, Turk, heathen or Christ's.³⁵

A further, more radical and outward influence, came from the Amish who adopted another culture to show their pietism. They wore different clothes, had beards, and their own way of cutting their hair. It was customary to say about those having long beards that they belonged to the sect of the Anabaptists.

34 Fritz, *op. cit.*, p. 93.
35 Fritz, *op. cit.*, pp. 101-06.

DIFFERENCES IN MOTIVES OF ETHICS

Later Pietism had its beginning with man's own depravity. At the root was a struggle with sin as Luther had experienced it. From here on, however, the later Pietism differed in that it believed faith had to be preceded by a long time of penitence. Walther said this was due to a false distinction between "spiritual awakening and conversion." The inability to believe was mistaken for not being permitted to believe or believing too soon. Hearers should not appropriate what did "not yet belong to them because it would prove a false comfort to them."[36]

These Pietists had three classes of people: the unconverted, the awakened and the converted. The Mennonites had only two, the unconverted and the converted. To the Mennonites the converted had to prove their conversion by their Scriptural walk. To the later Pietists spiritual awakening was accompanied by a consciousness of redemption and salvation which gave them great joy, having received forgiveness of all their sins. Their writings became edificatory and of joyous uplift and a means for "the practice of godliness." Following Christ in their daily obedience to the Scriptures (*Nachfolge*) was replaced by the *praxis pietatis* which meant that *Gottseligkeit* (the bliss of salvation) took the place of *Gottesfurcht* (the fear of God). Instead of the Anabaptist love they had friendliness and morality. Ethically they were much the same as the Anabaptists but the motives were different. Their moralism had its roots in an emotional goodwill of the regenerated whose conscience became the ultimate authority, resulting in the only recognition of the invisible church.[37] Gerhard Terstegen (1697-1769) tells us what it involved and how it expressed itself, when he says,

> Come ye through grace all purified souls to his untarnished service. Let the power of the Lord set us free from all that is visible: from all that which is intellectual, from all that which is rational, from all peculiarities: so that we as those who have truly separated themselves from that which may hinder, as simple, clean creatures may enter into our spirit and soul, so that God (who also is a spirit)

---

[36] C. F. W. Walther, *Law and Gospel*, reproduced from the German edition of 1897 by W. H. T. Dau (St. Louis, Missouri: Concordia Publishing House, 1928), pp. 363, 422.
[37] Friedmann, *op. cit.*, pp. 72-75.

may be found, seen, loved and that we may receive His spirit who is higher than all reason.[38]

Spener's aim also was "the deepening of the individual spiritual life,"[39] with a religion of emotions, focused upon edification and the actual experience of redemption from sin that was felt deeply. The restoration of a sweet relationship with Jesus was a part of conversion. Spener and Francke made it a point to acquaint people with the Bible so that this Christian experience could operate. The Mennonites could not accept this, believing that it led to a rationalism based on the knowledge of the Scriptures (*Schriftgelehrtentum*), orthodoxy and a confidence in the "natural light" of one's own wisdom which is taken for the Spirit. This rationalism usually ended in moralism, which to the Mennonites was not piety and therefore only a secondary level of ethics.

The pietism of Zinzendorf and Schwenkfeld was also spiritualistic. Even the Moravian *Abendmahlsgemeinde* (Communion Fellowship) was composed of individuals who had not the Anabaptist teaching that Communion is the partaking of the crushed kernel (Christ) baked into a new bread (the Church composed only of believers). Even if sin and the world crushed the Anabaptists they had Communion with Him who gave Himself for them. This conflict between the follower of Christ and a hostile world was of secondary importance to the Pietists.[40] In terms of ethics the Mennonites came to grips with evil, the Pietists with the emotional in the good.

The Mennonites judged that Lutheran pietism was neither to the left nor to the right. They went along with Geberding when he wrote to the pastors, "This piety . . . must have that trusting, resting, abiding, peace-bringing faith in a Saviour who has forgiven all sin. . . . He must have experienced justification by faith alone."[41] However, this statement, they said, did not go far enough. They maintain that trusting and resting faith is not enough, there must be more action; faith without works is not sufficient. This emphasis on works is often stressed to such an extent that one is led to ask, which comes first? It is

---

[38] Gerhard Terstegen, *Religion in Geschichte und Gegenwart* (Stuttgart: L. F. Riegersche Buchhandlung, 1844), II, 1343-46.
[39] Spener expressed these ideas in his *Ria desideria* of 1675. Walker, *op. cit.*, p. 497.
[40] Friedmann, *op. cit.*, pp. 78-87.
[41] E. H. Geberding, *The Lutheran Pastor* (Philadelphia: Muhlenberg Press, 1902), p. 89.

possible that traditions, non-resistance and other external criteria may be accepted as saving faith. In such cases ethics are motivated by the law, and the gospel is translated into the terms of the law.

Anabaptist piety, as did the Lutheran, began with a consciousness of depravity resulting in a deep remorse and struggle for freedom from guilt. Later Pietism was a recoil from this consciousness having deteriorated into dead and rigid orthodoxy.[42] Anabaptism struggled to put an unwritten ethics in the Scriptures into pious and sometimes even theologically acceptable practices. They found the gospel in the Sermon on the Mount and tried to obtain the wisdom of God by striving. This is impossible, says Barth, for man cannot of himself fulfill what God demands, it is disobedience (*Ungehorsam*) because Christ is the goal of the Law and this is for our justification.[43]

Later Mennonite tendencies to seek justification before God through works did not really spring from Menno's teaching. He preached deeds more than any other Reformer but he relied on faith to do those deeds. He learned this justification through faith in Christ from Luther.[44] Through faith and grace, he taught, one had to repent and obey the Scriptures as literally and completely as possible. This fulfillment of the Gospel became primary and the justification by faith secondary. It still is common in conservative Mennonite churches to accept a candidate for baptism upon recommendation of some elder who knows of his repentance and conduct. On the other hand it is also sound evangelical Mennonite ethics to refuse baptism until a candidate has given testimony of conversion to Christ and has given Scriptural proof of his sins being forgiven through faith in his Saviour.[45]

An integral part of Mennonite piety and ethics is the opening of the heart's door to Christ's love. When this love manifests itself through good deeds Mennonites have credence in such conversion. Philips says this "faith"

---

42 Mackintosh, *op. cit.*, p. 12.
43 Karl Barth, *Evangelium und Gesetz* (Kaiser Publishing Company of Munich, Germany), pp. 3, 18.
44 Harold S. Bender, "A Brief Biography of Menno Simons," *CWMS, op. cit.*, p. 6.
45 Mennonite Brethren Church of North America, *Confession of Faith*, translated by H. F. Toews (American edition; Hillsboro, Kansas: Mennonite Brethren Publishing House, n.d.), p. 45.

is a gift of God. It is wrought by God and produces His works of which love is the foremost. The main point in the law is that love comes from a pure heart, a good conscience and an unblemished faith. Out of such love come good works.[46]

In response to this obedience the love of Christ, great joy, peace and unselfishness come into the heart. This occurs in two steps: first is the experience of God's grace and mercy in forgiveness of sin and consequent justification before God and adoption as His child; second are the deeds such as: not offering resistance, complete obedience to the Master, being crucified with Him, and living in the world but not being of this world.

THE MANIFESTATION OF ETHICS AND PIETY

Mennonite ethics aimed at a total disappearance of everything personal and selfish in the practice of a true and brotherly reciprocity. Even in times of compassionless persecution they desired to be the seed that would fall into the ground to produce more fruit for Christ.[47] The spirit in which the world viewed them made them extremely practical and realistic. What was done to them was not a story of something that happened "once upon a time" or in a land "far away." It was not like mission stories sometimes are, distant and unreal. Family after family had to endure most severe hardships because the world found delight in inflicting torture upon them. Such experiences were desperately real, and so had to be their responses.

The result of this reality was a most practical expression of the truth, not a mere interpretation or debate. The Scriptures themselves were always interpreted and acted upon with naïve simplicity. Their spiritual sensitiveness disdained *Hochgelehrsamkeit* (scholarship for its own sake). Only the genuine self can make commitments; knowledge, rationality and the arts are only by-products. Spirit never plays the part of reason or emotion, only the gospel penetrates the innermost of total personality. Later "Pietism emphasized the seriousness of the moral life but unduly narrowed its sphere."[48] It took Wolff's philosophy, Schleiermacher's enthusiasm and the "enlightenment" to

---

46 Dietrich Philips, *EoH*, pp. 16, 17.
47 Friedmann, *op. cit.*, pp. 72-77.
48 Johann Michael Reu and Paul H. Buehring, *Christian Ethics* (Columbus, Ohio: The Lutheran Book Concern, 1935), p. 52.

broaden it. In the process, however, rationalism robbed scriptural piety of its genius. When there was nothing to be pietistic about rationalism created in itself such new objectivity. The objective in Mennonite piety was always beyond them; they remained only the medium.

In comparison it should be noted that this reality that motivated their ethics differed with leaders and churches. For Erasmus it centered in himself. He said it did not make much difference to him what happened to Luther or others as long as he could go on unmolested. He varied his loyalties and spoke in generalities to suit his interests. Never had he to face a court that tried him seriously like Luther had to. Far were from him such words "here I stand, I cannot and will not recant." For Luther the reason for such stand was just as real as his life. Again, the Catholics depended on their church, tradition and hierarchy; there was very little of that which gave reality to the individual. For the Mennonites the Scriptures and what they demanded were more real than their own lives. They suffered all the time for their convictions. That which made them do what they did was more real in many instances than their own existence. The demands of the Scriptures were above everything else and the symbols of their realities were incorporated in themselves.

The constitution that motivated the pietistical ethics of the Mennonites manifested itself in seven major ways. Of first importance was that "the Christian be fully surrendered or yielded to the will of God." This bordered on the fatalistic philosophy of the Catholics; we must accept God's decrees for us without question or murmur. But where the Catholics took God's imposition for them through the church, the Mennonites took it directly from God and His Word. They said, "The Word is given as a lamp to our feet and a light to our path. God gives us principles that apply to every circumstance of life." This docile acceptance of God's Word in every experience is not easy for anyone. Calvin sensed it in his citizenry when he said, "Let no one murmur that God might have made a better provision for our safety by preventing the fall of Adam. For such an objection ought to be abominated as too presumptuously curious, by all pious minds. . . ."[49] For the pious it is easier to

---

[49] John Calvin, *A Compend of the Institutes of Christian Religion*, op. cit., p. 44.

remain pious without asking for reasons than to seek out paths of reason that leave a troubled soul. The Mennonites soon arrive at the place where they have remorse about having been "too curious" about the ways of God.[50] Their story is filled with instances where they surrendered totally to the will of God and submitted to brutalities and injustices sooner than violate the dictates of their consciences.

Second, the Mennonites put a premium on the holiness of their earthly calling. Here the Catholic Church failed for the priests and monks remove themselves from their people. In the Mennonite Church it was and in many cases still is the custom to choose ministers from those who are good farmers or artisans. A main qualification for the ministry is that the candidate must rule well his own house and have obedient children. It is the minister's duty to make his ordinary earthly occupation holy before God and his people, and require of them the same stewardship he subjects himself to. Their relationship to God is a complete cycle; God looks at them through His Word, they look forward through the Word to man and again up to God. Never do they come to the Catholics' "blessed Sacrament" and other forms of Eucharistic piety.[51] In their midst everyone is in the presence of this piety at all times. In order to be eligible for the Lord's Supper the applicant must have walked peacefully with all men and must

> fear God from the heart, serve Him in truth, uphold unity, love, peace among the brethren, watch and pray; walk circumspectly, wage warfare against evil with patience, seek that which is good, be friendly, . . . submit and obey the elders and remember them . . . in prayer.[52]

All differences must be removed before the Supper for it is a "supper of harmony" (*Einigkeit* — being in harmony with their fellowmen — was the name they used for it), for all continued in the same piety and holiness of life To facilitate the supervision of this pious living they used to live in close communities with the church and school in the center. Present methods of communication and transportation have a great effect on Mennonite piety and there is in many cases, especially in urban areas, not much difference between them and others. Men-

---

50 *Appendix* II, w.
51 "Eucharistic Piety," *Tabernacle and Purgatory*, II (April, 1956), 355-56.
52 Menno Simons, *CWMS, op. cit.*, p. 1059.

no in his super concern for the holiness of the church practiced excommunication and avoidance for the purpose of maintaining this high ideal. Later Mennonite attempts to maintain this high standard of obedience and piety have had continuous difficulties.

Third, the Mennonites have a very high regard for the worth of the individual. They do not want to destroy any human life and set up such organizations as Voluntary Service, I-W Service and Mennonite Central Committee world aid. The teaching in this regard had its inception from the first days of the movement. Their life is to be that of service lived in a spirit of separatism, set aside to give rather than receive. Where Calvin wanted a theocracy in which to serve they said that they already belonged to Christ's Kingdom in which to serve. Their church was composed of holy members rather than a holy church.[53] Where the Reformed had Christian work the Mennonites were led through obedience into service for Christ. Their main service, piety and ethics were to make Christ's ethics known. This the Reformed did in their theocracy, which government was their mission work. Luther also had the view of the Anabaptists when even in his day he "recognized the duty of bringing the Gospel to the heathen, and Albrecht, Duke of Prussia, was anxious to Christianize those of his subjects who still worshipped idols." For the Reformed salvation of the individual depended directly on God, His predestination and majesty. The individual's worth was augmented by something vastly more important. It was "the will of that majesty as revealed in the Scripture as the unconditional law of all religious and moral development and how it stamped a legalistic character on the life of the individual."[54] The individual's worth was not destined by his service to others as a member of the Kingdom but was pre-destined by the divine majesty.

Fourth, Mennonite ethics depend on a high standard of self-refinement. Salvation to them means a pleading for grace, forgiveness and a pure heart. Menno describes his own conversion, saying,

> My heart trembled in my body. I prayed God with sighs and tears that He would give me, a troubled sinner, the

---

53 S. Hoekstra, *Beginselen en Leer der Oude Doopsgezinden*, vergeleken met die van de overige Protestanten (Amsterdam: P. N. Van Kampen, 1863), p. 31.
54 Reu-Buehring, *op. cit.*, pp. 47-49.

gift of His grace and create a clean heart in me, that through the merits of the crimson blood of Christ He would graciously forgive my unclean walk and ease-seeking life, and bestow upon me wisdom, candor, and courage.[55] "Justification is the act of God whereby He pronounces the sinner, who believes in His Son, free from all guilt and righteous in His sight. This occurs through grace, without any merit of our own, gives peace with God and all the other children of God, sets free from bondage of sin, perfects in holiness and inculcates a fear of God which controls and prompts constant soul refinement."[56]

Fifth, Menonnite ethics manifest a disregard for worldly power and political position. They contend that piety lacks almost always in worldly potentates and the politically exalted. In their eyes the Reformed (especially Zwingli and Calvin) "displayed the lust of the ecclesiastics for power and position and replaced the old democracy of the simple believers' band." This was not the "Medieval ethical criticsm of the hierarchy" but a description of their pietistic character. For Zwingli the Anabaptists were too radical[57] and Calvin did not realize that their pietism could be anything else than individual mysticism. "He made no distinction between the spiritualizing and the Biblicist wings of the movement." The Reformed, like John Dury (1596-1680), presented themselves as ecumenists. When they did not understand the Anabaptist position they became very severe, muzzled all dissent "so swiftly and brutally that only its echo was to be heard thereafter in the interiorized and socially often quite conservative form of Pietism."[58] The Reformed were so engrossed with their ecumenical vision that they did not have an appreciation of Anabaptist pietism nor Lutheran doctrine. When Pietism did come it "made visible the ecu-

---

55 Harold S. Bender, "A Brief Biography of Menno Simons," *CWMS*, op. cit., p. 12.
56 Board of Home Missions Southern District Conference of the Mennonite Brethren Church (P. C. Hieber, H. R. Wiens, A. W. Epp) *Fundamentals of Faith* (Third edition; Hillsboro, Kansas: Mennonite Brethren Publishing House, 1954), pp. 38, 40.
57 Hamlin Franklin Littell, *The Anabaptist View of the Church* (Second edition, revised and enlarged; Boston: Starr King Press, 1958), pp. 68, 146, 147.
58 John Ballie, Jh. T. McNeill, Henry P. Van Dusen, "Introduction," *Spiritual and Anabaptist Writers*, edited by George Hunston Williams and Angel M. Mergal (Library of Christian Classics, Vol. XXV; Philadelphia: The Westminster Press, 1957), p. 24.

menical reality of the Church in a manner entirely different. . . ."⁵⁹

The Anabaptists followed Luther in denouncing the rottenness of Rome for its ostentatiousness and aspirations for worldly power. Instead of a "congregation of believers" they erected huge cathedrals from which the hierarchy wielded its influence. Neither did the Anabaptists go along with any of the Reformers in regard to baptism and relationship of church and state. The Christian life for them was extremely serious business and a "matter of stern discipline and vigorous ethical living."⁶⁰ Where the Reformed Church over-emphasized other-worldliness the Catholic Church chiefly stressed visible mediations. Lutheran piety, on the contrary, reveals

> more the character of evangelical freedom; it fosters, not a stern and legalistic but an open, free and joyful spirit. It . . . is more favorable to the development of the inner life, is given more to contemplation, is richer in spiritual hymns, and shows a deep appreciation of art and culture. Lutheran ethics offers a greater latitude. . . .⁶¹

The Mennonites did not accept this as a full ethical requirement for them.

Sixth, Mennonite ethics manifest an intense desire to perfect Christ's Kingdom upon the earth; the kingdom here and now where its citizens reach out to be of assistance to other citizens. A citizen never takes the law in his own hand, he leaves it always to the Sovereign. Those not committed totally to the Ruler were not citizens of His Kingdom. The Gospel is the Sovereign's law for His citizens. "Christ is our Lawgiver," said Menno, "He is our Judge, our King."

It is inconceivable to the Mennonites how one can be a friend of the world and at the same time a member of the church. They say, "All who hear His voice, come to Him by faith, and follow Him as their Lord, are called out from among the world and their former associations." "It is impossible," said Andreas Castelberger, "to be a friend of both God and the world." They contend that those wanting to be friends of the world want to display self or escape the shame of Christ. Indulgence of any carnal kind is foreign to the Christian fellow-

---

59 Joachim Wach, *Sociology of Religion* (Phoenix Books; Chicago: The University of Chicago Press, 1944), p. 99.
60 Littell, *op. cit.*, pp. 69, 70.
61 Reu-Buehring, *op. cit.*, p. 46.

ship, and "personal display and aggrandizement are condemned strongly wherever they appear, all such tendencies among Christians are vigorously curbed by spiritual government.[62]

Seventh, the Mennonites consider their piety as a gift of new light. This light shone upon them when they were still in darkness. The devout bishop, Dietrich Philips, wrote that they had wandered far astray from the way of truth because the light of piety was gone and they sat in darkness. Since the sun of reason did not rise for them they were embroiled in wickedness and depravity. They trudged along very difficult paths for they did not know the smooth and easier paths of the Lord.

When talking about the light from heaven that stirs up piety mention must be made of the Zwickau Prophets. These were neither Anabaptistic nor Lutheran, because they used force to obtain their puritanical objectives and set aside the Scriptures. The Anabaptists used both Scripture and Holy Ghost direction. The former sought to force their light and social behavior on others where the latter limited their social reform to their own members, even excommunicated and shunned them if they refused to be reformed; the first were centrifugal and the latter centripetal. Luther likely gave the Anabaptists their direction in this regard when he said to Karlstadt who had left him and went to the Anabaptists, "I will drive and compel no one with force, for faith is to be voluntary, taken on without compulsion."[63] The Anabaptists did no more than give pietistic expression to the light they had received through the Scriptures and close fellowship with their Saviour and prayed that others might have the same experience and enlightenment.

EXAMPLES OF PIETISTIC ASPECTS

Giving three examples of Mennonite piety will prove helpful in understanding that which cannot so easily be put into words.

First, the Mennonite piety expressed by artists. Well-known Mennonite themes are "Cornelis Claesz. Anslo and Wife" by Rembrandt; "Gozewijn Centen Family" by C. Lubienietzki; "Bernese Farm" by Aurele Robert. Rembrandt in his pictures gives us some of the Mennonite characteristics he absorbed in his

62 Littell, *op. cit.*, p. 72.
63 Littell, *op. cit.*, p. 6.

associations with them. N. van der Zipp speaks of the "sobriety, inwardness, a turning away from outward things, and a concentration on the essential" here portrayed as a part of the Dutch Mennonite piety, especially of the Waterlanders."[64]

Second, the Mennonite piety as displayed by Mrs. Otelia Augsburger Compton, the mother of Dr. Arthur Holley Compton, former chancellor of Washington University in St. Louis and winner of the Nobel Prize for his research that led to the discovery of the atomic bomb. Her son Wilson writes about her:

> In my mother's room as long ago as I can remember were two books: A Bible, and Charles Scheldon's inspiring little book "In His Steps." The Bible she left to me and we have it in our home in New York. It is of an old-fashioned binding and was given to her by my father in 1885, the year before they were married. In it as she gave it to me was an embroidered bookmarker within which was encased an inscription in my mother's firm handwriting, undated but bearing the signature Otelia Catherine Augsburger, signifying that it was written before she was married. This inscription reveals my mother's inner active power. It was a simple compact.
> "I solemnly agree," she wrote, "as God shall help me:
> 1. To observe regularly seasons of secret prayer at least in the morning and the evening.
> 2. To read daily at least a small portion of the Bible.
> 3. To say a good word for Jesus Christ always and everywhere.
> 4. To try to save at least one soul every year.
> 5. To engage in no amusement where my Saviour could not be a guest."

Then in the dormitory are the family mementos which are typical of all Mennonite homes: "of interest perhaps by their very meagerness to girls of another day, as an evidence of the enduring values of life — the silent treasurer of family, home, community, and church. . . ."[65]

Third, the early Anabaptist hymns are another far-reaching example. Beyond the many Mennonite hymn-writers we do not know, there are, according to Bender, "at least 130 Anabaptist

---

[64] N. van der Zipp, "Rembrandt van Rijn 1606-1956," *Mennonite Life*, XI (October, 1956), 147.

[65] Wilson Martindale Compton, "Otelia Augsburger Compton," *Mennonite Life*, II (October, 1956), 176-79.

hymn-writers identifiable by name."⁶⁶ All these learned to sing about their experiences from the early Christian Church. "David formerly sang in Psalms," says Chrysostom,

> also we sing today with him; he had a lyre with living strings. Our tongues are the strings of the lyre with a different tone, indeed, but with a more accordant piety.⁶⁷

Many of the early hymns were written by prisoners and martyrs. One of the prisoners wrote, "We read and sing to the glory of God to pass our time." Like all Germans, the Anabaptists loved to sing and express their devotion to their Lord and Saviour. Then again singing helped them in their suffering, loss of home, family life. In their plight they sang the joys of the Lord over and over again. They found their only hope of life and peace in their Brother Sufferer, Christ Jesus in heaven. When they were deprived of the fellowship of their brethren they sang with them in their hearts. It was a repetition of the days of St. Ambrose of whom it was said, "The pious people kept guard in the church, prepared to die with their bishop. . . ." Or in the case of the persecution of Justin "it was instituted that, after

> the manner of the Eastern Church, hymns and psalms should be sung, lest the people should pine away in the tediousness of sorrow, which custom retained from then till now, is imitated by many — yea, by almost all of the congregations throughout the rest of the world."

An Anabaptist wrote in 1525,
> Should you desire to live with God,
> Eternal life inherit,
> Then steadily walk the Master's way,
> With him thou must be dying,
> Thy simple heart
> (With strong resolve)
> Must rest in God's forbearance.
> Thy earthly goods,
> Thy life and all
> Thy Father must possess them.⁶⁸

The Dutch were the first to produce a martyr hymnal, the *Lietboecken van den Offer des Heeren,* 1563. Of significance in

---

66 Harold S. Bender, "The Hymnology of the Anabaptists," *The Mennonite Quarterly Review,* XXXI (January, 1957), 5, 6.
67 Edward Dickinson, *Music in the History of the Western Church* (New York: Charles Scribner's Sons, 1902), pp. 55, 66.
68 "Editorial," *Mennonite Quarterly Review,* III (April, 1929), 90.

the expression of piety is the "outspoken martyr hymnal," the *Ausbund;* first edition in 1564, and still used by 15,000 Amish. Its full title is most significant.[69] At least twelve editions have been printed in Europe. All its songs tell in a most simple way about the piety and martyrdom of its authors. Number 10 has a note that says that it was composed by five pious people who were burned at Anttorff in one day. Especially rich in pietistic expressions is 101. Felix Manz who was drowned in Zurich writes "with pleasure will I sing: My heart doth joy in God," and closes with the words, "with Christ will I remain, who all my need doth know."[70]

Today much of this high regard for traditional piety is lost amongst the Mennonites. Dr. Bender believes this is because they have lost the martyr spirit and have been too much exposed to Lutheranism and Pietism. Mennonite piety consists today, rather obviously, of a mixture of traditional pietism and seventeenth- and eighteenth-century pietism. It is fitting to conclude this chapter with the pious words of one of the many Mennonite martyrs, executed shortly after writing,

> May the grace of the Lord be increased unto you, my dear wife. Be always subject to the Godfearing, and associate with the pious, and pray God to keep me in the truth; for truth abides and is strong forever; it lives, and will forever prevail. Greet all the saints with the kiss of love, and all who love the Lord Jesus, and tell them to be kind; for God is the Hero and Captain, who so faithfully succors in time of need. He is like a shower upon the parched earth in a dry summer. Thus he refreshes the afflicted souls . . . that thirst for him. . . .[71]

69 *Appendix* II, x.
70 Wenger, *Glimpses of Mennonite History and Doctrine, op. cit.,* p. 20.
71 B. Thieleman van Braght, compiler, *The Martyr's Mirror,* translated from the original Dutch edition of 1660 by Joseph F. Sohm (Scottdale, Pennsylvania: Mennonite Publishing House, 1938), p. 559.

CHAPTER VII

MYSTICISM AND MENNONITE ETHICS

THE QUESTION OF MENNONITE ETHICS

The Mennonite Encyclopedia makes no comment on the mysticism of Mennonite ethics. This omission may be due to an attempt to leave behind the stereotyped mystical piety so prevalent at the close of the Middle Ages. It may also have been felt that a comprehensive treatment of their pietism covered their mysticism, seeing that both are a "devotion or godliness of life, as distinguished from mere intellectual orthodoxy."

To the Mennonites religion has always been a way of life in which reliance was placed upon spiritual illumination believed to be transcending the ordinary powers of understanding.[1] When the movement began, Conrad Grebel wrote to Müntzer to rely on the power, the Word, the Spirit, and the salvation which has come to all Christians through Jesus Christ. In a letter to Vadian he says that he believes the Word of God "simply through grace, not skill." Since conversion there was something transcending the power of understanding that he acquired in Basel, Paris and Vienna universities.

Since pietism and mysticism are closely related, it seems as if the Mennonites were satisfied with the discussion of their pietism and leave mysticism to the Catholics. Even when they did this they were conscious that there was more underneath. They had the desire to grasp divine reality just like the Catholics but attempted it in a way all their own. Where the Catholics had a natural mysticism, the Mennonites had a simple brotherhood manifesting a feeling defying exact definition. Theirs was a religion of relying on spiritual illumination and experience, where the Catholics had a mystical religion relying on the hierarchy and tradition for its revelation. Both communed with the Highest and were opposed to rationalism, but where the Catholics had the church to mediate the Mennonites had the Holy Spirit.

[1] *The Century Dictionary and Cyclopedia,* prepared under the superintendency of William Dwight Whitney and Benjamin E. Smith (Revised and enlarged; New York: The Century Co., 1911), VII, 4480.

Qualben also believes that piety and mysticism together "caused them to sever relationship with the Lutherans."[2] Mysticism is not overt like piety and is therefore indifferent to the external church order. It is concerned with that faculty given to man by God which, through contemplation and transcendence, creates "striving after individual and conscious union with Christ."[3] Rufus M. Jones, the well-known Quaker mystic believes that Anabaptism is a form of mysticism. To this the Mennonite theologian, John C. Wenger, takes exception on the ground that the Anabaptists and Mennonites are Biblicists and that Pilgram Marpeck, Anabaptist elder (bishop) of South Germany, opposed the mystical Schwenkfeld, insisting that the Christian's obligation was to obey the written Word of God. Wenger, however, does not touch on the deeper causes that Marpeck, Philips, Franck and others had in common. He dwells on the externals and says, "The Dutch Mennonite elder, Dietrich Philips, opposed Sebastian Franck who had attempted to depreciate the external observance of the ordinances. The Anabaptists were not mystics, but Bible literalists."[4] Wenger does not make any allowance for the spiritualizing of these Biblicistic forms which gave them their strong tinge of mysticism and frequent provincialism.

Mysticism may operate independently of the Bible and when it does we have pagan mysticism. To what extent it is Biblical depends on the dominance it has over the transcendence of the ordinary power of understanding. The Anabaptists, Schwenkfelders, Münsterites and Hans Denck were all more or less controlled by Scripture. Also the Zurich Reformers, including Zwingli, were mystical because they placed Christian consciousness above the Scriptures.[5] They agree with Bainton when he

[2] Lars P. Qualben, *A History of the Christian Church* (Revised and enlarged; New York: Thomas Nelson and Sons, 1942), pp. 326-30.
[3] Albert Henry Newman, *A Manual of Church History*: Modern Church History (Revised and enlarged; Philadelphia: The American Baptist Publication Society, 1944), II, 4, 5.
[4] John Christian Wenger, *Glimpses of Mennonite History and Doctrine* (Third edition; Scottdale, Pennsylvania: Herald Press, 1949), pp. 8-9. By the same author in "Christianity and Mysticism," in *The Christian Ministry*, Vol. I (Oct., 1948), 207.
[5] ". . . stelde hij eigenlijk het christelijk bewustzijn boven de Heilige Schrift. . .": G. Keizer in "De geestelijke ontwapening der Christenheid in haar geschiedenis geschetst," in *Geestelijk Weerloos of Weerbaar?* Samengesteld Door J. H. De Goede, Jr. (Amsterdam: Uitgevers-Mij Holland, n.d.), p. 18.

says that "mysticism contributes by diverting attention from dogma to experience." He tells the story of the Anabaptists when he goes on to say that mysticism lies in "equating the way to God with the way of suffering, which comports more readily with martyrdom than with persecution."6

The question of Mennonite mysticism is better understood when taking a look at a few of their leaders. In 1522 Conrad Grebel laid the foundation of their obedience to the Bible. For him the Bible had to be known, experienced and accepted for control. He wrote to Vadian that the "doctrines of the Lord and the precepts have been given that they be fulfilled and put into practice." In this practice understanding came after obedience; the logical after experience. Scripture could only be understood through a spiritual illumination coming as a result of its reading. The Spirit clarified the Scriptures and prepared the heart to accept them obediently. In no case could the divine reality be grasped through traditional exercises prescribed by men. On the basis of what Scripture told them about baptism they knelt down and poured water on each other and derived a spiritual experience far beyond anything the churches and universities had given them. They could easily have anticipated that such non-conformity would heap wrath from church and state upon them but they were not much concerned. They did not define their actions philosophically. Why should they? They grasped the reality of the divine much more in their own direct way.

It is clear that Hans Denck, a leader of a certain group of Anabaptists, can hardly be called an Anabaptist or a true Mennonite. He was not non-resistant nor did he have the Mennonite understanding of sin and its teaching of the Word. Still he is considered, and rightly so, an Anabaptist and a mystic. His soul's experience of a painful insufficiency before God were the result of reading the Scriptures, spiritual insight and faith. For him "the Word was in human beings for this purpose that it might divinize them as happens to all the elect; the Scriptures (John 10:34) calls them therefore all gods."7 This direct communion with God through contemplation,

---

6 Donald H. Bainton, *The Travail of Religious Liberty*, Nine Biographical Studies (Philadelphia: The Westminster Press, 1951), p. 20.
7 Hans Denck, "Whether God Is the Cause of Evil," *Spiritual and Anabaptist Writers, SAW*, Vol. XXV of *Library of Christian Classics* (Philadelphia: The Westminster Press, 1957), pp. 91, 101.

vision and inner light, was of mystical making and importance. Typical of all Anabaptists and Mennonites was Dietrich Philips. In his description of his "rebirth" he describes his religious experience as a major spiritual illumination. His rebirth transcends the ordinary powers of understanding and moves the human mind to grasp the divine essence within and enjoys the blessedness of actual communication with the Saviour. Every conversion to Christianity through the acceptance of the Gospel is a mystical experience. It is possible that a religious experience, based only upon the "Biblicistical," may not reach beyond the law. Philips' rebirth was, like Luther's Gospel experience, through faith. Both men's "religious beliefs" were founded upon spiritual experiences, definitely a part of mysticism.

A simple act resulting from Anabaptist religious experience was foot-washing, which can only be mystically understood and evaluated. In the light of human understanding it is an almost irrational act; spiritually and mystically interpreted it is one that is indeed beautifully practical. This was so in the eyes of Menno. "Wash the feet," he says,

> of your beloved brethren and sisters who are come to you from a distance, tired. Be not ashamed to do the work of the Lord, but humble yourselves with Christ, before your brethren, so that all humility of godly quality may be found in you.[8]

Evans says that "Müntzer had . . . drunk deep of the German mysticism of the later Middle Ages."[9] Of this he gives evidence when he says that every part of the Word of God speaks to the soul. Perhaps the most real to him were the words about prophets, the return of the Lord and that all believers were priests and kings. Müntzer's anti-pacifism and insurrectionism were definitely not Mennonite but his mysticism was.

When Wenger writes, "The essence of mysticism is placing stress on an intimate life of fellowship and communion with God or Christ rather than be content as a humble believer on the Lord Jesus Christ, guided by the Word of God as interpreted by the Holy Spirit,"[10] it is difficult to accept that a newly con-

8 Menno Simons, "Admonition on Church Discipline," *CWMS*, p. 417.
9 Austin Patterson Evans, *An Episode in the Struggle For Religious Freedom: The Sectaries of Nuremberg 1524-1528* (New York: Columbia University Press, 1924), p. 41.
10 John Christian Wenger, *Introduction to Theology* (Second edition (Revised); Scottdale, Pennsylvania: Herald Press, 1956), p. 21.

verted Christian will remain emotionally entirely neutral and be only a "humble believer" without any mystical expression. Hoekstra, who was excellently versed in the history and teaching of the Old Evangelical Anabaptists and Mennonites, agrees with this when he says in his *Beginselen en leer der Oude Doopsgezinden vergeleken met die van de overige Protestanten* (Amsterdam, 1863) that the very heart of the "churches before Paul was the mystical Christ Himself." His kingdom and body He has taken up from the earth into heaven and there now is our citizenship. There are we seated with Christ where we now live the life that is hidden in Christ with God (Phil. 3:6; Col. 3:3). This is not a mere affection of the soul as influenced by the Divine Spirit but a mystical transcendence by faith into the concreteness that is laid down by the Word of God itself. The quality of the transcendence is spiritual and subjective but the motive is objective and heartening for it is based on the Word. There is that which is beyond the subjective and that which is felt.

Here De Bussy draws our attention to that which limits the mystical when he says that what we feel does not enable man's faith to penetrate the higher orders of the world. Biblical mysticism developed around the doctrine of the "revelation of the Evangelical truth." The Church of Rome and other Reformers were vigilant at all times to keep this Biblical mysticism from spreading. Rome made no allowance for faith other than its own. Only a few Anabaptist leaders had a faith strong enough to break through this barrier to arrive at the heart of the Gospel where faith dominated as it did in the case of Luther. It is not surprising to find Conrad Grebel write in 1524: "There are not twenty who believe the Word of God." The Mennonites have always stressed the faith of the Gospel; here may be the reason why they do not consider themselves mystics in the sense that some of the outstanding Anabaptists were.

Mennonite Biblical Mysticism and Ethics

Mennonite mysticism in its lead to an autonomy of Mennonite ethics had at times to follow secondary courses. Its progress could never be stopped because of the evangelical urge in all Anabaptists. Their vision of Christ's Kingdom on earth was a practical mysticism where that of the Spanish classical era was philosophic and speculative. Had their leaders been permitted to live, their plans would have materialized much sooner.

Mysticism and Mennonite Ethics 155

Christianity has always had its by-products. Starting with Rome we can continue all the way down to the smallest sect by way of by-products and find that the number of sects is directly proportional to the literalness of Scripture interpretation and obstruction. Spanish rule at The Hague closely watched and severely curbed all initiative in the Low Countries. Heresy abetted by Dutch nationalism produced radicalism everywhere. What form it had did not matter to the Catholics. Lutheranism and Anabaptism alike were subjected to fire and water. In the Lutheran agitation David Joris, one of its members, hung up scurrilous sheets against the pope on the church doors. They all believed that the pope was the Antichrist, and all whipping, tongue-boring, banishment, hanging, drowning and burning alive, ordered by the court at The Hague, could not stop it. The "Anabaptism of The Netherlands," says Bainton,

> assumed highly ecstatic forms. The movement was already ten years old and the soberer leaders had been liquidated. The direction fell in consequence to less balanced spirits. All of them spirit-filled, able through dreams and visions to declare the mind of the Lord.[11]

Here a by-product of Lutheranism fed into the stream of Anabaptism, swelling it to an above-flood stage.

David Joris left the Lutheran Church and joined the more mystical Anabaptists and became their leader with the results of extreme literalism and fanaticism. His movement became so radical that, at a meeting at Bocholt in 1535 to clarify matters, the reactionaries, later the Mennonites, withdrew. Basically their faith was the same but in expressing it they differed greatly. According to Blesdijk, Joris' doctrine was typically Mennonite for he touched people's hearts so powerfully that they withdrew "from the love of vanity, self-wisdom, arrogance, and impurity" and directed them to "the true wisdom which is the fear of God, simplicity, chastity, and righteousness." His approach was prevailingly mystical in that his picture of God was "impartial and unrestricted, extending his grace to all creatures and refusing to be bound by all man-made lines of land or sect."[12]

Joris' words became the heart of Mennonite mysticism. To be a Mennonite, professing doctrine alone is not enough. Wen-

---

[11] Roland N. Bainton, *The Travail of Religious Liberty, op. cit.,* pp. 126, 127.
[12] Bainton, *op. cit.,* p. 132-135.

ger says that the right spirit of conduct must also be in evidence. This involves non-resistance, non-swearing of oaths, non-conformity, a simple life, obeying the Bible literally and taking up the cross of Christ in obedience. This all revolves around the Christians' attitude to the Bible, his estimation of the ideal church and his Christian life and ethic.[13] For Joris' mysticism the objective was the union with the "boundaryless God, to be God with God himself." He says,

> This way of union is the way of inward transformation through a re-enactment in personal experience of the incarnation and passion of Christ, neither of which is of any avail unless thus inwardly appropriated. What does it help me to know that Christ was conceived of the Holy Ghost, and born of the Virgin Mary, if he be not born in me? If you have missed the nature and spirit of the love of Christ, all the outward physical blood of our Lord Jesus will not help you, however firmly you believe that it has been shed for you. Listen to this, you slaves of the letter, who teach that we are justified by faith which consists in holding firmly that Jesus Christ died for us.[14]

With these evangelical principles Joris helped to blaze the path to the biblical conversion experience position in Mennonite ethics. Every baptismal candidate had to give evidence that he had accepted Christ as Saviour and Lord of his daily life.[15] Accepting a conversion experience as genuine would have been comparatively simple had mysticism not played a part. To Joris the Holy Ghost talked Dutch and the external Bible was a rather nebulous standard. He maintained that the most controverted points dealt with externals whereas the inward alone mattered. Denck and others also substantiated this by contending that the Bible was not a "visible book written by the hand of man," but was "living, eternal, and potent. None was worthy to discover, open, teach, confess, or read it"; it was "a sevenfold light shining in the faces of men and angels."[16]

All other Anabaptists accepted the conversion experience and the Holy Spirit's operation in the life of the believer, but in the way they experienced it they differed, depending on the prom-

---

13 Wenger, "Glimpses of Mennonite History and Doctrine," *op. cit.*, p. 147.
14 Bainton, *op. cit.*, pp. 135, 136.
15 S. F. Pannabecker, "Conversion," *The Mennonite Encyclopedia*, edited by H. S. Bender and C. Henry Smith (Scottdale, Pennsylvania: Mennonite Publishing House, 1955), pp. 704-05.
16 Bainton, *op. cit.*, pp. 136-138.

inence they gave to the written Word of God. They also differed with the Medieval mystics in that they made no special effort to please Rome. Those outside looked upon them, and often with good reason, as enthusiasts who depended on "private revelation" and the direction of an "inner light," stigmatizing "obedience to Scripture as letter service (*Buchstabendienst*) making private revelations the norm of their faith."[17]

When this is said about the Anabaptists and Schwenkfeldians it is imperative to cite Menno Simons at some length and look at the ingredients that eventually and permanently went into Mennonite ethics. He took an opposing view to Joris and the other radicals. He was a Biblical mystic in that the Bible was his norm of faith, and through the knowledge of the Word alone could the ideal Christian and church be realized. The following longer statements from his writings tell what Menno taught about the written Word.

> Brethren, I tell you the truth and lie not. I am not Enoch, I am no Elias, I am not one who sees visions, I am no prophet who can teach and prophesy otherwise than what is written in the Word of God and understood in the Spirit. . . .
> I shall write or speak nothing but that which I can prove by Moses, the prophets, the evangelists and other apostolic Scriptures and doctrines, explained in the true sense, Spirit, and intent of Christ. Judge ye that are spiritually minded.
> Once more, I have no visions nor angelic inspiration. Neither do I desire such lest I be deceived. The Word of Christ alone is sufficient for me. . . . There are but two Davids contained in the Word of God [referring to David Joris]. Whosoever poses as a third is a falsifier and a blasphemer against Christ. Let every soul take heed, lest he err in his faith.
> . . . I repeat that I have formerly acted shamefully against God and my neighbors . . . and I still do sometimes think, speak, and act recklessly, which, however, I sincerely hate. What am I that I should boast, seek, and teach anything else than the ever blessed Christ Jesus alone, His Word, sacraments, obedience, and His God-pleasing, virtuous, and unblamable life. He is the only one of whom it is written that He was begotten of the Holy Ghost; that He knew no sin; that guile was not found in His mouth; and that His

---

17 John Theodore Mueller, *Christian Dogmatics* (St. Louis, Missouri: Concordia Publishing House, 1955), p. 95.

doctrine, Word, will, and commandments are life eternal. Therefore take heed and watch over your soul . . . remain in a humble walk before God in the true measure of his faith. . . . Let no man deceive himself. Let spiritual pride and vain boasting be far from you, for God resisteth the proud, and giveth grace to the humble. I Pet. 5:5.[18]

In spite of these vast differences, the Mennonites are often wrongly put into the same camp with the radical "enthusiasts." But, says Littell, "the reputation of the Anabaptists is in fact changing because newly published documentary materials and certain German monographs have made imperative a thorough revision of still prevailing judgments regarding those called 'Anabaptist.' A reassessment of the entire movement is timely and feasible."[19]

Menno Simons' genius imprinted Biblicism with a warmth, love and sacrifice for the fellowship. Until his time it was more a sacrificing for the truth. In the expression of truth in fellowship was the uniqueness of Mennonite mysticism. Human value is so vivid that non-resistance and foot-washing come naturally. Indeed only the Word of God literally interpreted could be accepted as *bona fide* prescription of human relationship. This ideal of fellowship had not been reached in the prior Anabaptist movement. In their floundering their momentum was spent on the individual.[20] Mennonite mysticism uniquely applied to Biblical Christian principles produced a new way of life and tried to move the life of the Apostolic Church forward into the sixteenth century.

At this stage the question arose whether the Mennonites were mystical or spiritual. It was difficult to think of a "spiritual" way of life. A life had to be real as it was lived within the bounds of society. Mennonites believe that their way of life must be extremely real because it must literally express Biblical principles. Reality is given to all details as practiced in Bible times in the belief that religion is the same at all times. Nor do they spiritualize the demands made in the Sermon on the Mount. In the Lord's Supper the real part is

---

[18] Menno Simons, "Why I Do Not Cease Teaching and Writing, 1530," *MSCW*, pp. 310-11.

[19] Hamlin Franklin Littell, *The Anabaptist View of the Church* (Second edition, revised and enlarged; Boston: Starr King Press, 1958), pp. xii-xiv.

[20] J. Harder, "Das Mennonitentum als gemeindliche und gesellschaftliche Erscheinung," *Der Mennonit*, internationales mennonitiches Gemeindeblatt, XI (Juni, 1948), (Karlsruhe: Buchdruckerei Heinrich Schneider), 69.

not Christ but the person partaking it. "The Real Presence" is a real symbol pointing to a new way of life made real by obeying the Scriptures. The life they live here is governed by the life they have from God. The problem of their ethics is to harmonize the demands of the Scriptures, the church and society. They carry on as other people but live a life motivated directly by Christ.

A new ethos results from a life with Christ and non-conformity to the world (those people who ask not Christ to lead them in their daily walk and do not unreservedly submit to Him as Lord). Mennonites say, "If we yield in full submission to God, making no provision to fulfill the lusts of the flesh . . . we will overcome the world." To help in this overcoming they used to settle in closed communities and the ministers closely watched the deportment of every member during the week. Their various mutual-aid plans made insurance unnecessary. The command of the cross to follow Christ and serve one another still has a tremendous mystical power over them and produces a dynamic with which to triumph in difficulties. This results in much more than only a "spiritual religion"; it is a mystical union with Christ that produces a definite way of life. Their mysticism is exactly the opposite of what the so-called mystics had during the Middle Ages. Those had a "union of essence, which destroyed distinct personality and subsistance of either Christ or the human spirit."[21]

By definition the spiritual relates to sacred things of the church and not to the temporal. According to this the Mennonites are not spiritual for they have nothing that is "sacred." One such example is their cemeteries which receive no particular care. Earlier they insisted that their dead be buried anywhere since no burial place was holy. Outside influence has changed this but many congregations still have a semi-forgotten, weed-covered cemetery. The Amish do not even have separate buildings for their church services and many Mennonite churches are very plain and often barnlike. Their ministers do not wear robes but the same clothes as their members. Neither has God's Word only a spiritual control over them. No portion of it is exempted from being put into the practice of everyday living. "When I find myself assailed by temptation," says Wenger, "I forthwith lay hold of some text of the Bible."

21 Henry Bancroft, arranger and compiler, *Christian Theology* (Johnson City, New York: Johnson City Publishing Company, 1946), p. 167.

To the mystic the intangible acquires a tremendous reality. This in no wise is a speculative or philosophical reality which the Word through the Holy Spirit brings near. The spiritual counsels, the mystical gives expression to the counsels. If the Mennonites were liturgical the Kyrie would be the part of the service that would suggest a place where much of the biblical mysticism could be expressed. Now they rely on the Word presented in the simplest rigor. They say, "The curse of theology today is its reduction to abstract theory and philosophical speculation and system, rather than the simple presentation of the express counsels of God as revealed in His Word."[22]

MENNONITE SPIRITUAL MYSTICISM AND ETHICS

The Mennonites have always had a deep, spiritual longing which never is satisfied in this world. Their piety attempts to compensate for this. It seems more liturgical worship services would give their souls needed opportunity for expression. Suppressed mysticism always erupts unexpectedly some place. That which God put into man must be expressed. Reed in *The Lutheran Liturgy* makes the striking observation of how the mystical operates in the human soul. "The Kyrie," he says,

> tersely and poignantly voices the collected petitions and longings of the worshipers. A somewhat more mystical point of view is expressed in the idea that the Kyrie represents our deepest spiritual longings and hopes, which can never be fully realized in this world. . . . Pious devotion has suggested numerous other mystical explanations. . . . Liturgy is woven in by . . . sacramental . . . contrasting moods and . . . rhythmic succession of adoration, praise and petition. . . . Upon these two wings of humility and confidence all liturgical prayer rises to the throne of grace.[23]

Through the years of intolerance, the streamlets of mysticism have channelled their own ways around obstructions in the sands of time and sought to refresh by shifting emphasis from a liturgical worship service to a unique way of life.

Mysticism always maintains that spiritual truth cannot be apprehended by the logical faculty nor can it be adequately expressed in terms of understanding. Mennonitism does this when it expresses itself in a mystical religious way of life rather

---

22 Wenger, *Introduction to Theology, op. cit.*, pp. 19, 20.
23 Luther D. Reed, *The Lutheran Liturgy* (Fourth printing; Philadelphia: Muhlenberg Press, 1947), pp. 255-56.

than in worship or spirituality. Among the Amish, Hutterites and very conservative Mennonites this is frequently carried so far that even Mennonites who are not so much acquainted with them do not fully understand their way of life. The early Anabaptists, who were very sensitive in their mystical discernment, knew without many words when a person was of their kind. This is still quite evident among the Hutterites who live in closed communities. Some Mennonites also feel that it is essential to live in close communities to preserve faith and sensitivity to mystical spirituality. Their mysticism is nourished by an "otherness" apart from spirituality. It is for this reason that they are not so-called pacifists. Their life, which they have directly from God to make known to all men, is a way of non-resistance. This was especially the case in earlier mysticism. It is striking that the Waldenses and the Franciscans were gripped simultaneously by the desire to take this message of the new life to the world. This mysticism of the Waldenses was carried on later by the Anabaptists of which Blaurock is a typical example when he says, "We know through the Spirit that we are sent by God." Muralt questions this when he asks, "Do these assertions really prove that the Anabaptists have revelations through the Spirit independent of the Word of God?"[24] Here is a dynamic which spirituality never imparts, a dynamic beyond all traditions, an intensity that touches the smallest space of human existence.[25]

The Mennonites, Amish, and Hutterites have perhaps asserted their way of life more than any other people. The Hutterites have stayed with their communes and grown so fast that neighboring communities have become alarmed. Their life is still a part of strong German mysticism which occupies the center of the stage with the minor actors always waiting in the wings. According to Tauber and Eckhart this mysticism carries over into religious motives with the result of depreciating with bitterness and humiliation all temptations in other expressions.[26]

---

[24] Leonhard von Muralt, *Glaube und Lehre der Schweizerischen Wiedertäufer in der Reformationszeit* (Zürich: Kommisionsverlag Beer & Co., 1938), pp. 28, 29.
[25] J. Garder, "Das Mennonitentum als gemeindliche und gesellschaftliche Erscheinung," *Der Mennonit*, Internationales mennonitisches Gemeindeblatt, Vol. xi, No. 6 (June, 1958) Karlsruhe: Buchdruckerei Heinrich Schneider), 69.
[26] Erich D. Seeberg, *Luthers Theologie in ihren Grundzügen* (Zweite Auflage; Stuttgart: W. Kohlhammer Verlag, 1950), pp. 27, 29.

Inwardly they assert themselves not by prescribed ways. Some of the Anabaptists were so independent and strong in their sensitivity that they thought they could get along without Scripture, even to the point of refusing theological knowledge that offered restraints. Denck and Hubmaier relied especially on their own interpretation of Scripture and set it on paper which many did not even care to do. Müntzer and others conferred directly with the Spirit and depended on it.[27] This was just what Hegel tried when he resorted to the mystical on the level of his own rationality and made "sin luminous intelligence."[28] Related to this is the mysticism advocated by Rufus Jones when he takes no recognition of "human depravity and the need of a divine Mediator."[29] The Mennonites in turn are motivated by the same mysticism but after that they are made very much aware of their need of a personal Saviour.

In later years, according to Peter M. Friesen, the glow of this mysticism was fanned into flame among the Mennonites in Russia by the Pietism of the eighteenth century. The Mennonite Brethren Church in Russia during the middle of the nineteenth century and later, with little theological schooling, was led to excess in religious expression and one-sided views. The Libenau church wrote, "All are very happy and elated in the Spirit and the church life is in good order." Or in the words of Newman, "When they say about us that we shout and dance that is the truth." Such perturbations rooted in a mystical background resulted in excessive moralistic striving without resorting fully in faith to the mediations of Jesus Christ to self-engendered goodness, and the lifting of self into God's presence; all directly in opposition of Karl Barth's conviction that God reveals Himself to man in Jesus Christ.[30] Mysticism without the mediating Redeemer Christ Jesus is a semi-pelagian form of religious expression which, according to Horton, "seeks to elevate above the world."[31] Horst, the present-day Mennonite promoter of doctrine, accepts this "elevation" with proviso that "there are two kingdoms — the kingdom of God and the king-

---

27 Hoekstra, *op. cit.*, pp. 98-99.
28 De Goede, *op. cit.*, p. 52.
29 *App.* II, y.
30 Otto Weber, *Karl Barth's Church Dogmatics*, translated by Arthur C. Cochrane, (Philadelphia: The Westminster Press, 1953), pp. 35-49.
31 Walter Marschall Horton, *Christian Theology: An Ecumenical Approach* (Revised and enlarged edition; New York: Harper & Brothers Publishers, 1958), p. 206.

dom of this world — and all of us belong to one or the other." To him there really is no "elevation"; there is only a separation from the world. To conform to the world "means to follow the forms of fashions of the world and to be in harmony and agreement with the standards of the world."[32]

This mystical Mennonite way of life, however, does not assert itself in an esoteric manner. In a most unique way Mennonites wait to be called up higher. As biblical mystics they separate from the world and try to live a life "of heaven" and wait as thousands of their martyrs did "to come up higher after their sojourn here is completed." When reading of the awful tortures they endured one wonders whence their heroic strength. This, they say,

> all depends on the place where one lives, whether on the side of the world or on the side of God. In this and only in this lies the reason for all the heavy suffering we are subjected to in this Western world.[33]

One of their oldest books, *Güldene Aepffel,* is entirely devoted to a description of this dwelling place.

All mysticism went through the stages of purification, enlightenment, and ecstasy, writes Wenger. Instead of these definite stages the Mennonites have the "conversion experience" and a life free from deliberate sin. "The first birth of man," says Menno,

> is out of the first and earthly Adam, and therefore its nature is earthly and Adam-like, that is carnally minded, unbelieving, disobedient, and blind to divine things; deaf and foolish; whose end, if not renewed by the Word will be damnation and eternal death. If now you desire to have your wicked nature cleared up, and desire to be free from eternal death and damnation so that you may obtain with all true Christians that which is promised them, then you must be born again. For the regenerate are in grace and have the promise as you have heard.[34]

The biblical "new birth" is a mystical experience based on the Word. At this time the new citizen of the Kingdom of Heaven promises fealty to Him for the rest of his days. The Holy Spirit now directs his life and makes him aware of a biblical mysticism that he has in common with all believers.

32 Horst, editor, *op. cit.,* pp. 72-73.
33 *Appendix* II, z.
34 Menno Simons, "The New Birth," *CWMS,* p. 92.

Besides this, mysticism may have this anchorage in an intense reviving experience independent of the Word and be based on an entirely pagan foundation. In either case it is a soul-stirring and captivating event that cuts across all avenues of life and chains the individual to the essence of his new being. Perhaps some of the greatest "soul experiences," says Dr. C. Noordmans, were found with the Manicheans who had not a Christian origin.[35] This psychological phenomenon has the same effect in pagan and Christian. What the Mennonites and all others that believe in a religious "new birth" experience do, is to give this psychological personality remaking a biblical, Christ centered prerogative. "Many Christians," says Wenger, "who are evangelical, some Catholic and some Protestant, have had moments of great spiritual intensity in which they have come into a tremendous awareness of the immediate presence of God. Charles G. Finney would be a good example of this type of mysticism."[36] Other examples are the Exodus of Israel (Exodus 13), Gideon's victory over Midian (Judges 7) and David's praise for the deliverance from all his enemies (Psalm 18). Newman believes that it was a reformatory force even during the Middle Ages.[37] According to Seeberg, when it emerged again it left neo-platonism and pantheism behind and taught that outward forms were of no account. We have to unite with God, "God being in us and we in God. By contemplating God we become one with God. By contemplating Christ we become one with Christ."[38]

In conclusion it is essential that we compare this "new birth" mysticism with classical mysticism which paid no attention to human depravity, the Word of God, or a Christian experience. Schleiermacher (1768-1834) as a mystic deprecated obedience to the Word and postulated feelings. The Anabaptists and Mennonites aimed to be under the control of the Word and the Spirit of truth. How else could Blaurock and many others have asked to be baptized when they knew that they would be brutally murdered for making such request, Even if the majority of the Reformers made allowance for error in understand-

---

35 G. Keizer, De geestelijke ontwapening der Christenheid in haar geschiedenis geschetst," *Geestelijk Weerloos of Weerbaar?* Samengsteld Door J. H. De Goede, Jr. (Amsterdam: Uitgevers-Mij Holland, n.d.), p. 52.
36 Wenger, "Introduction to Theology," *op. cit.*, p. 22.
37 Newman, *op. cit.*, II, 4.
38 *Ibid.*, pp. 5, 26.

ing, the Scriptures remained right and real to them. Perhaps never tolled mysticism clearer than when Luther said, "*Ich kann nicht anders*" (here I stand, I cannot recant, so help me God). What made it the message that it was? It was the Holy Spirit operating by faith through man's mystical powers. Never had it occurred to such an extent since the days of the Apostles. Followers of George Fox had similar experiences to a degree. "There was nothing unorthodox about this," says Hordern.

> Christians have always believed that the Holy Spirit speaks to the heart of man and guides him. Both Luther and Calvin laid a great emphasis upon it. But there was a tendency in sectarian circles to find the ultimate authority in the Inner Light rather than in the Bible.[39]

This criticism expresses the lesson that Anabaptists were unacceptable to the other religious bodies. The expression of this mysticism and ethics needs to be discussed to determine whether the judgments passed upon them by the other Protestants and by the Catholics were correct.

MENNONITE EXPRESSION OF MYSTICISM AND ETHICS

Basically all Anabaptists accept that man is a mystical being because he is able to think, feel and live on a higher plane where the atmosphere becomes rarer and the soul is less hampered. Whether such rising is sane or not depends on the extent that the Holy Ghost is permitted to lead.

All Reformers had trouble in charting this mystical process from death to life. Too often they looked upon original sin as a part of the conversion process which made it difficult to deduct a plan of salvation that was sufficiently explainable. Often, too, since their objectivity was obscured by legal terms, they had to make a leap of faith in order to reach the Gospel. The deep truth had to be grasped not negatively through the corruption of a person's nature but positively through a peculiar consciousness of divine presence in which they worshipped.[40] They all accepted the rise of the soul but where some stressed the negative and legal others dwelt practically only on the positive and on the gospel. No one was as clear on this point as Luther when he gave the law and the gospel their proper places.

When Latourette says that "religious geniuses," who combined

---

39 William Hordern, *A Layman's Guide to Protestant Theology* (New York: The Macmillan Company, 1957), p. 42.
40 Hoekstra, *op. cit.*, pp. 61-63.

mysticism with practical achievement appeared in the Catholic Church, we must include the Anabaptist leaders, seeing that almost all formerly belonged to the Catholic clergy. This combination of practical religion and German mysticism was always expressed subjectively[41] in the form of the *Jesumystik*[42] of St. Bernard. In trying to bring about practical achievement and nourish the life of the spirit, the state of the soul was carefully analyzed with an almost uncanny application of psychological principles.

It is highly significant to observe here that the Catholics who emphasize the practical religious achievement in mystical utterance and the Jews who do not accept Jesus Christ as the world's Messiah rely much more on psychological analysis than the Anabaptists and the like. The latter use mysticism as the gateway to a "decision for Christ" followed by an obedience to Him based on His word. Their intimate relationship with God finalizes their actions based on an analysis of what Jesus would want us to do after He has taken our guilt of sin from us and placed it upon Himself. The former starts with a psychological analysis with the objective of getting along without implicit obedience to Christ where the others attempt to look at the life of the soul and learn to know it and the inner life through denial. In a way it was a reaction to the height of power and glory of Innocent III. This spectacular program of subjectivity and denial was instigated by two men, Peter Waldus at Lyon, and Francis of Assisi in Italy. Anabaptist mysticism was in a large part a duplication of Waldus' "practical achievement," only mountains and time separated the movements.

As one would expect, Waldus and the Anabaptists had much in common with the Franciscans and other orders. Mysticism characterized thousands of Spaniards and gave rise to scores of writers and a vast literature. It was not confined to any one religious group but was found in several of the existing orders and now again produced a new one. The Moravian Milicz of Kremsier

> canon and vicar of the Cathedral of Prague . . . carried his message among the lowly and the humble. As Saint

---

[41] Philip S. Watson, *Let God Be God!* and *Interpretation of the Theology of Martin Luther* (London: The Epworth Press, 1947), p. 13.
[42] Seeberg, *op. cit.*, p. 26.

Francis, he began by renouncing all privileges, offices and riches. This conduct won for him great popularity and captured the imagination of the people. . . . He was a mystic, an Apocalyptic, who prophesied the imminent coming of the Antichrist and the end of the world between the years 1365 and 1367. . . . His apocalyptic tendencies were reproduced even in the works of the painters.[43]

These apocalyptic prophecies and mystical manifestations were soon expressed by Catholics and non-Catholics alike. At least this one hope of relief from the rigours of the time could not be taken from the chafing peasants. In the church several post-Thomistic religious leaders swung away from fine-spun speculation of holy living and with St. Hilary,

held that the Lord was not placed to save His people by means of subtle points of theology. They were founders of the mystical movement which flowed most profusely during the fourteenth and fifteenth centuries in the Rhine valley and the Netherlands.[44]

These influences soon showed up rather strongly among the *Wederdoopers*, who were numerous in this area. Karl Rembert describes how these different streams flowed in various directions with various results. The mystical spirit appealed to the common man especially when there was a leader with enough schooling to make his particular message of simple, pious and mystical expression tasteful. Where the church did not satisfy the longing of the soul it was sought elsewhere.[45] With Menno it was an "inner soul-struggle which did not cease until he broke the bonds which bound him to the Catholic Church and stepped forth in the faith and liberty of the Gospel."[46] To him and Luther the chief pontiff of Rome was no longer the servant of Christ but his opponent. Where Rome made repentance objective the Anabaptists made it also subjective; they wanted to see the fruits of repentance. Mysticism did not stay in its own original form and where it could not be expressed it was felt.

Among the Mennonites in the Netherlands it expressed itself in a desire for freedom. Cranmer and Pijper have 250 pages

---

43 Benito Mussolini, *John Huss*, translated by Clifford Parker (New York: Albert & Carrless Boni, 1929), p. 20.
44 Matthew Spinka, editor, *Advocates of Reform*, Library of Christian Classics (Philadelphia: The Westminster Press, 1953), XIV, 14.
45 Karl Rembert, *Die Wiedertäufer im Herzogtum Jülich* (Berlin: R. Goertners Verlagsbuchhandlung Herman Heyfelder, 1899), p. 5.
46 Bender, "A Brief Biography of Menno Simons," *CWMS, op. cit.*, p. 5.

on the topic of *"Der Leken Wechwyser"* (the course charted for the lay people). Here the Anabaptists participated everywhere in wide-spread unrest. Under *"freyheyt"* (freedom) he mentions that the Christians are free from ceremonialism and articles made by men.[47]

Mysticism viewed the end of religion as the union of man with God....[48] "The subduing of the flesh was ... wholesome discipline and any suffering imposed from without was to be welcomed."[49] "I wrote this," says an Anabaptist imprisoned for his faith, "in Creeffen's house from where we expect any day to make our sacrifice. We are sincerely satisfied that God considers us worthy for this."[50] Another writes that Christ had told them long ago that they would have no peace upon earth (Matt. 10; Mark 13). They had to be persecuted as He had been and they had to follow in His footsteps. He was free but did this for them. Why should not they, too, suffer as those of His household. They were not above Him.[51] They felt very strongly that they were called from the world of sin to be the Bride of Christ. Their life was separate from that of the world. This was a very significant teaching of all the Anabaptists, and still is among the Mennonites.

The Anabaptist Joannes Anastasius lets us know how mystically they viewed the *"Avondmaal"* (Lord's Supper) when he begs his listeners to "feel themselves" before the supper: examine their words and works, and see how they feel. "Do this," he says, "so that the Spirit of Christ may dwell in you and not the evil spirit." In another place he stresses the blessed improvement independent of all ceremonialism.[52]

Several mystical currents impressed the Mennonites in the sixteenth century. One of them Doctor Pyper sets forth in the book *Van den Gheloove* (About the Faith) when he points out that it is not enough to speak much about the Word or carry

---

[47] Auth. Ioan. Anastasio Valuano, "Der Leken Wechwyser," *Bibliotheca Reformatoria Neerlandica*, Opnieuw uitgegeven en van inleidigen en aanteekenigen voorzien door S. Cramer, en F. Pijper ('s-Gravenhage, Martinus Nijhoff, 1906), X, IV, 123-376.
[48] G. G. Mannhardt, "Corpus Schwenkfeldisnorum," in *Geschichte der Mennoniten*, compiled by Cassel K. Daniel (Philadelphia: J. Kohler, Nr. 911, Arch-Strasse, 1890), p. 57.
[49] Bainton, *op. cit.*, p. 57.
[50] *Appendix* II, (1)
[51] *Appendix* II, (2)
[52] *Appendix* II, (3)

it, we must have it in the spirit that believes the book (Word) and that it has changed and renewed us. That the Lord has done a glorious work in us must be believed in the spirit.[53] The external ceremony is only an occasion or opportunity to express the feeling that is within. The spirit and the heart must eat and not the mouth only.[54] According to Bergson, such statements are mystical for "now," he says,

> if you distinguish this metaphysical system from all others by saying that it compels our assent . . . then we are dealing with mystic experience. True mystics simply open their souls to the oncoming wave. Sure of themselves, because they feel within them something better than themselves, they prove to be great men of action, to the surprise of those for whom mysticism is nothing but visions, and raptures and ecstasies. That which they have allowed to flow into them is a stream flowing down and seeking through them to teach their fellow-men; the necessity to spread around them what they have received affect them like an onslaught of love. . . .[55]

DELINEATION OF MENNONITE MYSTICISM AND ETHICS

In the confession of Thomas van Inbroeck at Cologne in 1558 we have the key to the whole matter of mysticism and ethics when he says the Scriptures "cannot be broken, neither are we to take away from, or add to, the Word of God (which) abideth for ever."

Three Anabaptists of outstanding ability in thought, dialectics and leadership were greatly responsible for laying the foundation and shaping of Mennonite ethics in this area. These were:

(1) Dr. Balthasar Hubmaier, an ardent student of the Scriptures. Even if he wavered in times of extreme inflicted suffering, he always regarded the Scriptures "as the final authority and best guide." He permitted himself to be influenced by Müntzer and cast unjust reflections upon the Anabaptist cause which harmed his influence as a leader. However, when the validity and use of the Scriptures were in question "he main-

---

53 *Appendix* II, (4)
54 *Appendix* II, (5)
55 Henri Bergson, *The Two Sources of Morality and Religion*, translated by R. Ashley Audra and Gloudesley Brereton with the assistance of W. Horsfall Carter (Garden City, New York: Doubleday & Company, Inc., 1956), p. 99.

tained that all customs and traditions must be subject to the Bible."[56]

(2) Hans Denck was one of the radical mystics among the Anabaptists. It is perhaps true when Kielstra writes: "All kinds of untruths are said about him. His writings amply vouch for this." Denck's stress was not outward but inward. Proof of being in possession of the Word of God was its operation within and consequent outward ethics, an ethics that fitted into the formulae of the Scriptures. He asks: "What is faith? Upon what does it rest? What is its foundation and fountain? Is it innate and produced as the fruit of hearing the Word only outwardly? I am a poor being and hunger for the better things. Can outward faith bring inward peace? No, not belief but only obedience to God can do this. Unbelief is disobedience, selfishness and sensuality."

Denck found it difficult to agree with Luther, who held that man cannot exert any effort towards good. Through the Holy Spirit man is able to produce a life witnessing of Christ's power from within. He taught the *"Doopers"* that no one was predestined to be saved and others to be damned. He said that everyone has the potential to be good. In all cases there must be fruit of obedience. What Denck combatted was the outward churchly operation and its application of the Word. To him that was not the life that a Christian had from Christ. He counted the outward beliefs of the church as useless. Many preachers as builders erect a very shaky structure. Preaching peace when there is no peace is tempting God. Obedience to God leads to wonderful comfort and light amidst deepest suffering.

Besides Denck we have Jakob Kautz, who came in contact with him and Ludwig Haetzer in Worms when they translated the Prophets from Hebrew into German for the first time. Since his conversion from Lutheranism to Anabaptism in 1526 he was feared by the Reformers, banished repeatedly and imprisoned. He published the complete Bible in German five years before Luther's Bible. As a typical mystic he urged the spiritual life in union with God and made no allowance for outward forms. His central theme was an inner obedience that forms the objective of all Christian effort. "The Word," he says,

[56] J. H. Langewalter, *Christ's Headship of the Church According to Anabaptist Leaders Whose Followers Became Mennonites* (Pernem, Indiana: Mennonite Book Concern, 1917), pp. 75-77.

that we speak outwardly with our mouth . . . is nothing living, nor the eternal Word of God, but only a witness or indication of the inner Word, so that the inner Word may be rightly understood.[57]

(3) Kaspar von Schwenkfeld was not a Mennonite but his relation to them is important. His statements are especially fitting in determining the relationship of Anabaptist mysticism to the other Reformation movements. From his correspondence with the Dutch Mennonites we see that after repeated meetings with Luther, Melanchthon and Uchenhagen in Wittenberg he agreed with them in all main points including infant baptism and the Lord's Supper. He did not disregard the *Confessio Augustana* but did not want to accept it as the Gospel of Christ nor swear by it. He could not accept Melanchthon's statements any differently than the Lutherans accepted the writings of Augustin and Hieronymus.[58]

Mystically, if not in all points doctrinally, the Schwenkfelders' ethics stood in close relationship to those of the Mennonites. They said the Anabaptists were closer to them because they were more concerned about Biblical truths than some of the learned. Daniel K. Cassel, the compiler of Schwenkfeld's correspondence points out that the main points of Fox's teaching of the "inner light" agrees with the customs of the Mennonites and that he likely got it from them. Schwenkfeld desired that the Reformation take place in every heart through faith in the Scriptures. Other historians also make this connection between the Quakers and Mennonites. Closer relationship must be sought in results. Since emotions always ran high in the Reformers, enduring qualities had to be proven with time. In perspective we see Schwenkfeld as a religious enthusiast, Hans Denck a rationalist, and Menno as one who changed the Münsterites into a harmless sect. The ethics emerging from these mystical concepts can best be defined from what the Mennonites did.

---

57 Wilhelm Wiswedel, "The Inner and the Outer Word," *The Mennonite Quarterly* XXVI (July, 1952), p. 179.

58 A. B. "Kaspar von Schwenkfeld und die Correspondenz der Schwenkfelder mit der holländischen mennonitischen Societät in den Jahren 1725; aus dem Archiv der Mennoniten-Gemeinde zu Amsterdam," Daniel K. Cassel, compiler, Geschichte der Mennoniten (Philadelphia: J. Kohler, Nr. 911 Arch-Strasse, 1890), p. 366.

The "Inner Light" and Mennonite Ethics

No one stressed the "inner light" more than Hans Denck (1527). Modern Mennonites do not want to consider him in their discussion of their faith because he had his own "brand" of mystical Anabaptism. Wiswedel replies,

> Denck not only promoted the authority of the Holy Scriptures, but he also made abundant use of them. To him the Holy Scriptures are true and constant and reveal nothing but what God in truth wills.

Following Wiswedel's discussion of Denck's "inner light" philosophy in the *Mennonite Quarterly Review*[59] we see how he planted and promoted his ideas among them and how influential they are today.

(1) From Anabaptist writers we see that they do not deny all historical objective means of salvation other than the "inner light." The order would perhaps be: first, an inner capability to interpret Scripture by means of the Holy Spirit that God gives to those who ask Him; second, the Word; third, the admonishing that it requires for undivided obedience.

(2) In this fuller interpretation and obedience the Holy Spirit has to be in control. To have Christian and Anabaptist ethics, obedience must be given to His dictates. The life-giving Spirit of God turns the written and proclaimed Word into God's Word. There is an inner inspiration to co-work with God. This inner word sharpens the inner spiritual eye and gives it a true comprehension of the truth revealed in the written Word. This inner light is at all times present in the believer and guides him in all his actions.

(3) Preaching the living Word does not consist only of speaking and interpreting it to an audience. Ordination does not make a preacher. No one was more versed in the Scriptures, accepted and recognized than the Pharisees and yet they were far from the knowledge of God and Christ. Denck was not far from the spirit and life of the monks. The outward was the total result of the inward from which it rose. He repeatedly cites II Cor. 3:6, where the apostle warns against worshiping the letter, countering such adoration with the fact that the letter of the Scriptures can become a living word only through the Holy Spirit. Here Denck permitted himself to become a Biblicist under the influence of Luther. He speaks much about

---

[59] Wilhelm Wiswedel, "The Inner and the Outer Word," *The Mennonite Quarterly Review*, XXVI (July, 1952), pp. 179-83.

discipleship which can only come through the gospel, freedom of the will and divine light in the human soul.

It is difficult to believe that Denck was indifferent concerning the written Word when he in his day was foremost among the Reformers in translating the Prophets from the Hebrew into German. In the acceptance of this "inner Word" as the most dependable ethical guide, neither he nor the Mennonites at present separate it from the outer Word. When they choose their ministers today they do not call them "ministers" or "preachers" but "servers of the Word" (*Diener des Worts*). Their main responsibility is to make God's Word known and be examples to their flocks in obeying it. They are not "pastors" nor "canons" nor "reverends" nor "priests" but "servants of God's Word." The outer Word always receives the required attention to avoid its detachment from the Spirit. Peter Rideman, in his *Confession of Faith,* speaks of those ministers who "go through the country and establish through the Word" groups of believers and followers of this Word.

When the ministers of the *Kleingemeinde,* a small but one of the oldest Mennonite groups, met at Meade, Kansas, in 1957, they called it a *Diener-Konferenz* (servers conference). It is of significance when they state in one of the opening sentences that these meetings were attended by thirteen teachers (ministers, preachers or "teachers of the Word" —*Lehrer des Worts*). In connection with this they say:

> The contained twenty-three questions were discussed with prayer and considered in the light of present-day problems. They were viewed in the light of the Holy Scriptures and when the inner light, after much deliberation, gave dependable understanding these were recorded in the form of resolutions. The purpose of this Conference was not to add or subtract from the Scriptures. It was much more the purpose to find the best way how to apply the Scriptures to the problems our churches face. Rom. 12:16. . . .[60]

The discussions in the *Kleingemeinde* about the "inner light" do not indicate detail and extent. There is a danger in every such instance of putting one's own teaching into the Word instead of extracting from the Word its teaching. It appears that not using electricity, telephones or cars, as some Anabaptist extremists do, is putting preconceived notions into the Word.

[60] Diener-Konferenz der Kleingemeinde vom 23. zum 28. Oktober 1937 in Meade, Kansas.

As every other Protestant branch, Mennonites today accept, with discretion, modern ways and knowledge. They have their colleges, seminaries and a number of graduate students in state and other institutions. In spite of their various training they do not admit that the validity of the Word and its required obedience is thereby lessened. Liberalism and modernism in theology is removed from them to a much greater degree than from some of the non-Mennonite confessions. But for the Mennonites, says Wenger

> Christian truth is eternal and unchanging. They accept the entire Bible as the inspired Word of God, inerrant in its counsels and authoritative in its commands. Those who want theological relativism will not find it in the Word of God. The church cannot teach the commandments of men as the law of God, nor can it ignore for men what the Word of God asks of them. The message of the church must therefore be the Word of the Lord without addition or subtraction. The principles of the Scripture must be brought to bear upon twentieth-century life. To this end the church invites all those who are willing to abandon their sin and to live for God to unite themselves with the Body of Christ.[61]

Coming back to Wiswedel, he says that Anabaptist preachers desired that church members have a religious experience and upon this faith and repentance baptism be administered. When the masses by their consent to the printed and proclaimed Word had become church members without becoming new creatures then more emphasis was given to the inner Word. Occasionally the emphasis became disproportionate but never was the Spirit separated from the preaching of the Word.

(4) The Anabaptists drew a sharp line between Biblical faith and that which was commonly called "faith." Biblical faith was that which worked deeply in the soul by the Holy Spirit, while the common faith went only as far as believing the Bible. Thus Stadler said,

> It does not suffice to confess: I believe the written word and consider it God's Word. Such faith does not save and is not followed by improvement of conduct. Biblical faith is a work of grace of the Holy Spirit and brings to life the read or heard Word, so that it becomes a power in man to live righteously and to suffer patiently. Indeed,

---

61 J. C. Wenger, *Who Are Mennonites?* (Scottdale, Pennsylvania: Herald Press, n.d.), p. 10.

suffering becomes for those who believe from the heart a means of strengthening faith, but not the means by which a man comes into possession of the Spirit or of the "inner Word."[62]

(5) That there was occasional evidence of unwholesome concomitants of the inner illumination cannot be denied. It did indeed occur that the supposed voice of the Spirit was simply the brain. But does that not still happen among the Christians today? Yet this phenomenon does not necessarily discredit the valuable content of the insight gained by the idea.

(6) The Anabaptists believed in the immediate work of the Spirit of God. God can speak directly to the soul; the Bible is not His only revelation. If this were so we would have to deny miracles. But all other revelations of God to man must be proved by the Holy Scriptures which are in a sense the absolute measure that can alone be normative. That which does not agree with them cannot be God's Word.

(7) The Anabaptists share the idea of the "inner Word" with several others. George Fox said: "Upon the Spirit, upon the inner Word everything depends." Gottfried Arnold quotes a rhyme by Anna Orvena Mayer: *"Aber Gottes Wort, Jesus Christ, ist Geist und Leben, redet inwendig"* (the Word of God and Jesus Christ are spirit and life and speak inwardly). Tersteegen wrote: *"Von Kreatur, Vernunft und Sinne abgeschieden, im edlen Seelengrund macht sich die Gottheit meinem Geiste kund"* (Independent from the creature, the intellect, and the senses, the Godhead reveals Himself to my spirit in the pureness of my soul). Spurgeon said: "I have prayed that the Holy Spirit may disclose to you the meaning of the words of Scripture." George P. Schultz, one of the recently deceased older Mennonite evangelists, wrote:

> It is the work of the Holy Spirit to guide the people of God through their uncertainties, dangers, and duties of this life to their home in heaven. . . . Our first duty toward the Guide is that we must remember to surrender to him and follow Him all the way. . . . So many people have too little confidence in the divine Guide and think they can guide themselves better. Poor souls, but finally they must understand the language of the Guide. This is the sweetest voice that comes to a human being.[63]

---

62 Wiswedel, *op. cit.*, p. 189.
63 G. P. Schulz, *Short Talks on Live Themes* (Scottdale, Pennsylvania: Mennonite Publishing House, 1924), pp. 76-78.

MENNONITE HYMNS AND ETHICS

The ethics of Mennonite mysticism is also prevalent in the songs they use. Shifting to American customs, dropping the German language and being under the influence of other denominations have been the major reasons of their disuse. Nevertheless, their content still describes Mennonite Biblical mysticism.[64]

64 *Appendix* III, a.

PART THREE

CHAPTER I

THE APPLICATION OF MENNONITE ETHICS TO OTHERS

IDEALISM AND MENNONITE ETHICS

When Hoekstra says, "All faiths rest upon an ethical foundation," he expresses a well-recognized Mennonite principle. The "Christian faith," observes Wenger, "also involves a longing to please God and if one has been truly converted he will desire . . . to do the things . . . which God desires" and with St. Paul will "always take pains to have a clear conscience toward God and toward men."[1] For the Mennonites this means an ethical activity that induces outsiders to note that they take religion seriously and emphasize practical piety. It is a purely spiritual activity endeavouring to know the will of God through the Gospel of Christ and subjecting to it in obedience and trust.[2]

Simultaneously with the movements of Luther and Zwingli appeared an independent group, the Anabaptists. They had no outstanding single leader, no state help or even protection, and no organized clergy. The Sermon on the Mount was the core of their movement, furnishing organization and motives. They placed great reliance on the ethical portions of the Epistles of the Apostles, especially the Epistle by James with its emphasis of "doing."

Translating the Scriptures into action was extremely simple to them. No formal worship, no specially formulated creeds, no confessions or agreements were necessary. Those who believed in doing what the Scriptures required simply banded together. They drew up their first confession of faith in 1527 but before they had an opportunity to see it function its author and helpers were already brutally tortured to death.

Being creedless, non-liturgical and literal, they sought religious expression elsewhere. The emphasis was so much on put-

[1] John Christian Wenger, *Introduction to Theology* (Second edition, revised; Scottdale, Pennsylvania: Herald Press, 1956), pp. 274-75.
[2] Reinhold Seeberg, *History of Doctrines*, translated by Charles E. Hay (Grand Rapids, Michigan: Baker Book House, 1954), I, 41, 42.

ting the Scriptures into action that Anna Brons says, "No one can be justified by faith alone without doing the first works which the Gospel requires. . ."³ In later years, this frequently led these reactionaries into rather emotional and expressive religious denominations. During the 1930's a number of conservative Old Colony Mennonites in Saskatchewan joined the so-called Pentecostal Assemblies. It was John Holdeman in the last quarter of the previous century who swayed Mennonite religious thinking drastically when he started his own group on the basis of teaching "the whole truth." Today his followers distinguish themselves by "practicing a more spiritual child training, disciplining unfaithful members, scriptural avoidance of apostates [this includes persons who wear neckties and shave themselves] and avoiding world-minded churches . . . etc."⁴ Another typical example is Canon Theodore Wedel, who left his father's Mennonite church at Newton, Kansas, and became an outstanding liturgical Episcopalian. Another group that looked for more outward religious expression were the Templars. These left the Russian Mennonite churches and went to Turkestan and Palestine to be on hand when the Lord Jesus would return for His own. Class Epp, their leader, had extravagant opinions concerning his own mission and calling and claimed to be a divinely commissioned prophet. Later they moved to Palestine and were finally pillaged and made homeless during World War I.

For those remaining with their traditions, the main norm of religious expression is their relief work. They have portable and permanent food-processing plants for the sole purpose of relief and mission work. Another is teaching and Christianizing the Indians in the Chaco of South America who even speak the Mennonite Low German. They have a Voluntary Service Organization that provides, among other services, leper help and teachers for neglected areas in Northern Canada and Newfoundland. Every branch has its missionaries. The Evangelical Mennonite Brethren have one missionary for every 29.65 members.⁵

3 John Horsch, *Mennonites in Europe* (Second edition, slightly revised; Scottdale, Pennsylvania: Mennonite Publishing House, 1950), p. 16.
4 P. G. Hiebert, "Church of God in Christ, Mennonite," *ME, op. cit.*, I, 598.
5 Sam J. Schmidt, General Secretary, *The 1958 Annual Report* of the Evangelical Mennonite Brethren 64th Annual Conference session (Omaha, Nebraska: E.M.B. Headquarters, 839 Pine Street, 1958), pp. 17, 41.

The motive for such spending of money and effort is obedience to God. For them neither "Hegel's idealistic conception of the world" nor his "optimism about social process" are the answer. They agree with the topic of the Second Assembly of the World Council of Churches at Evanston in 1954: "Christ — the Hope of the World." Their ethic is the practical application of Christ's principles and were it not for their frequent disagreement among themselves and wasteful dissipation of energies resulting from it, they would accomplish much more. Partially their spirit of separation from the "world" carries over to undesirable separations among themselves. However, this ideal of being "saved to serve" they have all in common.

This practical love idea dates back to the Early Church. During the Reformation "non-resistance, spiritual government and sharing" appeared "in vivid form in all Anabaptist areas instead of a philosophical and theological ideal.[6] The heart of Menno's message was a church composed only of believers who participated in the practical issues of the New Testament. In going back to the Primitive Church they met the recurring appeal to follow the example and direct teaching of Christ. It was a form of love that demanded constant denial on its paths of duty. It was for this reason that the early Swiss Brethren asked their baptismal candidates "whether they would when necessity required," give all they had to help their brethren, and let none be in want if they could help it. Capito wrote to Zwingli about this unselfishness and "praiseworthy sincerity of the Anabaptists."

In spite of this sincerity and high ideals this unselfishness was misunderstood. In "religious toleration and liberty of conscience" they were too far ahead of their day. To them, like to Erasmus, truth expressed in word and deed became the principal object. They totally relied on it to endure and vindicate itself. To Melchior Hofmann's fantastic idea of his kingdom and being one of the "prophets" they paid little attention for they were confident that it would soon prove its own worth. As expected, many of his newly baptized followers defected when persecution arose. The truth for them was what a woman said under torture about a meeting where about

---

6 Hermann Nestler, *Die Wiedertäuferbewegung in Regensburg*, ein Ausschnitt aus der Regensburger Reformationsgeschichte (Regensburg: Druck und Velag von Josef Habbel, 1926), pp. 32-41.

thirty-six persons assembled at night in a forest. . . . One brother, named George Bastian, was reading the Scriptures and speaking for three hours. When he was done, they all knelt and prayed for a quarter of an hour for all authorities and for their persecutors. After that, all partook of a common meal for which some had brought food. Then one of them admonished those who were not yet baptized to lead a quiet Christian life. Some had need of clothing and tools, and were supplied.[7]

In order to be able to help others they had to keep their own needs to a minimum. This help, however, was never only for Mennonites. Almost all present Mennonite Central Committee help goes to non-Mennonites. G. G. Kornelsen writes on Aug. 1, 1934 in the *Steinbach Post* in connection with the sixtieth anniversary of the coming of the Mennonites,

A number of Lutherans had settled near Edmonton, Alberta, Canada. These in their poverty were compelled to send one of their pastors to seek outside help. In his travels he also visited the Mennonite settlement east of the Red River in Manitoba. Here he received copious help in the form of clothing, food and livestock.[8]

According to Nestler the early Anabaptists and Mennonites were laborers mostly with very little theological training. Even if their thinking about religious and social questions happened to be frequently confused, nevertheless in their practical assistance to others they had good judgment. They understood that they had to be frugal to sustain themselves amongst an unfriendly people and had to reject all wearing of costly clothing and ornaments, and many asked their tailors and seamstresses to hold to plain and simple custom and make nothing at all for pride's sake.

Ritschl thinks the Anabaptists shared this puritanical view with the Calvinists. They often met in Strassburg, he says, and took to each other's opinions. This "Calvinism," says Smyth

has much to answer for on the aesthetic score; Puritanism has followed the arduous path of duty without looking to either side. . . . (It) went straight on and carried man's burden; it lifted by main strength the whole world to a

---

[7] Horsch, *Mennonites in Europe*, op. cit., p. 128.
[8] G. G. Kornelsen, K. J. B. Reimer, J. G. Toews et al. *Das 60-Jährige Jubiläum* (1874-1934) (Beiträge zur mennonitischen Geschichte, Heft I; herausgegeben vom Warte-Verlag, Steinbach, Manitoba), p. 41.

higher order, and opened a purer and grander prospect for humanity.⁹

Whence the motives for such unselfish acts of "purer and grander prospects?" Among several the following five are outstanding:

First, Keizer points out, "the people were electrified by the power of the Word as preached by the itinerant lay preachers and the patience and strength with which they endured appalling torture."¹⁰

Second, they taught that through the Holy Spirit came the potential to discern and pursue the right. This discernment took place in three stages: 1) facing evil with a simple ignorance and avoiding it, 2) believing the truth with the strength of youth, 3) applying mature wisdom and experience in diagnosing situations.¹¹

Third, they said: "We are saved by grace as the plan of salvation: we are saved by the blood of Christ as the ground of it; we are saved through works which include repentance and faith, as the condition of it."

Fourth, they looked upon themselves as the "light of the world." The leaders aimed to be examples in every way to the flock. They exhorted their congregations to follow them. Two such outstanding leaders were Dietrich Philips and Menno Simons.

Fifth, they taught: "Be sober, be vigilant: because your adversary, the devil, as a roaring lion, walketh about, seeking whom he may devour; whom resist steadfast in the faith, knowing that the same afflictions are accomplished in your brethren that are in the world." These verses form the core of many sermons.

RADICALISM AND MENNONITE ETHICS

With this idealism expressed toward others came also an extravagant radicalism. In every serious reach for higher ideals there is great possibility for radicalism because extremists always "attract other extremists."

---

9 Newman Smyth, *Christian Ethics* (New York: Charles Scribner's Sons, 1892), p. 139.
10 G. Keizer, *Geestelijk Weerloos of Weerbaar?* Samengesteld Door J. H. De Goede, Jr. (Amsterdam: Uitgevers Mij. Holland, n.d.), p. 38.
11 Friedrich Otto zur Linden, *Melchior Hofmann*, (Haarlem: De Erven F. Bohn, 1885), p. 16.

The Anabaptists were strongly influenced by Hussite radicalism and its two resulting factions, the Adamites who held that "the Holy Spirit was enough to create sons of God," and, opposed to them, the Taborites, who fought the civil war. These point directly to the fanatical Münsterites later. Fanaticism and barbarous excesses were perpetrated by Catholics and fanatics alike. Even Calvin took such a position when he was instrumental in the burning of Michael Servetus.[12]

Radicalism is a form of impatience attempting too much, too soon, too differently. Müntzer was a glaring example. He gave ample reason for being called a dangerous revolutionary when he sought to overthrow "all oppression in the world, both secular and religious." Peter Friesen believes that the Mennonites have always been inclined to be radical and given to separation. Our fathers were contentious, he says, and let us not make the mistake and believe that they were "angels."[13]

Zwingli turned against them because they gave him trouble in the Zurich government. This did not mean that the Anabaptists who followed Menno were resistant; their teaching was that the government could not be resisted with force in any way.[14] Hubmaier's position was that of the Baptists today; he baptized by immersion and used the sword. Vedder and others are of the opinion that the Evangelical Anabaptists had their origin in Zurich rather than in Wittenberg.[15] In an intolerant and violent age it was regarded most radical for anyone to refrain from all coercion and physical resistance and rather submit meekly to persecution than soil conscience.

Justus Menius (1499-1558), Urbanus Rhegius (1489-1541), Philip Melanchthon (1497-1579), Andreas Althaser (1500-1539) and others "struck out against the ideology, practice and radical

---

12 Benito Mussolini, *John Huss*, translated by Clifford Parker (New York: Albert & Charles Boni, 1929), pp. 120, 122, 152.

13 Peter M. Friesen, *Die Alt-Evangelische mennonitische Bruederschaft in Russland* (1789-1910) *im Rahmen der mennonitischen Gesamtgeschichte* (Halbstadt, Taurien, Russland: Verlagsgesellschaft "Raduga," 1911), pp. 46-69

14 Johann Loserth, *Doctor Balthasar Hubmaier und die Anfänge der Wiedertaufe in Mähren* (herausgegeben von der historish-statistischen Section der k.k. mähr. Gesellschaft zur Beförderung der Landwirtschaft, der Natur- und Landeskunde; Brün: Verlag der hist.-statist. Section, Druck von Rudolh M. Rohrer, 1893), pp. 84, 97.

15 John Christian Wenger, *Glimpes of Mennonite History and Doctrine* (Third edition; Scottdale, Pennsylvania: Herald Press, 1949), pp. 142, 149, 162, 163.

dissent"[16] of the Anabaptists. Several authorities believe that it is a serious "unfamiliarity with the primary sources of Anabaptism" when "revolutionaries, nonresistants, mystics, Biblicists, Hutterites and spiritualists are lumped together in one common condemnation."[17] Neither did Calvin make any distinction between the spiritualizing and the Biblicistic wings of the Reformation. To him they were all radicals of the same kind. Bullinger's judgment of their radicalism is perhaps most commonly accepted; he believed that they were irresponsible followers of Müntzer who resisted every conformity.[18] The large amount of new material that is found today on Anabaptism makes possible the formulation of honest, modern and unbiased opinions about their radical principles of non-resistance and obedience to the Spirit of God.

When examining the movement closer we find four main streams of radicalism. The best known was the fanatical Müntzer insurrection. Another was a doctrinal revolution as expressed in the *Schleitheim Confession of Faith*. Other articles of faith were produced after Schleitheim, the best known being those adopted at Dordrecht, Holland, in 1632. Among the items in the Dordrecht confession are: "the holy kiss, the washing of the saints' feet, taking no office with the civil government, no defense by force, no swearing of oaths"[19] and other similar literal biblistic statements. In comparison to the usual ordinances these are extremely radical.

The third has a sectarian prominence. Sects within the Anabaptist camp became numerous. Groups were started, says Johannes Weisenkürcher, by "grabbing" members from outside; especially guilty of this were the non-Mennonite Anabaptist Hutterites who later disintegrated into many sects.[20] Much of this was also due to a suspiciousness in connection with infant

---

16 Franklin Hamlin Littell, *The Anabaptist View of the Church* (Second edition, revised and enlarged; Boston: Starr King Press, 1958), pp. 73, 145.
17 *Ibid.*, p. 146; Bender, *Conrad Grebel c. 1498-1526 the Founder of the Swiss Brethren Sometimes Called Anabaptists* (Scottdale, Pennsylvania: Herald Press, 1950), pp. xiii and xvi; George H. Williams and Angel M. Mergel, *op. cit.*, p. 15; Robert Friedmann, *Mennonite Piety*, Through the Centuries Its Genius and Its Literature (Goshen, Indiana: Mennonite Hist. Society, 1949), p. 3.
18 Carl Pestalozzi, *Heinrich Bullinger* (Elberfeld: Verlag von R. L. Friderichs, 1858), pp. 40-43.
19 Wenger, *The Dordrecht Confessions of Faith*, op. cit., p. 214.
20 Menno Simons, "Reply to Gellius Faber, 1554," *CWMS, op. cit.*, pp. 625, 781.

baptism. In a letter, Menno Simons accused Callius Faber of slander and asked him
> whether it was true that when they baptized infants in Regensburg they used exorcism? The statement of this read: "I adjure thee evil spirit to come out of this child." The Anabaptists maintained that this was done and had thus caused many Lutherans to leave their faith.[21]

Fourth, was the radical attempt to produce an ideal Christian Church. The ban gave Menno an endless amount of trouble. In a letter to his brother Menno opens "his heart to reveal his sorrow over the ban trouble in the church."[22] The harshest conception of the ban was voiced by Leenaert Bouwens which led to several divisions.

For Mennonites as well as others it has been difficult to give these expressions of their radicalism proper complexion. Qualben thinks that they are a part of the Müntzer incident. Those approaching all social adjustments through social-economic views, such as Karl Kautsky (1854-1938) and the sociologist H. Richard Niebuhr (1894—), write about them in terms of socialistic nomenclature. These are partially right but do not state the whole involvement. When the Münsterites, due to severe persecution, relinquished proven Anabaptist sobriety, they yielded to Chiliasm and became useless to the Mennonite cause.[23] Beckerath does not class the Zwickauer Prophets with Grebel because he differs radically with Müntzer in that he strictly adhered to the Biblical basis of nonresistance. Even if most of them were peasants and artisans their radical ideals shone through. They were more radical than Thomas de Stitny (1325-1400), who, as did Luther later, said, "It is the faith which saves souls," but, not wanting any schism, did not step out of the church.[24]

Neither lay the radicalism of the Mennonites in the economic field. A later expression of this was the Hutterite *Gütergemeinschaft* (common property) in one direction and the Münster insurrection in the opposite direction. King Wenceslaus feared

---

21 Nestler, *op. cit.*, p. 139.
22 Menno Simons, "Letters and Other Writings," *CWMS, op. cit.*, p. 1055.
23 Gerhard von Beckerath, *Die Wirtschaftliche Bedeutung der Krefelder Mennoniten und ihrer Vorfahren im 17. und 18. Jahrhundert* (Abhandlung zur Erlangung des Grads eines Doktors der wirtschaftlichen Staatswissenschaften der Rechts- und Staatswissenschaftlichen Fakultät der Rheinischen Friedrich-Wilhelm-Universität zu Bonn, 1951), pp 2, 4.
24 Mussolini, *op. cit.*, pp. 27, 57.

that the propagation of Wyclifism, accentuated by Hussite preaching, might lead to civil war and communism. "That there actually existed among the plebeians the hope of a radical change in the institution of property is shown," says Mussolini, "by all the rural and agrarian insurrections that broke out in the thirteenth, fourteenth, and fifteenth centuries." Religious reforms preceded popular revolts. They disregarded what others claimed as "cherished possessions." Their Christianity was like a motor that is too powerful for the body. If their judgments had been less radical the measures against them would have been less severe. "Their conception of the church," points out Herschberger,

> as a gathered body of the redeemed, their way of love and non-resistance, their rejection of responsibility for the social and political order, their separatistic depreciation of the forces of cultural synthesis, their pure Biblicism, and their general disregard for the claims of historical continuity made the clash with the culturally entrenched traditions of the Reformation enevitable. In fact, the tension between Anabaptist absolutism and historical realism, including modern democracy, is a permanent implication of this radical type of Christianity.[25]

For them the Reformation proceeded too slowly and cautiously. Their main contention for ignoring the orders passed against them was that no secular court according to the Scriptures had the right to judge in religious matters. The early Anabaptists accused Zwingli of not doing justice to the cause of God by advocating that religious matters had to be decided by the state.[26] When the Swiss Brethren saw that Zwingli, as an earnest Reformer, remained "cool and practical" without a "profound sense of sin," they proceeded to interpret the Bible for themselves and to determine what it demanded of them.

Even if the Anabaptist fathers appeared very radical in their day, they are not considered so today. Their views on separation of church and state and the freedom of conscience are highly prized legacies by every Westerner in our time. Their radicalism at first made vigorous effort to know the Word and when this was opposed in every way they became radical. "The common, unlearned man turned either to personal Bible study or to

---

25 Guy F. Hershberger, editor, *The Recovery of the Anabaptist Vision* (Scottdale, Pennsylvania: Herald Press, c.1957), p. 137.
26 J. C. Moerikofer, *Ulrich Zwingli*, erster Theil (Leipzig: Verlag von S. Hirzel, 1867), p. 279.

criticism of the monks, ceremonies and images.²⁷ When Zwingli remained indifferent to their appeals for more Scriptural practices, Grebel began to lean more and more to the iconoclasts, the potential radicals, and with Mainz "led in a radical movement that went far beyond Zwingli."²⁸

The University of Basel made Grebel a radical. "Here" no attempt was made to latinize the student "in the spirit of the old scholasticism and to lead him to an unconditional acceptance of traditions of the old church."

Glarean and Vadian indirectly carried a large share of the responsibility for the independence and radicalism of the Anabaptist movement.²⁹ They taught their students of whom several later were Anabaptists, to think radically and independently and gave them Luther and Humanism to influence their Bible reading and gave them enthusiasm and "zeal toward the goal of a renaissance Christianity."

The main point of difference revolved around baptism. Here they found their jumping-off place for their subjectivity which proved so potential later.³⁰ "We should expect," says Latourette,

> that in a time of religious ferment and of rebellion against the Roman Catholic Church such as was seen in the sixteenth century when the Bible was being widely read in the vernacular and salvation by faith and the priesthood of all believers were being preached, Anabaptists would emerge independently and without collusion in several places and would display marked variety. This indeed, was what happened. Some groups interacted on one another.

In their experience they developed a certain type of mutual enthusiasm, social action and attraction. The common peasant saw visions and had dreams similar to what we find in our present "Communism." There emerged a religion of action which rooted in forgiveness, and was marshalled by God to separate itself from that which was only sham Christianity. No power on earth could deprive them of their experiences. They believed that they were destined to finish what Luther and others had

27 Bender, *Conrad Grebel* . . ., *op. cit.*, p. 87.
28 Kenneth Scott Latourette, *A History of Christianity* (New York: Harper & Brothers, c.1953), p. 780.
29 *Ibid.*, pp. 9-24.
30 "Wiedertäufer," *Meyers grosses Konversations-Lexikon* (sechste gänzlich neubearbeitete und vermehrte Auflage: Leipzig und Wien: Bibliographisches Institut, 1908), XX, 595.

only begun. The future will reveal, states Mark Cattepoel, whether those were great man who invented the atom bomb for the destruction of innocent life or those who acted according to their conscience in the preservation of peace in their souls. The results of the clashes in such "religious ferment" usually acquire permanency in some form or another. Hans Hut did not participate in open hostilities but was even then considered more radical than Hubmaier who also was a "Schwertler" (one using the sword). The Count of Nürnberg describes him as a *"finsterer, ausschweifender, grübelnder Phantasier"* (a gloomy, excessive and hypercritical visionary). Their conference at Schleitheim in 1527 was partly an effort to bring various convictions together. Hans Denck, the Humanist, demanded exemplary Christian conduct. His contact with Erasmus and Aventin supported his radical views.[31] In 1519 Hubmaier's pupil, Eck, stirred up the peasants to drive out the Jews, destroy synagogues and cause disturbances in the procession to the "Schöne Maria." Hubmaier himself, as the well-known *Domprediger* at Rattenberg, openly debated with Zwingli the question of infant baptism. When it is said that Menno Simons taught "strict nonresistance" because he was tired of radicalism, that cannot be accepted because the Swiss Brethren in 1527 at Schleitheim already said that "the sword is ordained of God outside the perfection of Christ." In spite of his radical idealism he never relaxed in the teaching of his original convictions even if a martyr's death followed him like a shadow. It was unheard-of radicalism to depend only on the New Testament and not on the *Obrigkeit* (magistrates of the state). Deviating so drastically from the Medieval pattern of the parish church still presents itself as ludicrous to many. To them it was beyond reformation, it was restitution.[32]

The Anabaptists have always had a strong social direction. The reason for this, according to Troeltsch, was their attempt to revive the "theological theory of the Primitive State," and express it according to "the strict law of the Scriptures, the radical law of Nature and monasticism." They read their radicalism out of the Scriptures where Zwingli, in a much milder manner, resorted to the historical and traditional. "Even alongside Paulinism," continues Troeltsch, they found

[31] Nestler, *op. cit.*, pp. 14-15.
[32] Dietrich Philips, *EoH, op. cit.*, p. 315.

a radicalism which was indifferent and even hostile to the world; it appeared in the form of the love-communism of the Primitive Church and in the Chiliast-Apocalyptic rejection of the world; similarly, Radicalism existed alongside of the social development of the Early Church which carried on the Pauline tradition in the Montanist and Donatist sects, and, above all in monasticism.[33]

Zwingli influenced Hubmaier before he met Grebel in 1524 to spread out politically with great zeal.[34] The Swiss Brethren were against these radicals, later especially against Melchior Hoffman. Waldshut and its "evangelical radicalism" was known far and wide. Erasmus stirred up Hubmaier when he said that it was terrible to baptize infants. Luther, too, had fired him on when he said for six years that the mass was of no avail without faith. In many neighboring places Hubmaier's demands were well known and directly led to the peasant's revolt.[35] It was natural after listening to evangelical sermons about the same blessings to everyone. When Campus went along and began to deal with the social ills of the time he was imprisoned.[36]

It was partially through the work of the Anabaptists that the radical Reformation entered the social field of ethics. There was a theological undergirding of "democratic political pluralism."[37] The Swabians, claims Keizer, are a people inclined to dream and "mysticise" (*een volk tot droomerijen en mysticisme geneigd*"). It was from their territory that the stress of social radicalism had its beginning. From Mähren we get the Hutterites with their *Gütergemeinschaft* (brotherhoods living in communes). We find as early as 1528 that they had a mutual-aid plan which provided help for those in distress. Anabaptist refugees arrived in increasing numbers from Switzerland and Tyrol who had to be assisted with essentials until better days would come. This went on until the Tyrolean hatmaker, Jacob Hutter, in 1535 established his Hutterite Brotherhood Communes called *"Bruderhöfe."* These followers of Hutter are not Mennonites but Anabaptists who went through the

---

[33] Ernst Troeltsch, *The Social Teaching of the Christian Churches*, translated by Clive Wyon (Second impression; London: George Allen & Unwin, Ltd., 1949), pp. 335, 329.
[34] Loserth, *op. cit.*, p. 72.
[35] Nestler, *op. cit.*, p. 19.
[36] Karl Rembert, *Die Wiedertäufer im Herzogtum Jülich* (Berlin Gaertners Verlagsbuchhandlung Hermann Heyfelder, 1899), p. 176.
[37] Thomas Müntzer (1524), Sermon Before the Princes, *SAW, op. cit.*, p. 25.

same persecution as the Mennonites. It is common for the ignorant to look upon the Mennonites as Hutterites.

This Anabaptist-Hutterian practice still appears to be rather radical. It was a radical way of trying to recover man's true value. The Anabaptist contention for tolerance, freedom of conscience and being one's own priest simply meant that everyone was worthy to possess them. The authority for this was the Bible. It was like solving an equation and finally arriving at the value for "x," standing for the worth of the individual. The words of Würzelburger, a simple *Schulmeister* (village teacher) of that day, are enlightening: "This is my religious conviction, based upon the Scriptures. I will give up my views as soon as I'll be assured of and taught something more true." In the midst of his tortures he said, "It is exceedingly brutal and cruel that I am treated this way and am not supposed to stay with the truth. I do not want to live if I am not permitted to be a Christian." The reason for this torment was that he believed in adult baptism and refused to confess to a priest. In his eyes the individual declared his own worth, knew when he was worthy of baptism and when he was absolved of his sin by none other than Jesus Christ. When the sacraments of repentance were offered to him before his execution he refused them.[38]

Descarte's conception of God consisted of a clear and distinct ideal given to man through His immediate acts for knowing the object. The Anabaptists knew the worth of man directly from simple contact and what God said. They needed really no "religion" to know God. Philosophically and Scripturally they were not radicals but radical realists. They accepted Jesus' words that He was the end of the law in that He had fulfilled all demands of the law. Not exterior religion but their inner witness determined their worth. Of this baptism was a sign in two ways, of conversion and of acceptance — being worthy of acceptance. In no case was baptism only a "sign." What made this radicalism still more real and vivid was the edict of "the Reichstag of Speier, composed of Protestants and Catholics, in 1529, i.e., four years before the rise of the Anabaptists of Müntzer, that every rebaptized adult should be put to death without trial, either by fire or sword, as convenience offered."[39]

Mennonitism is also radical because the times in which it

38 Nestler, *op. cit.*, p. 19.
39 Nestler, *op. cit.*, p. 26.

had its origin were radical. The corrupt condition of the church was such that they had to seek comfort, confidence and understanding amongst themselves. Calling those outside their circle "the world" and shunning them did not make for friendship and mutuality.

Gottfried Keller, an admirer of Zwingli, called them *Tazzelwürmer . . . Ratten und Mäuse* (glow-worms, rats and mice) in the midst of such *Kristallgeistern* (crystal-clear spirits) as Zwingli and others.[40] Luther in the *Deutsche Messe*, 1526, stressed the organized fellowship of committed believers, and Free Churchmen of both the sixteenth and twentieth centuries have regretted that he "did not have the courage or conviction to actualize his ideal."[41]

This matter of putting their ideals literally into practice was, and perhaps is, the greatest factor in their radicalism. It was their constant aim to "form a church on the basis of the principles used in the Apostolic Church." Christianity still considers this extreme. In their own build-up to face such judgment the Amish and more conservative Mennonites still have the custom of singing their religious convictions over and over. Their way of putting their beliefs into practice was most obvious and therefore they received the brunt of persecution. The Anabaptist hymns of the sixteenth century, says A. J. Ramaker,

> have a clearly defined religious and doctrinal significance, for they contain the religious ideals and convictions of one of the reformatory parties in that revolutionary age when the Medieval Church was breaking up in the lands of middle and northern Europe, and when a number of programs were being offered they were hotly contended. The program of the Anabaptists was the most radical of any proposed and therefore drew the fire of resentment and persecution from all the other parties, including the Old Church.[42]

The religious ideals for which the Anabaptists and Mennonites contended meant a radical reconstruction of the Medieval Church. They realized that this was difficult with all the radical cross-currents among them. They opposed these but since the very nature of Anabaptism was radical it was difficult to

---

40 Nestler, *op. cit.*, p. 32.
41 Littell, *op. cit.*, p. 163; he also cites, William A. Mueller, *Church and State in Luther and Calvin* (Nashville: Broadman Press, 1954), pp. 24-25.
42 A. J. Ramaker, "Hymns and Hymn-writers Among the Anabaptists of the Sixteenth Century," in *MQR*, III (April, 1929), 93, 98.

clarify their stand. Hoekstra seems rather optimistic when he writes that the Mennonites had a big task of removing all kinds of *"onnutte spinnewebben"* (useless cobwebs) and limitations of the written Word of God, but now in later years he "found no trace of these questionable prophetical inspirations."[45]
It was a herculean task for the Mennonites in their enthusiasm to go beyond the Reformation. What they aimed at, continues Ramaker, was "revolution

> for the Medieval Church had been allied and firmly united with the state for more than 1200 years, whereas the Anabaptist position meant a sharply defined voluntarism which separated the baptized believers as well from the world as from the state churches. The converts to Anabaptism therefore found themselves in a two-fold opposition: to the mixed churches of the European Christian World and to the state authorities which were by law required to uphold the constituted order.[44]

Berkouwer also faces the question whether the awakening in the beginning of the sixteenth century was a "reformation" or a "revolution."[45] Rome speaks of a revolution because the Protestants revolted against its authority. This is true of the Anabaptists, because, as he says, they "were individualistic, spiritualistic and anarchistic." The "anarchism," however, should be applied with much reserve, for their sense of obedience to authority was even much more sensitive and developed than in any of the others.

To what extent was it revolutionistic? Rome says this revolutionary spirit led "to the revolution of 1795 and later on to the revolutionary century in which we are now." Accordingly there is a "historical connection from the Reformation to the revolution." If this is so then the "Reformation is thus accused of being the preparatory work for the secularization of the modern world."[46] The Anabaptists refused at the time to accept the authority of the State over their conscience. In no wise though were they without authority for they obeyed the Scriptures more literally than the rest. They claimed to be free in

---

43 I. J. L. C. de Bussy, *Ethisch Idealisme* (Amsterdam: H. H. de Bussy, 1875), p. 102.
44 Daniel Williams, *What Present-Day Theologians Are Thinking* (New York: Harper & Brothers, c.1952), p. 99.
45 C. C. Berkouwer, *Modern Uncertainty and Christian Faith* (Grand Rapids, Michigan: Wm. B. Eerdmans Publishing Company, 1953), pp. 40, 41.
46 *Ibid.*

the interpretation of Scripture and putting it literally into action. In the promotion of this liberty they stood in principle where the existentialists stand today. Their common high regard for the value of the individual they have in common inherited from the Humanists.[47]

In theory the Marxists also put a high value upon the human being. They want no class system which puts one person above another and none is to be deprived of what belongs to him as a human being. In principle this is Anabaptistic even if this group anchors it to the Scriptures as did Luther. Zimmerman, a Marxist, says,

> Müntzer cannot be taken for an Anabaptist, he never baptized nor were his secret disciples Anabaptists. He used baptism to advance his own ideals and plans as the leader of the most fiery element of this sect.[48]

With Müntzer baptism was a cultic rite rather than a religious symbol of regeneration. His baptism was based on philosophy whereas the Mennonites have a theologically ethical baptism. In baptism, they say that they enter into covenant and agree to associate with

> every one truly believing in Jesus Christ and penitently seeking refuge in Him to lay hold of the hope set before them through the washing away of sins by the blood of Christ.

Müntzer's *zweckmässiges* (means to an end) baptism served him "*sich zu bedienen in derselben Freiheit die er auch sonst für sich und seine Sache in Anspruch nahm* . . . (took to baptism with the same sense of liberty as he did elsewhere). For him God was in man's own spirit and enlightened reason, the only manner in which God revealed Himself to men.[49] He, according to Zimmerman, radically departed from Luther and the Anabaptists who saw God and His Son Jesus Christ revealed in the Scriptures which form the very norm of their ethics. Where he promoted his own spirit and person Menno remarked,

> This is my only joy and desire of my heart, that I may extend the borders of the kingdom of God, publish the truth, reprove sin, teach righteousness, feed the hungry with the word of the Lord, lead the stray sheep into the right path,

---

47 *Ibid.*, p. 67.
48 Wilhelm Zimmermann, *Der Grosse Deutsche Bauernkrieg* (Volksausgabe: Berlin: Dietz Verlag, 1952), pp. 211-12.
49 *Ibid.*

and win many souls to the Lord through His Spirit, power and grace. . . .⁵⁰

According to this, Wenger, a present-day Mennonite theologian, is right when he points out that

some historians have imagined a connection between the radical Zwickau Prophets or the fanatical Thomas Müntzer and the founders of the Mennonite Church. But for this supposed connection there is no historical foundation.⁵¹

The question whether Müntzer was an Anabaptist in the true sense is still debated, especially in non-Mennonite circles. Those who think of Mennonites as social and religious radicals say he was. Others, like Wenger and all Mennonite historians, say he wasn't because of his non-Anabaptist views on resistance, baptism and discipleship. This is an important item in the problem of Mennonite ethics. Even Marxism is vitally interested in it.⁵²

SECTARIANISM AND MENNONITE ETHICS

The expression of Mennonite ethics as related to others also showed itself in sectarianism. In their first years they were so engrossed with the spreading of their religious ideals and practices that they did not bother much to learn to know the beliefs of others. In their zeal they pursued a proselytism which virtually destroyed the last cord which might have united them with other Reformation bodies.⁵³ This was more the case among the radical Anabaptists; the Mennonites and allied Anabaptists "as a rule . . . lived quietly for themselves."⁵⁴

Menno Simons abhorred not only Müntzer's sect but looked upon all sects as abominations. "I was not called," he says, "by the Münsterites nor any other seditious sect. . . . (Our) people (are) not (of) such perverted sect as they are made out to be, but true Christians, though unknown to the world. . . ."⁵⁵

Dietrich Philips also avers that the Mennonites are not a sect but of the true church comprised of believers. He speaks

---

50 Menno Simons, *The Complete Works of Menno Simons*, translated from the original Dutch or Holland (First part; Elkhart, Indiana; Published by John F. Funk and Brother, 1871), p. 75.
51 Wenger, *Glimpses of Mennonite History*, *op. cit.*, p. 4.
52 Zimmermann, *op. cit.*, pp. 211-213.
53 Ramaker, *op. cit.*, p. 99
54 Fritz, *op. cit.*, p. 84.
55 Menno Simons, "Reply to Gellius Faber," *CWMS*, *op. cit.*, p. 671.

at length about the ban, the means with which they tried to keep the church pure and from becoming a sect. If all churches did this then according to the Gospel all Christians would belong to the same church.[56] This is a constant problem in the exercise of their ethics. Principally it is operating in the opposite direction of sectarianism. Practically it might be said that just the application of such a principle tends towards sectarianism.

A statement from 1526 says directly that they were not a sect and describes their relation to other Christians as "another group."[57] Those who are outside of Christ and His Word and "try to make valid their positions, faith, and conduct with the sword," says Menno, are sects.[58] Hoekstra, on the other hand, says that Heberle rightly called the Anabaptists a sect because they united the radical elements of the Reformation in themselves. Schaff agrees with this for, he says, they promoted the continuance of the pre-Reformation heretical sects.

No doubt the word "sect" came to be applied to the Anabaptists and later to the Mennonites because of their idealistic views and actions. In many instances the word has, and still gives, erroneous impressions. Ernst Troeltsch describes it well when he says,

> Originally the word was used in a polemical and apologetic sense, and it was used to describe groups which separated themselves from the official Church, while they retained certain fundamental elements of Christian thought. By the very fact, however, that they were outside the corporate life of the ecclesiastical tradition — a position, moreover, which was usually forced upon them — they were regarded as inferior side-issues, one-sided phenomena, exaggerations or abbreviations of ecclesiastical Christianity. That is, naturally, solely the viewpoint of the dominant churches, based on the belief that the ecclesiastical type alone has any right to exist. Ecclesiastical law within the modern State definitely denotes as "sects" those religious groups which exist alongside of the official privileged State Churches, by law established, groups which the State either does not recognize at all, or, if it does recognize them,

---

56 Phillips, *EoH, op. cit.*, pp. 232-371.
57 *Anno MDXXVI III Fol CXVIII* (no author, date nor publisher).
58 Menno Simons, "Foundation of Christian Doctrine," *CWMS, op. cit.*, p. 175. He lists those groups as sects that do not stand firmly and exclusively on the Word of God but establish their respective systems of doctrine partly on human authorities.

grants them fewer rights and privileges than the official State churches. . . .
Very often in the so-called "sects" it is precisely the essential elements of the Gospel which are fully expressed; they themselves always appeal to the Gospel and to Primitive Christianity, and accuse the Church of having fallen away from its ideal; these impulses are always those which have been either suppressed or undeveloped in the official churches, of course for good and characteristic reasons, which again are not taken into account by the passionate party polemics of the sects.[59]

It is perhaps safest today to agree with Littell when he says that we should recognize Anabaptism "as a third type" of the Reformation quite distinct from both Roman Catholics and Protestants[60] and not designate it as a "sect" without further analysis and closer description.

ESCHATOLOGY AND MENNONITE ETHICS

Another matter that involves the ethical problem of the Mennonites is their eschatological views. When this unique Mennonite way of life is finished, then what? Through the years of martyrdom they were taught to look to the beyond, their only place of hope and rest. Braght's *Martyr's Mirror* is still read in many of their homes with the purpose of not becoming attached to the world but rather having their affections set upon that which is in heaven. With the intense revival of the New Testament Church came the "yearning after another world" which had even been a potent factor in Greek philosophy before the Christian era. In dire times these prophetical and eschatological hopes drowned out the pains of their earthly existence. The court of Nürnberg wrote in 1527 that Hans Hut said that angels had revealed to him much about the last judgment, when the Lord would gather His dispersed flock. Here they were compelled to worship Him in *Winkelgottesdiensten* (worshipping in hidden places) but in His presence He would wipe their tears from their eyes. Their worship services were extremely simple but desperately real.[61]

The Scriptures told them that the final judgment would re-

---

59 Troeltsch, *op. cit.*, p. 334.
60 Littell, *op. cit.*, p. 1
61 Georg Tumbült, *Die Wiedertäufer*, Vol. VII of *Monographen zur Weltgeschichte* (in Verbindung mit anderen herausgegeben von Cd. Heyck; Leipzig: Verlag von Velhagen & Krasing, 1899), p. 21.

veal all deeds, the good as well as the bad. They spared no efforts to be placed on the right-hand side of God at that time. This fitness did not come only through profession and confession, it had to come through deeds. Their eschatology was rigorously concrete. The Dordrecht and subsequent confessions were not influenced by Millennialists. The deeds the Lord required of them were very simple and needed no explanations and speculation. To this point Bender writes,

> Under modern outside influences particularly since 1900 Chiliastic views such as premillennialism and even dispensationalism have won considerable acceptance in nearly all Mennonite groups in North America except the radically conservative groups such as the Old Order Amish, Old Order Mennonites, Old Colony Mennonites, and Church of God in Christ Mennonite. . . .[62]

In general, the groups that have stayed more by themselves have been less affected by popular eschatological views.

In Anabaptist and Mennonite eschatology the suffering of Christians always plays a role. The wicked never cease doing the evil deeds which Scripture does not permit. The kingdom of Satan is in opposition to the Kingdom of God and we must wait patiently for our final triumph with Christ. From our manner of waiting can be judged to which kingdom we belong. The denouement for the Mennonite lies in his direct relationship to his kingdom.

The Amish, Old Order Amish and the more conservative Mennonites speak more about taking the cross of Christ upon themselves than about Christ's cross and redemption. The hope of those towards the right lies in the ultimate victory in union with Christ. Those in the middle and towards the left receive Christ as Saviour from sin as all other evangelicals. The conservative groups teach that we cannot have the assurance of salvation; all we can do is only to "hope." This "is in radical contrast," says Bender further, "to the joyful assurance of the early Anabaptists, including the martyrs for whom such a doctrine would be inconceivable."[63]

This radical form of Christianity is very obvious in their ethics. They go about trying to be as perfect in their actions as possible. They avoid speaking about their salvation for fear of being "proud." According to I John 2:15-17, in their judg-

---

62 Harold S. Bender, "Eschatology," The *ME, op. cit.,* I, 248.
63 Bender, "Eschatology," *ME, op. cit.,* I, 248.

ment, they must avoid living as the world does. Examples of this are their objections to modern conveniences such as cars and electricity, garments and haircuts. To them mere thought and profession are "unchristian and futile."[64]

Such expression in society is negative and directly opposed to the thinking of about four-fifths of the Mennonites who try to do the will of God by helping others by way of Voluntary Service, The Mennonite Central Committee, or missions. With all it is a waiting for the return of Christ when everyone shall receive the rewards according to his deeds.

64 William Hordern, *A Layman's Guide To Protestant Theology* (New York: The Macmillan Company, 1957), p. 2.

CHAPTER II

MENNONITE ETHICS IN RELATION TO SELF

THE BASIS OF SELF AND ETHICS

The early Anabaptists were strong personalities. Religion flowed from them to society, not the other way around. Their break with Rome forced them to be intensely original. The paradigm for their lives lay in the Scriptures and not in the disclosures of men. What knowledge they had of religion came directly from the Scriptures, their conversion and religious experiences later. Their joys of salvation constituted the main content of these experiences.

Mennonite religious sturdiness was of an inner emotional nature. Around them was no inducement to be an Anabaptist or Mennonite. If they wanted any greatness at all it had to be within. Where Rome and the Reformers could make a display of their religion they were forced into seclusion and quietude (*die Stillen im Lande*). Seldom could Anabaptists and earlier Mennonites live in peace and according to the Scriptures as they knew they should. Non-resistance, a literal exegesis of the Scriptures and a *Nachfolge* (implicit obedience to the Scriptures united with discipleship) had to come naturally. Their entry into a conscious Christian life by means of repentance, conversion and baptism was the biggest event of their lives and no further embellishments were needed.

Luther's words, "The church is indeed a great mystery," impressed them and they felt that the responsibility for a pure church was upon every individual. There was nothing of Rome's salvation through the church; just the inverse was the case. This idea of separating the believers in the church from the unbelievers outside came from the Scriptures, not from man. "The teaching of man, ceremonies, long coats, the doing of the bishops, and all priestly pomp," said Luther,

> lead not to the church but to hell. The church should never teach such things. So, the church is composed of naked children, men and wives, peasants and citizens, those who

are without clerical garb, a cardinal's hat or garments in which to perform the mass.¹

To Anabaptists and Mennonites this meant that everyone had to look into his own heart to determine whether he was a Christian. The proof of true church membership was *Nachfolge*. Luther and Menno taught that every believer was his own priest. It is striking to find that the men in the Mennonite Church (Old), the Amish, Hutterites and smaller conservative groups wear suits that resemble those of some clergymen in non-Mennonite denominations. Amish women particularly use bonnets that are much like those worn by nuns in the Catholic Church. It is frequent that Mennonites garbed in this manner are addressed as "father" by those who do not know the Mennonites. Again, Luther influenced the Mennonites in forming their own type of character when he taught that penitence and faith must be combined.²

Mennonites shared this with all the earlier Reformers, and Berkouwer in our own day says that only a positive thesis and a positive faith will be of any fruit.³ In the same sense they aimed not to subtract from the religious greatness of others but strove to add to their own faith and inner magnitude. Grebel wrote to Vadian, ". . . I shall not accept the person of man and I shall not make God equal to man. The doctrine of the Lord and the precepts have been given to the end that they be fulfilled and put into practice."

In his reaction to the Catholics, Luther once more made the greatest contribution by maintaining that no lesser sharpness than Paul's teaching about the righteousness before God would do. Early the Swiss Brethren recognized that God was primarily concerned with the salvation of man through his own individual faith and that the faith of the church or any outward religious exercise never saves anybody. Men of sturdy character and independent spirit can afford to rely on God alone in their worship, their way of life and in their combat with evil; which in this case is not overcome with the sword and more evil but

---

1 Martin Luther, *Luthers Werke* herausgegeben von Pfarrer D. Dr. Buchwald, *et al.* (Volksausgabe in acht Bänden, erste Folge, Reformatorische Schriften; Berlin: C. A. Schwetschke und Sohn 1898), II, 285.
2 D. A. Schlatter, *Das Christliche Dogma* (Zweite Auflage; Stuttgart: Calwer Vereinsbuchhandlung, 1923), p. 581.
3 G. C. Berkouwer, *Modern Uncertainty and Christian Faith* (Grand Rapids, Michigan: Wm. B. Eerdmans Publishing Co., 1953), p. 43.

with love and the sword of the Spirit.⁴ Here Grebel wrote to his sadly faltering friend, Thomas Müntzer, "Stand by the others like a hero and champion of God." In worship this heterogeneity led to an avoidance of all external ceremonies and requirements⁵ and a drastic non-conformity that others often wrongly interpreted as bigotry in spite of its appeal and felicity to their own inner needs. At times they found its acceptance and following astounding, because, says Horsch,

> the non-resistant Brethren were so utterly different, telling of a new learning, conversion of the soul, a holy life, separation from the world, a congregation of truly converted souls, freedom of conscience, and a Christianity based on the Bible and love of God and all men, that their doctrine spread with a rapidity that was phenomenal. This notwithstanding that the laws of the countries required every individual to belong to the State Church and made separation from it punishable with death.⁶

This inner magnanimity gave rise to an outer intrepidity. This does not include that they appeared great in the eyes of others; what mattered most to them was that they were great in their own faith and in the manliness depicted in the Bible. In quality this fortitude was no different than that of others but in degree it was subjected to much greater severity. It was like steel that is hardened under severe heat. For a keen cutting edge it was good, but otherwise it was too brittle. Such hardness has proven time and again to be limited in usefulness. One frequently hears the remark that Mennonites and their kind are exclusive, unconventional, and in manner avoid sociality. Their withdrawal is not from sin only but also from those of other camps.

With Luther, the Mennonites accepted the directness of Scripture and combined it with a soundness of faith and irreproachability in conduct. Those admitted to their communion services were not screened as much for doctrine as for conduct. Menno sought in his communicants inner greatness through faith, purity, and a richness of soul that constantly benefited others. In his

---

4 Belfort E. Bax, *Rise and Fall of the Anabaptists*, Pt. III of *The Social Side of the Reformation in Germany* (London: Swen Sonnenschein & Co., Ltd., 1903), p. 11.
5 Henry Wace, *Principles of the Reformation* (N. Y. American Tract Society, n.d.), p. 104.
6 John Horsch, *The Mennonites, Their History, Faith and Practice* (Elkhart, Indiana: Mennonite Publishing Company, 1893), p. 15.

view greatness of goods or prestige never gave assurance of religious possessions. For him a dependable ethics was the surrender of self to Jesus Christ and accepting Him as Lord. "The sum of the whole matter," he writes,

> is that he who would with the disciples and guests of Christ sit at the Lord's table, be he rich or poor, high or low, must be sound in the faith and unblamable in conduct and life. None is excepted, neither emperor nor king, prince nor earl, knight nor noblemen. Yea, as long as they err in doctrine and faith, and are in their lives carnal and blameworthy, they are by no means to be permitted with the pious to partake of the communion of the Holy Supper.[7]

Communing with those who did not adhere to Mennonite faith and practice was a serious deviation. Luther, the champion of freedom of conscience, also refused fellowship with Carlstadt and Zwingli. The Anabaptist fathers not only refused fellowship with Luther and others but excommunicated their own members who were not in full harmony with them. Deeds in the name of religion were above profession and expected from everyone purporting a religious experience.

The rules for Mennonite deportment are an etiology of Scripture. They aim at a total avoidance of Pelagianism and legalism but seemingly are not entirely successful. Peter Friesen repeatedly refers to the quarreling and bickering among the Mennonites over rules and ordinances and how their high ideals were shamefully dragged into the mire. He laments that their love to prescribe and demand obedience has degenerated into mere form of showing authority and pride. Among them is more obliquity and clannishness than in their neighbors.[8] What Friesen wants to convey is better understood when reading Gerhard Wiebe's account of the reasons for the Mennonites leaving Russia and settling in Canada rather than the United States. He calls for much more stringent rules and obedience in Russia and the first decades in America.[9] Even during Menno's time his brotherhood became saturated with legalism. Wenger, however, in our day does not accept this, for the "Mennonite Brotherhood," he says,

> with its ordinances and restrictions may seem like a neo-legalism. It is not so intended. The obedience of love is

---

7 Menno Simons, "The True Christian Faith," c.1541, *CWMS, op. cit.*, p. 150.
8 *Appendix* III, b.
9 *Appendix* III, c.

never legalism; it is loveless conformity to a code which is legalism. A joyful awareness of the centrality and foundation of Christ's redemption and of God's grace will prevent this simple and earnest obedience to Christ's Word from degenerating into a formalistic legalism.[10]

Mennonite church members are made aware that they must be obedient to those who "have the rule over them." Such obedience can never be forced, it must be voluntary. This is in extreme contrast to the practice of the Catholics and Reformers who killed Anabaptists because of their disobedience for conscience' sake. All that the church can do, and must do, is to set forth duty in general principles

where specific mention is absent. Home, civil and church government must be obeyed.[11]

Throughout the story of the Anabaptists we find that profession without the fruit in deeds is looked upon as mere hypocrisy. "Truly you will be saved," says Hans Denck, "in so far as you in truth believe and not hypocritically." No man can save himself, God is in all. "Salvation is in a person but not of a person." In his judgment a person has to be sensitive to the Spirit who directs to the Scriptures to which he must submit his will. Every word of the Bible must be accepted as inspired and the standard of life be no lower than that of the Scriptures. Daniel Kauffman of the Mennonite Church has compiled a book stating side by side the Bible standard and the standard of those not accepting the Bible as final authority. In the introduction he asks that the book be read carefully for "it will be a means of helping the reader to contend more earnestly for the historic faith of our fathers, the Church, and the Bible."

The Mennonites allege that when a person comes in conflict with the church he does not violate the church's rules but Scripture. Individual interpretations of the Bible always vary and here is the reason for so many divisions amongst them, the Amish and Hutterites. They all agree though that their members must live a quiet and humble life and refrain from the ways of the "world." Hans Denck was lauded because he was a quiet, gifted man of friendly appearance and unblamable in conduct.

Some groups apply the promise of obedience of incoming mem-

10 Wenger, *Glimpses of Mennonite History and Doctrine, op. cit.*, p. 162.
11 George R. Brunk, Jr., *Ready Scriptural Reasons* (Scottdale, Pennsylvania: Herald Press, 1954), pp. 89-90.

bers directly to their own little Mennonite division, looking upon it as the only true church of God. One such is The Church of God in Christ, Mennonite. "Many boast," says John Holdeman, the founder of this church, "of being born again and children of God but their conduct does not vouch for this."[12] Shaving and wearing of neckties are not permitted; women worship with a particular head covering; musical instruments are not used. A prospective member promises to stay in the church and when he joins another he is excommunicated and shunned. The excommunicated are said to go back into the world, for they have left the only true Apostolic Church which can be traced back to the day of Pentecost.[13] No outside baptism is valid. No other Mennonite group demands obedience in such a narrow sense. Shunning is practiced by some Anabaptists and one or two conservative Mennonite factions. Ethical responsibilities are exceptionally far reaching in such instances.

All Mennonite groups want their converts to have the conversion experience and the conviction that they must follow the ethical principles of love as practiced in the Apostolic Church. Their lives must be kept free from sin through confession, penitence, and moving within the confines of the church. Faith in God and love towards their fellowmen are sometimes stressed even more than the redemption and atonement of Christ for man's salvation.

QUIETISM AND PATIENCE

Being a Mennonite has always required the practice of patience and love. At no time are the members absolved from the obedience promised at the time of conversion and baptism. At that time all guilt is removed through repentance and forgiveness; joy and hope take the place of remorse and gloom. What modern psychiatry is trying to do for the unadjusted, Jesus, as the great Mediator who takes away the sin of the world, does for them. Psychological tension and personality disintegration are infrequent due to the acceptance of sin and its removal through Christ's atonement and a way of life in church, home

[12] Johannes Holdeman, *Der Alte Grund und Fundament Aus Gottes Wort Gefasst und Geschrieben* (Lancaster, Pennsylvania: Gedruckt für den Verfasser von Johann Där's Söhnen, 1862), p. 91.
[13] P. G. Hiebert, "Church of God in Christ, Mennonite," The *ME, op. cit.*, I, 600.

and school based on a program of conservation of energy rather than its dissipation. Patience and quietism in this connection have always proven a great remedy in times of stress.

In the face of extreme persecution all the founders of Anabaptism found it indispensable to direct their followers to a life of renunciation and patience. Michael Sattler (1495-1527) wrote to his adherents that they should continue in all truthfulness and godliness with great patience and love. Dietrich Philips (1504-1568) says that we must admit that we are sinners and even after we have become Christians our flesh is still inclined towards evil and deserves the wrath of God. Because of this depravity we must submit to the control of God's law. Felix Manz (1480-1527) who was drowned in Zurich said, "I sing because my heart is filled with His joy." "Our suffering is severe," says Blaurock (1480-1529), "but we thank the Lord and pray that we can do so joyfully." "The Scriptures . . . require of us true repentance," writes Menno, "and the sacramental signs . . . signify, represent and teach to all true Christian believers a penitent and unblamable life."

At no time did the Anabaptists and Mennonites promise an automatic Christian security after conversion like the Calvinists provided for. The convert always remains ethically responsible towards God and man. Where there is teaching of "eternal security," that comes from outside.[14] Braght exhorts, "Let us be patient . . . till the day come, which, if we remain faithful unto the end, will assuredly bring us that which we here wait for in hope." Never were they allowed to strike back at their tormentors. Müntzer and his horde were most un-Anabaptistic. In fact they considered themselves so little that way that they were judged to be queer, odd and incongruous. Their ethic of the liberty of conscience took them far beyond any of the other Reformers. They were constantly taught to give up their will and submit unreservedly to the will of the Father. Ethically they developed an attitude of offering and giving rather than demanding. The world let them know in no uncertain terms that it would not have any of their "heresy." They withdrew more and more until they finally acquiesced to be no more than *"die Stillen im Lande"* (the quiet in the land).

After the Reformation the *Wiedertäufer* had lost much of

---

14 C. K. Lehman, "Eternal Security," *ME, op. cit.*, II, 254.

their enthusiasm for the propagation of their faith. The severe times had dulled their cutting edge and they were content to be left alone and live quietly for themselves. Like the others, they formed a denomination but here they were far behind because their strength could not be used in construction but had to be spent in warding off the enemy among whom were the Socinians in Holland. Being on the defensive is still an outstanding Mennonite characteristic. Today this quietism is found, says Littell, "not in people (like at the time of Müntzer) but rather in places, not in ethical prescription but in Biblicism, not in formality (like *Geldprediger* — preachers who preach for the money that is in it) but in piety."[15] Evidence of this is the twentieth-century emigrations to South America, Mexico and Honduras.

We can get another view of the situation when we note that at the peace of Westphalia in 1648, at the close of the Thirty Years War, religious liberty was granted to the Lutherans and Reformed as well as Catholics, but not to the Anabaptists, who had, according to their principles, persistently refused to bear arms. It is time that "we Mennonites," says Hoekstra, "as members of society, as individuals give ourselves to society. He who wants to gain must lose his life. . . ."[16] Evidence that this opinion is taking hold of the Mennonites in our day is their revival of world-wide conferences, numerous recent European peace organizations, the reorganization of a number of Mennonite denominations in all European countries and mission fields, and a revival of interest in Anabaptist literature and history.

Conservatism

It is logical that the Anabaptists with an ethico-conversion and a spirit of quietism, endurance and defense should arrive at a distinctive conservatism. Their "tendency towards conservatism," points out Troeltsch,

> was prepared by Paulinism, and it was continued in the combination of radical and conservative elements which was achieved in the Thomist social doctrine, in the form

---

15 Franklin Hamlin Littell, *The Anabaptist View of the Church* (Second edition, revised and enlarged; Boston: Starr King Press, 1958), pp. 30-82.
16 S. Hoekstra, *Beginselen en Leer der Oude Doopsgezinden, vergeleken met die van de overige Protestanten* (Amsterdam: P. N. Van Kampen, 1863), pp. 71, 72.

of a structure of Christian civilization upon architectonic-evolutionary historical lines.[17]

Conrad Grebel observed that there was falling away in the march of Christianity from the conservatism based on the Word. The church had structured its own conservatism along "evolutionary-historical lines." Its ethics were moulded by an hierarchy according to tradition and not by a brotherhood in conformity to the Word. The organization of the former was based on priority where the latter relied on the originality of the Primitive Church. The conservatism of Rome used the devices of man; the Anabaptists joined Zwingli and other Reformers in ridding themselves of all human means. "Just as our forebears fell away," says Grebel,

> from the true God and from the one true, common divine Word, from the divine institutions, from Christian love and life, and lived without God's law and gospel in human, useless, unchristian customs and ceremonies, and expected to attain salvation therein, yet fell far short of it . . . so every man wants to be saved by superficial faith, without baptism of trial and probation, without love and hope, without right Christian practices.[18]

The Pauline evangelical urge of conservatism was felt by all Reformers. The Anabaptists found, like Tillich in our own day, that they were "a mixture of being and non-being."[19] Their "non-being" always followed them like a shadow and this made it necessary for them to conserve all their being for emergencies. They, like everyone else, desired to have a destiny, a future. This question becomes much more consequential when lives are insecure. The idiosyncrasy of Mennonite conservatism designs at all times a most comprehensive exploitation of the resources invested in their concept of destiny. Their slogan might well be: You are what your destiny is to you, and your destiny will be to you what you are in the light of its conservatism.

This conservatism has always been approached through the life of Christ, His reality, the prayers of the martyrs, and has been absorbed to become a part of their personalities. During the last two World Wars Mennonite conscientious objectors be-

17 Ernst Troeltsch, *The Social Teaching of the Christian Churches*, translated by Clive Wyon (Second impression; London: George Allen & Unwin, Ltd., 1949), p. 329.
18 Conrad Grebel, "Letters to Thomas Müntzer," *SAW, op. cit.*, p. 75.
19 Paul Tillich, *Biblical Religion and the Search For Ultimate Reality* (Chicago: The University of Chicago Press, 1955), p. 11.

came spectacles as non-participants. Especially during the first, they were publicly decried as "huns." Sincere conservatism does not mean to do something better than it has been done, but do it more truthfully. The whole Reformation was a consciousness of a need for the truth.

The Mennonites have from the time of their inception sensed a need in their conviction to ally Christian and social principles. In their attempt to do this they were radical, but in the interpretation of the Scriptures as to what had to be done they were very conservative. According to Scripture they felt the Divine imperative to separate from the world and on the other hand they had to be in the world to help it. In trying to find a solution in this ambivalence they arrived at a certain degree of *Eigengesetzlichkeit* (a striking amount of self-imposed ethical legalism).[20] Where the Reformation gave evidence of a conservative attitude toward ancient dogma, Anabaptism disclosed an attitude towards simple Biblicism. To all appearances their teachers knew not much else than the story of the Cross, the accounts of deeds of love and how to help carry one another's burdens.[21] Always reverting back to this simple knowledge was to many not only conservative but naive.

Mennonite conservatism has always looked for the lost paradise. Repeated emigrations of certain groups through the years point in that direction. Exemptions from military service and state control of their schools have been given as the main immediate reasons. More distant perhaps but just as real is the reason given on the basis of Scripture that we have no abiding place here and seek a better country. Instead of being led by the spirit of this world they aim to follow only God's Spirit. To keep away from the voices of the world they band together and live in their own villages or even closed communes like the Hutterites. When they clash with the cultural, political and religious views of their neighbors they base their reactionary, unconventional and conservative actions on the literal interpretation of Acts 1:14 and 2:42-47. Their judgment is correct when they say that they do not "belong to this world."

This persistence in their ways conserved their energies for their own enterprises. They have developed a frugality, sobriety, honesty, truthfulness and an all-embracing dutifulness which,

---

[20] G. J. Heering, *The Fall of Christianity*, translated from the Dutch by J. W. Thompson (New York: Fellowship Publications, 1943), p. 75.
[21] Bax, *op. cit.*, p. 15.

in the form of mutual aid, goes to all continents. "As one studies the history of the Mennonite Church," says Byler,

> it becomes apparent that relief service is inherent in its faith. This is likely due to her unusual history of persecution over a long period of time. As early as 1710 the Dutch Mennonites generously assisted Swiss Brethren to migrate to America. . . . There are many other examples of relief service recorded in the annals of Mennonite history.[22]

Of note in this connection are the *Doopsgezinde Societeiten* and the Mennonite Central Committee with their extensive mutual-aid programs.

The ethical problems related to such conservatism in our day are augmented by improved facilities in communications and transportation, and extended urbanity. The Mennonites have become like the other members of society. They join other denominations when their churches are too far away and when they form their own denominations their services are so much like those of non-Mennonites that an interflow of members is frequent. The characteristics of the village peasant so vital to conservative Mennonitism are gone in urban areas and a new era for Mennonite ethics has already been ushered in.

The more outward conservative Mennonites attempt to stay by themselves. Those with a greater evangelical emphasis feel that all born-again Christians belong together; especially those who profess the Scriptural ideals of peace and brotherly love. What belongs to the "world" is an open question and subject to constant reassessment. In their vocabulary, everything, man included, belongs to the world until it is re-created. The "born-again" person is not of the world but continues to live in the world. The religious experience, or being born again according to John 3, is the first step of re-creation. The experience of this step is comprised of: acknowledging of guilt and sin; seeking their removal solely through Christ's act of the atonement through repentance, confession and application of His grace; accepting Christ as Saviour and Redeemer from the works of Satan and as Lord at all times; to live a life of non-violence to our fellowman and of unequivocal obedience to the Scriptures.

The movements and actions of the unrecreated belong to the world. The actions of the recreated are separate from the

---

22 Irvin B. Horst, *A Ministry of Goodwill* (Akron, Pennsylvania: Mennonite Central Committee, 1950), p. iii.

world. Referring to the ways of the unregenerated they speak of "worldly." Then, too, especially with the Amish, the ways of those not connected with their immediate faith are judged as "worldly." This is again in the sense of being still unregenerated. "There is a great, wide and wonderful 'world' of God's creation for the welfare and happiness of man," writes George Brunk,

> not for his abuse but for his use. There is a "world" of human souls that we are to love and seek to save. There is a great, dark world of sensual, satanic error which the Christian must hate and avoid."[23]

In the light of this we can understand when Philips says that "what the world thinks of us must not be our concern. We submit to the judgment of all true Christians, speak with Paul, and believe all that is written in the Law and in the Prophets." Hans Denck admonishes, "All who truly fear God must renounce the world," and, "we cannot continue," says Menno, "to live in splendor and pomp." Holdeman in later years went even further when he said that our withdrawal from the world must reveal itself in the simple clothes that Christians must wear. At no time, he rules, may anything be worn beyond the essential. Jewelry and other fineries are an abomination in the sight of God. When Müntzer set up two copies of the Ten Commandments reminding the people of God's law, Grebel wrote to him to abolish the tablets for they would lead to idolatry. "Theirs was an ethical as well as a religious urge," says Latourette, for they "endeavored fully to live up to the ethical demands of the Sermon on the Mount."[24] "The ascetic ideal of the sects," observes Troeltsch over against the Catholic way of striving for Christian perfection and "the sense-life of the monasteries were a union in love which is not affected by the social inequalities and struggles of the world."[25]

OBEDIENCE (*Nachfolge*)

The ethical demands in the Sermon on the Mount bring everyone face to face with the problem of obedience. To the Mennonites it has always been an obedience that required nothing less than following the Master's footsteps at all times. They

---

23 Brunk, *op. cit.*, p. 115.
24 Kenneth Scott Latourette, *A History of Christianity* (New York: Harper & Brothers, c.1953), p. 779.
25 Troeltsch, *op. cit.*, pp. 332-33.

spoke with Tertullian, "That which is from God is not so much extinguished as obscured," and with Irenaeus, "To be good is to obey God, to be evil is to be disobedient to Him."[26] "It is our duty," says Kierkegaard, "to give our life over to the most High unquestionably and irrevocably for obedience"; and they with him, because of defying all ecclesiastical convention, are "stamped as a people of lonely courage."[27]

The Mennonite fathers chose obedience "rather than foreknowledge." They did not specialize in fore-knowledge for comfort, for "whoever had yielded himself had in a measure tasted the sweetness of the bitter cross." With Denck the vision of the cross led them through obedience to eternal life. Such obedience is a natural consequence of accepting Jesus Christ as Savior and Lord. It involves the entire Trinity, the Father above speaks through His Word, the Cross of His Son marks every place and is dominant in every decision, the Holy Spirit from within directs ethically into every phase of practical daily living.

About the origin of this life of *Nachfolge* Alexander Prieur at the 1956 Mennonite World Conference said,

> This life of "Nachfolge" has its potential in the Word of God which is brought near to men by the Holy Spirit. The authority of this Word is the death of Jesus on the Cross and His resurrection. This Word leads to true repentance and faith. It is the seed of the new birth and brings about a new life of obedience in Christ Jesus.[28]

Before conversion man serves the devil and the flesh, after conversion the authority of the Scriptures. In the words of Prof. Benjamin Unruh, "The poison of our own will has to be extracted before we can practice obedience."[29] No one can follow God except he who has previously learned to know Him (*erkennet*).

To the Mennonites the commands of the Bible concerning Christian living are very simple. Hans Denck says, "Whosoever does not testify thereto by his manner of life, God will judge

---

26 Seeberg, *op. cit.*, I, 122.
27 Hugh Ross Mackintosh, *Types of Modern Theology*, Schleiermacher to Barth (Reprinted; London: Nisbet and Co., Ltd., 1954), pp. 218, 223.
28 Theo. Glück, compiler, *Das Evangelium von Jesus Christus in der Welt*, Report of the 6th Mennonite World Conference (Karlsruhe: Druck und Verlag: Heinrich Schneider, 1957), p. 20.
29 Benjamin H. Unruh, "Die Botschaft des Evangeliums in unserer Zeit," in *Botschaft und Nachfolge*, Bericht und Vorträge der mennonitischen Studententagung auf dem Thomashof, 1947 (Karlsruhe: Ev. Sort. & Verlagsbuchhandlung Flügel & Co., 1947), p. 38.

along with others who are perverse." In the words of John Holdeman, a very severe Mennonite elder of a small faction, he who transgresses and does not abide in the teaching of Christ has no God. He who is obedient to the teaching of Christ has both, the Father and the Son. It seems as if his followers are primarily concerned with the fulfilling of the law (plus the rules of the church) and give it a sort of precedence to the preaching of the Gospel.

The essential character of the Anabaptists from their beginning was that of obedience to the Word rather than ceremonialism, church fasts, pilgrimages, adoration of relics, making the sign of the cross, using the rosary, and the like. After Menno had decided to follow the Scriptures he had terrible conflicts as long as he wanted to stay in the good graces of the church. This continued until he surrendered to God and publicly submitted to baptism and ordination to preach literal obedience to the Bible. Obedience to him was nothing less than Christ in him and he in Christ. He said, "We must be moved by His Spirit," and "abide in His holy Word outwardly and inwardly." What this cost him he expressed in a poem eleven years after his baptism,

> My God, where shall I wend my flight?
> Ah, help me on upon the way;
> The foe surrounds both day and night
> And fain my soul would rend and slay.
> Lord God, Thy Spirit give to me,
> Then on Thy ways I'll constant be,
> And, in Life's Book, eternally!
>
> When I in Egypt still stuck fast,
> And traveled calm broad paths of ease,
> Then was I famed, a much-sought guest,
> The world with me was quite at peace;
> Enmeshed was I in Satan's gauze
> My Life abomination was,
> Right well I served the devil's cause.

The Mennonites still regard Menno and hundreds of martyrs as examples of the words of Paul: "Therefore, my beloved brethren, be ye steadfast, unmovable, always abounding in the work of the Lord, forasmuch as ye know that your labour is not in vain in the Lord." Obedience and worthy citizenship of Christ's Kingdom became Menno's greatest possession. No price was too great; good fortune, fond hopes, prized families and homes, unsullied names, life and blood, all were given up for it.³⁰ Magistrates can only be obeyed "to the extent that they do not militate against the supreme authority of Gods Word (Acts 5:29)." In times of war such principles lead to "conscientious objection." These problems are different today than when Anabaptism began. The Mennonites are conscious of this and a goodly number render non-combatant and even combatant military service.³¹ This of course is stamped as disobedience to the Word and Anabaptist concepts. Their answer is usually one of caution: "Let him that thinketh he standeth take heed lest he fall (I Cor. 10:12)."

Early in the Anabaptist movement Matthiä Cervas realized how easy it is to believe that through obedience we may try to obtain righteousness before God. He wrote early in the sixteenth century,

> I wrote to you that we may learn to know God's ways, and why He created us. Why we should love and obey Him and not seek our righteousness and salvation through our own works. Through obedience other than coming to Him for salvation no one will be saved. Through works of the flesh none is made righteous before God (Rom. 3).³²

Anabaptist obedience has always embodied the observance of "former ways," submission to authority based on the Bible, non-resistance and resignation in persecution. This fealty is best expressed in their prayers and songs which were spoken and sung over and over again in their simple worship services and while waiting to be executed. One of their earliest prayers reads,

> But now our compassionate Father, Thou knowest that no good dwelleth within men and that he is unable of himself to perform anything good. But Thou, O God, art through grace the author and finisher of all our works. We pray now, dear Lord, to lift Thy compassionate countenance upon Thy creation and Thine own.³³

When Hans Denck (1500-1527) had finished translating the Old Testament Prophets from the Hebrew and was prepared to expound them regardless of the cost, he prayed, "O Lord my

---

30 Samuel Geiser, *Die Taufgesinnten-Gemeinden* (Herausgegeben im Auftrag der Konferenz der Altevangelischen Taufgesinnten-Gemeinden (Mennoniten) der Schweiz; Karlsruhe (Baden) Karlstrasse 26: Druck und Verlag: Heinrich Schneider, 1931), p. 19.
31 Ernest Crous, "Non-resistance," *ME, op. cit.*, I, 897-907.
32 Sattler, *op. cit. Güldene Aepffel in Silbern Schalen*, n.d.
33 *Ibid.*

God! Let me be obedient unto thee and do to me whatever thou wouldst through thy most beloved Son, Jesus Christ, through whose Spirit the world should and must be chastised."

Two of the earliest hymnbooks were the *Ausbund* and *Gesangbuch*. In the introduction of the *Ausbund* (1570) we read, "The following pages give us a record of a few praiseworthy Christian deeds performed in true faith, which each speaker sealed with his own blood." In connection with the first hymn we have the note that here the Christians are taught how to sing and pray in spirit and truth. Almost all songs are very long, telling usually the story of imprisonment, trial and admonition to those left behind. Number 6 and 119 are typical of the obedience stressed in almost all songs.

No. 6 by Jörg Wagner (1527)
Christian obedience (*Nachfolge*)
Does not permit that we be affected
By the shame that the world puts upon us;
We have to take His cross upon us.
There is no road to heaven
That is without it.
This I have been taught from the days of my youth.

No. 119:
Let us sing from the depths of our hearts,
In peace and harmony press on to perfection
That we may please God
For that is what He wants of us;
Let all the pious take this to heart,
That we may do our Father's will,
For that we must on earth fulfill
Like it is in heaven.
Thus Jesus Christ teaches us
That we become perfect
As our Father in heaven is perfect.

The *Ausbund* belongs to the earliest Anabaptists. The later Mennonites used the *Gesangbuch*[34] where we find the same exhortation to obedience in numerous songs. Here are three examples:

No. 510:
Destroy the will of the flesh within me
And make me submissive;
Through Thy love urge me on
To walk after Thee through my life.

---

34 *Appendix* III, d.

No. 272:
Man's nature and the flesh find it difficult
To remain with the teaching of Christ
But this has to be obeyed
When we want to go to heaven.

No. 274:
Submissive Lord Jesus,
As thou gavest over thy will into the Father's hands,
Make me also obedient that I may submit unto Thee
My whole life.
Make me quiet as an obedient child,
   Humbly do Thy will.

Beyond this teaching of obedience directly to the Word of God follows an obedience to the church, which is a part of the former. The *Ausbund,* now used only by Amish, says, "It is our resolution to abide with the practice that has proven to be the right one. We should not transgress the rules by which we are governed." As long as the church is a "living church," such rules promote true Christian living, but this lacking, its members merely "obey rules." Of the latter are evidences in the Mennonite and other Anabaptist churches. True Mennonitism places all church obedience on the Word and disobedience to it is disobedience to the Bible. Sound training of Mennonite youth centers on obedience to the Bible and where this is the case juvenile delinquency is almost unknown.

When Mennonites speak of obedience to parents they do so not in terms of obligation or affection. It is between these two that modern psychology places such child-parent relationship. "One of the obvious ways," points out Stagner

> in which the child affects the parent is as the object of a certain obligation. Traditionally this obligation has been greatly emphasized, although more recently there seems to be a more healthy emphasis upon the affection rather than the obligation which is the child's right.[35]

The Mennonite answer to this is,

> The true motive of obedience is not force or outside pressure but love within the heart for the person to whom obedience is rendered. The proper child will obey its parents because it loves them. We will obey the laws of

---

[35] Ross Stagner, *Psychology of Personality* (Second edition; New York: McGraw-Hill Company, Inc., 1948), pp. 376-77.

the land . . . and God for the same reason. . . . If we fail to obey His commandments it is idle to say that we love Him.[36]

The primary point of child guidance is that child and parent love and fear God. But since guidance cannot come without knowledge every Christian is obliged to learn the will of God and "follow Him wherever He may lead." This is very important and only through prayer and giving an ear to the Holy Spirit's guidance at all times can parents and church succeed.

Such uncompromising demands of obedience lead to an "either-or" ethic. On the facade of its behavior one can read in bold letters the resolution of obedience or disavowal. When disobedience is chosen the church is nevertheless bound to obedience and must relentlessly separate from the transgressor. Disolving these difficulties is not easy because the question of interpretation is always in the foreground. Mennonites are aware of this and in order to avoid compromise they are frequently inclined to postpone and delay the decisive action. They say that the decision is not crucial and go on without noticing it. Their leaders warn them against embarking on the road to secularization of their religion and against closing their eyes to their deepest and most reliable insights.

This aloofness from current religious practices always leads the Mennonites to the application of the law. They are concerned about the deeds of the individual whose discipleship is foremost and fundamental. A most frequently used term is *Nachfolge Christi* which reflects the drama of the Cross. Christianity to them is the "imitation" of Christ in the context of the Kingdom of God.

Discipleship to the Mennonites is not an adaptation to compromise at the expense of the pure Gospel. When they excluded those who had not been born again and who openly flouted the principles of the Gospel, they were called *Umstürtzler* (upsetters). Instead of having an all-embracing religious and social culture they excluded everything contrary from their society. Their Biblicism fearlessly disregarded the traditions that dominated the Reformation and made its own substitutions. For this reason they were called "enthusiasts," "syncretists," or "*Schwärmer.*" For them baptism came when a person was able to comprehend the tremendous requirements of the Gospel. This

---

36 Horst, *op. cit.*, p. 65.

faith had to sustain them in good and bad times for they knew whom they believed and through whom they were able to remain steadfast and unmovable. "Truly their faith," Strasser exclaimed, "is an independent growth."

PART FOUR

CONCLUSION

THE PAST

When considering the dissertations that have been written about the Anabaptists and Mennonites since the Second World War one is impressed with the preponderant attention given to the sixteenth century. It has been felt in these pages that there is a need for further blending of the beginning of Mennonitism with that of the twentieth century. No re-suffering of the past lends the future a helping hand.

Mennonitism that wants to be convincing in our day must be without bias and extenuation. Questions relating to them demand answers that are applicable to our present social and religious problems; its repertoire has to include late renditions. In the face of a steady increase of goods, and repeated new findings in psychology, sociology and theology, there must be a re-thinking of their whole gamut of convictions and expressions.

That Mennonitism has its ethical problems is most obvious. Sometimes those living outside their natural habitat don't want to be called Mennonites because too much present-day Mennonite radicalism belongs to the past. It belongs either only to the past or only to the present. There is an involuntary disassociation and apprehension of distance. This is untenable for the present as well as for the future. In their search for belonging they are never fully satisfied.

THE PRESENT

No independent, Hegelian type of mental structure can give the Mennonites what they need. They must build in this modern age as everybody else does. Their building material must be carefully examined for Mennonite soundness. There is no need of using material of questionable quality; recent Mennonite writings convince that there is an ample and dependable supply.

Mennonites in their modern building must avoid current grotesqueness. The greatest reason for modern contortion is fear.[1] Unforgettable are the late President Roosevelt's words,

---

[1] Joachim Wach, *Sociology of Religion* (Phoenix Books; Chicago: The University of Chicago Press, 1944), p. 281.

"Our objectives are clear, namely establishing and securing freedom of speech, freedom of religion, freedom from want and freedom from fear everywhere in the world." To this adds Robert E. Speer, "Fear is the ruling motive of the human race." Only the truest Mennonite material and structure will contribute to peace in home and state, nationally and internationally. Mennonites face the new problem of fitting into society since they have "eventually achieved a social status which was to effect . . . the privileged groups." The result is that their problems of ethics are mounting. And more, what will they do in view of current "tendencies toward unification?" They will have to admit that such exist and that they are of great significance. "Definitely positive are the co-operation in social, charitable, and to some degree, educational work," says Wach, "among the denominations and the growing awareness of the significance of the central issues in the field of faith and order."[2] Mennonites must reckon that their young people read and accept this.

Looking at their camp, will those twenty divisions of Mennonites that participated in the Sixth World Mennonite Conference in Karlsruhe in 1957 come closer together? Will they close ranks or will they permit foreign architects to influence their structuring? To the outside world their ethics are becoming more and more felt and meaningful. But their actions towards each other also are acquiring greater significance through modern facilities and inter-action.

GUIDES

Proper turns in the road can only be made safely with a warning light at the back and a dependable direction light in the front. To serve as such in the approach to the problem of Mennonite ethics the following five points are suggested.

1. Greater integration of the findings on Mennonite ethics written during the last half century and expressing them in the terms of principles duly applicable to modern times.
2. Mennonite leaders (religious, educational, social) to converge at regular intervals and determine further the answer to the question already brought into prominence in Europe as early as 1911, viz., *"Was ist Men-*

---

2 *Ibid.*, p. 286.

nonitisch?" or *"Wat is ons 'Doopsgezind'?"* (What is Mennonite?)
3. A meeting of Mennonite leaders for learning to know each others' ideals and work towards closer internal union.
4. Continue to implement in world conferences these ideals as fast as possible.
5. Develop and teach a consistent Mennonite ethic in their schools and use such profiles in expressing their relations to non-Mennonite thinking.

This joint action in conferences and special meetings cannot be stressed too much. As has been shown, Mennonites have the tendency to be independent and immovable in their convictions. This has frequently led to strife and small reasons causing lasting divisions and separation. Perhaps one such movement was the Templar exodus from Russia to Palestine and Australia where it practically disappeared like the Australian rivers in the dry sand. These people sought to know directly the will of God in truth, beauty, perfection and godliness.

Sound Mennonitism must base its teaching on the works of its originators such as Menno Simons and Dietrich Philips, who have been repeatedly quoted. It must agree with the latter when he says the Word of God must be our authoritative guide. Only here will it find the foundation for its ethics. It must purge out the old leaven of malice and wickedness and be unleavened to form a lump having sincerity and truth. It must demand of its followers that they present themselves as "a chosen generation, a royal priesthood, an holy nation, a peculiar people, that should show forth praises of him who hath called them out of darkness into his marvellous light."

ETHICAL STANDARD

As in the case of Kant, theistic arguments did not satisfy the Mennonites. The moral argument from the Scriptures (philosophy in Kant's case), was above all rationalizing. The fundamental Mennonite principle is that the moral qualification comes through the experience of accepting Jesus Christ as Saviour and Lord in our daily life and promising unreservedly to obey Him at all times as He gives grace. In case of failure only repentance can restore to full fellowship with God and believers.

Mennonites teach that Christians must follow the "higher ethical standards" of the New Testament. Professing to be a

Christian and not live up to the full implication of New Testament ethics is merely accepting a sub-Christian ethic, something similar to what God gave in the Old Testament. The New Testament demands a fulfillment of the old laws. How this is to be done is clearly set forth in the Sermon on the Mount. There we find that the new standard for killing is to bar all anger, for adultery to be removed even from all thought about illicit relations with the opposite sex, for divorce only one reason, viz., adultery, for dependable truth make only such statements that require no oath, and to obtain one's legal rights never resort to the law courts but have love for everyone.

The law of the Old Testament was never annulled. The New Testament affirms that the moral law of God is permanent and valid for all time and men. Paramount for all ethical instruction in the Scriptures is the love for God and the love for mankind. The first takes place when man is saved through faith and the second is the result of the first. No more can Christians dispense with the law of God than could Kant ignore the moral law. The law of God is their ethical guide for which Christ Himself is the righteousness. Righteousness for Christians comes only through union with Christ, the only Mediator. Never can it be obtained by approaching God through the philosophical and psychological. Early Protestantism had no moral autonomy, only at "the mercy seat God dispensed atonement for sinful men and Himself." From such atonement flowed the Holy Spirit into the redeemed and gave divine guidance. Only when present-day Mennonitism pledges unwavering loyalty to these basic principles will it prosper. Closer examination of original materials reveals that just here lies the heart of the entire movement.

The Mennonites are in danger of becoming as those against whom their fathers rebelled. Selling Mennonitism demands ethical principles that possess originality and appeal. Prattling after others convinces no one. Neither is there attraction in antiquated or excogitated methods. Their ethics must agree with modern knowledge and that Mennonitism which fire, sword and drowning could not quench. Thomas Kelley saw the same danger in Quaker circles when he wrote, "Many of our Quaker brethren have become as conventional as the people against whom our forefathers rebelled."

The high inherited moral standards of Mennonitism are in jeopardy today because of modern shrinkage of distance and need of re-evaluation and adjustment. Their homes are exceptionally strong. To keep them that way they cannot afford to relax their former vigilance and sturdiness. The piety and devout church life for which they are known must be idealized in every "unequal yoking." The church as the center of all family and social activity cannot make room for interests in more material provision and worldliness. I John 2:12-18 never has gotten out of date. In fact, today much greater demands are made on young Mennonite couples to live these in true traditional form. As we have seen, Mennonites were good stewards, frugal and willing to provide others with essentials. They had to be thorough and even excel to remain in existence.

ETHICAL PROBLEM

The problem of Mennonite ethics is aggravated by a "Fundamentalism" and "evangelism" that repudiates non-resistance and church membership. Their sense of belonging has always been very strong and given them inward security in a hostile world. Besides this they constantly face the problem of accepting other cultures and remaining Mennonites. In a society in which the melting of various social and ethical elements has proceeded far, being "different" becomes an ever greater problem. The distinctive Mennonite way of life is more and more lost sight of by Mennonite and non-Mennonite alike. The heart of the problem is how to retain the Mennonite Scriptural principles in a non-Mennonite environment.

Muralt, the recent Swiss historian and authority on Anabaptism, poses two important questions which the Reformation has placed before us. The first: "Just what relationship is there between the Christian and culture, people, state, and the world?" The second: "Is it essential that those who seriously attempt to do the will of God band themselves together in isolated communities?" In conclusion he makes the statement that "the Anabaptists and Mennonites have the Word of God in their favor" when answering his questions. In doing this it is observed, though, that the greater their sincerity the less will be their exclusion of others.

But here again is evidence of weakness and strength at the same time when Mennonites and non-Mennonites in their zeal accept each other. The former cannot afford to cast away that which has proven to be a common good and the latter cannot afford to pick up that which belongs under the bushel. Dosker maintains that their peculiar "Weltanschaung," their puritanical and almost ascetic view of life, has led to endless differences and divisions and at the same time to a sublimity of courage. Here we have a description of a faith that aims to be free from human design, expressing itself in fellowship and the preaching of simple Biblical truths, in opposition to dead dogmatism and clericalism. Their fathers had the special mission of promoting "most vigorously a faith independent of human invention and churchianity." The early Anabaptists refused to affiliate with any "organized" church and its non-essentials, but rather resorted to a simple and unadorned preaching of the truth. Christ's aims to them were not set forth in humanly defined statements.

During the sixteenth century and later their leaders often depended on the doctrines of the church on a legalistic basis. Often there was little relation between dogmatism and human personality. Shortly after Menno even such things as whiskers, buttons and pockets became matters of faith. An endless battle, which still exists in areas, over meaningless, dogmatical and pietistic questions ensued. During the first quarter of the present century these divergencies culminated in an exodus of the radicals to Mexico and South America. This differs with early Anabaptism which did not seek to realize its aims in escape. Its adherents became wholehearted members of the movement and in it proclaimed a "Christian social order within the fellowship." The proportions of their influence mushroomed to such extent as to alarm pope and Protestant.

Because of the persecution they met with during the last two World Wars, present Mennonite leadership is in danger of keeping its thinking too much in the past. They forget that the whole world at present tries to forget its victories and defeats. The big task is to solve the many sorry problems that are left. The once sheltered faith of the Mennonites has been radically exposed to the "radiation of the world" through schools, services and modern means of communication. The one task for them is to recognize the universal need of "a Balm in Gilead," and do all they can to satisfy that need. Elmer Ediger, present administrator of Prairie View Hospital at Newton, Kansas, and director of Christian Public Service for the Mennonites during the Second World War pointed out recently that the Mennonites today should become more aware of the total human needs. It is their responsibility to share that which they have with those who have not. Their churches must transplant themselves through evangelism and material and spiritual aid. Pietism is only truly such when it reaches out. Until it does that it is only mysticism trying to escape from responsibility. This is undesirable in Mennonite thinking.

VALUE OF LIFE

Professor Roy Wood Sellers, a modern religious liberal teacher, declares that "religion is loyalty to the values of life." To Mennonites these "values of life" exist not because of divine immanence but because God says that man has eternal status and destiny. Dr. Benjamin Unruh, the Mennonite professor at Karlsruhe, points out that when we stop to look alone at the world for a *Weltanschauung* we are sorely disappointed. "Civilization," according to Albert Schweitzer, consists of giving ourselves to the perfecting of the human race. Mennonites view this value of human life as these men but for them it lies in "the foundation of Christian assurance which is God's Word confirmed by Christian experience." Human life is precious because it is so in the sight of God. Taking human life is wrong; God alone is the giver and taker of life.

Our age is confronted ethically on a larger scale than ever before. According to Schweitzer this is so because of the disregard of the spiritual which makes men ethical. The value of man lies totally in the spiritual and ethical, not in the material where we have tried to place it. This perversion has caused mankind to drift into the doldrums of ethical vigor. Materialism has grossly misled man in his grasp for possessions. When he lets go of life, to his dismay he finds that he has only chaos and ruins left. Now historical positivism waits for favorable winds with which once more to sail and chart new ethical areas. So far according to results it has been an abortive attempt. The Mennonites with many others have sincerely tried to avoid hopeless stagnation and possible retrogression. They have attempted, at least, to apply the simple and unconventionalized practical teaching of the Sermon on the Mount and put forth a concerted effort to bequeath oncoming generations with a more worthwhile legacy.

Händiges points out that the Mennonites have been forced to abandon a defensive position and become offensive. It is imperative that they make their ethics known. It is like drawing a map of areas successfully traversed before with great casualties and no previous charting. Statements of their ethics have become more and more indispensable.

Due to the last two World Wars and the Russian Revolution thousands of Mennonites have been uprooted and dispersed in all continents. Last summer the Evangelical Mennonites in North America affiliated with the Evangelical Mennonites in South America as a result of the southern brethren's appealing for spiritual and moral support. Here was another ethical challenge combined with an overwhelming number of practical, religious and moral issues. One example is an entire village having only two fathers who escaped the rigors of war and "Sovietization."

In later years strong recourse has again been taken to Mennonite Biblicism, frugality and actions of love. Even the Indians in South America who live close to them sensed the deeper Christian principles in action and many have become Christian Mennonites. Hostile tribes have killed some of their settlers and leading missionaries. Nevertheless, this cannot deter them; many before had to pay the supreme sacrifice for the truth. According to Händiges the attention of the world once more is focused upon their deeds, not through sensationalism but through the re-enactment of deeper Christian principles based on the direct application of the Scriptures. The press comments on their manners, pietism and peculiarities which do not fit into the usual religious denominationalism. Never before has a non-resistant religious group engaged an eleven-hundred-passenger boat to transport refugees from a Europe in ruins to the primeval and uninhabited Chaco of South America.

During the summer of 1958 when the Mennonite disaster organization helped El Dorado, Kansas, get on its feet again after a tornado destroyed a large part of the city, the *Wichita Beacon* wrote editorially:

> This town has had acquaintances with the Mennonites before. . . . That acquaintance stresses the fact that the Mennonites live their Christianity — and devotedly practice the precepts of the Golden Rule. As a sample of the neighborly philosophy animating the Mennonite sect, the following paragraph is taken from a report prepared by Dr. J. Winfield Fretz, chairman of the Mid-West Mennonite disaster organization, about the Eldorado mission:
>> This is the tornado season. Let's be on the alert and ready to go again if disaster strikes. If we can't extinguish the hatreds and fightings abroad let's not

grow weary of ministering the needs of our neighbors who may fall victims of disaster at home.

This is rather idealistically spoken and may contain ulterior motives. Nevertheless, in the light of the fundamentals discussed, one must accept, to a degree at least, some genuine Biblical love and urge of practicing Christian principles of peace.

PRESENT EMPHASES

Pertaining to future world peace Mennonite ethics are a-millennial. They live in peace now above the law of the state. In regards to the coming "Kingdom of the Lord" they try not to put off until tomorrow what they can do today. State and church are separated and the kingdom is in their own heart. Man was created strong and has need that this strength be constantly renewed by the Lord.

They aim to be governed by the laws written in their hearts by the gospel message. Their Central Committee spreads its efforts over the entire world as a means of peace. "In the Name of Christ" is the slogan of its banner and is put on "their arrows" instead of deadly poison. In spite of "wars and rumors of wars" their peace efforts now find more favorable response than ever before. Human futility and fear logically have come to their assistance. "Witnessing such anguish," they say, "it behooves Christians not to waste time arguing at length about details associated with the coming of Jesus," but exhorts us to be engaged in the evangelization and nurture of the lost.

Muralt focuses our attention on two outstanding ethical issues, the unhindered spreading of the Gospel and vital concern to live one's convictions. Dietrich Philips saw this four centuries ago when he said that Christ commands us to preach the Gospel to all creatures and teach obedience without equivocation. Just this has always added to the problems of Mennonite ethics. According to Latourette, "Originally vigorous missionary persecution caused them to withdraw within themselves and to perpetuate themselves by birth rather than conversion."

It is possible that the underlying anxiety of our times will help us in overcoming inhibitions and obstructions. According to our psychologists there is a dearth of "belongingness" in our day. One wonders how far Mennonite traditions will serve as a reward to those who attach to them. Rapid change and insecurity create a demand for the re-establishment of unshakable principles and direction that leads back to sanity. Even Mennonite "queerness" with all its stifling negativism is called on to give positive service. "In spite of all their crudities and mistakes," says Walker, "they were prophets of a freedom to come." The Mennonites believe that Walker's "freedom to come" is now here. Doubt and fear must be chained hand and foot to biblical principles and an ethics demanding unreserved compliance.

From the time of Menno the Mennonites have tried to keep their doctrine free from dogma, the wisdom of man and the pride of life. With Menno they say that man has always tried to appropriate some of the glory and honor that only belongs to God and that he must learn repeatedly that he must preach God's doctrine "unwaveringly, regardless of the dignity of any man, fearing no man's tyranny nor yielding to any of the learned ones." It is contended that Jesus taught the lesson of humility, equality and service by washing the disciples' feet (John 13:4-17). Usually in connection with the communion service they wash each other's feet as Jesus directed. In some churches they say to each other after the washing, "The Lord be with us, preserve us in peace and strengthen us in love." In the light of present emphases this rite is very significant. It has taken on a threefold meaning: towards the heavenly Father it is a divine knowledge; towards their neighbors an evangelical truth; and towards themselves a fruitful and active faith.

THE BURDEN OF ETHICS

The Mennonites, according to the teaching of their fathers, begin to feel their burdens of sin when arriving at the years of accountability and understanding. At such times they are invited by the Scriptures to call upon Jesus Christ for confession and forgiveness. They become converted by accepting the Lord Jesus Christ as their personal Saviour and Lord of their daily lives. Having thus received by regeneration and justification by faith the peace of God for their conscience, they receive the assurance that they are members of the Kingdom of God. The Holy Ghost now inhabits them and fills them with a divine love and desire for the things belonging to Christ and God. The outward symbol of this transformation is baptism.[3]

After conversion a Mennonite embarks upon a life of disciple-

---

3 *Appendix* III, e.

ship and separates from the world to conserve his resources with which to fulfill the requirements of this new life. This separation means turning the back on the world and the face to a life with Christ which shows itself outwardly in piety, meditation, service and religious exercises. No part of Scripture is omitted just because it is outdated or impractical. "The greatest element in the Anabaptist vision was the ethic of love and non-resistance as applied to all human relationships."

SUPPORTS IN DIFFICULTIES

All obedient Christian walk in this world has its difficulties. Mennonites for encouragement and mutual support band themselves together in fellowship with those of like convictions and experience. Jesus Himself as author and helper walks with them and "washes their feet" as described in John 13. This rite, as they practice it in their churches, substantiates to them that His love and humility are shed abroad in their hearts and create a willingness to serve. It is mystical, extremely practical and humbling, and the symbol of spending and receiving love. The uninitiated have no appreciation for it; it is totally foreign to them. For the experienced Jesus Himself shows how to love and how to be loved and produces a joy which is above everything that the world can offer. This together with baptism and communion rendered in full obedience to the Scriptures produces a citizenry beyond anything this world produces. It is not a trying to be different, it is being different. It is comprised of those who have entered through the narrow gate and continue on the narrow way. When they confessed their sins and promised obedience they were convinced by the Scriptures that the way of the world was far too broad.

This curtailment of worldly interest centers its vision first upon its own fellowship (church) and, second, upon Christianity as a whole in the world to which it owes everything it possesses. Christians are only stewards of their goods and talents. To feed the hungry and clothe the naked is their responsibility. Never do they make any demands for state aid of any kind. This is considered being unequally yoked with the world and inviting its rule in spiritual matters. As early as 1527, when the Swiss Brethren asked Zwingli to abolish the mass, this became an important issue. When Zwingli refused to take steps to prohibit its further practice on the grounds that the city council had to decide, Simon Stumpf cried, "Master Ulrich, you have not the right to leave this decision to the council. The matter is already decided; the Spirit of God decides it."

With such teaching this law of Christian deeds is always a vital issue and irrevocably planted in the heart. This is what happened also to Peter when Jesus came to wash his feet. Jesus likewise teaches the same lesson now, "washes their feet" and remains by their side when He dispatches them on their missions of goodwill. Their ethics are simply the responses to His commands. In an age where the permanent seems to be unhinged they attempt to restore its stability and permanency. In this venture they always encounter a spirit of gross misunderstanding which is a leftover from those years when nonconformist "buds" were picked off early and cast into the fire. It is their joy, however, that they have the assurance that they will eventually "blossom" with Him and none shall pluck them out of His hand. The world will pass away but His word will not pass away. With the world will also disappear all warfare, hate and violence. Until such times, however, they must continue in obedience to Him for He says, "Ye are of God, little children, and have overcome them; because greater is he that is in you, than he that is in the world."

In the times of the Apostles and Reformation the people were imprisoned, beaten, exiled and killed because of their faith. Today subtler forms are employed except in time of war when violent persecution also breaks out. But "more often" they feel that "it is in the form of ridicule, opposition on the part of members of the family of friends, and being dropped from certain social circles." All instruction classes are acquainted with the words of Paul when he says, "All that will live godly in Christ Jesus shall suffer persecution."

Ethics on such a high, uncompromising and positive level are bound to meet in our present social setup with ever increasing difficulties. Various cultures and non-Mennonite ways now flood previously closed Mennonite communities and their young people live no longer sheltered lives. Their high ideals have to exist side by side with those of other Christians whose ideals may be just as high and sometimes higher. Their youth attending non-Mennonite institutions see this and learn to appreciate other views. For many it is difficult to be an out and out conscientious objector when a friend or classmate gives his all for a great cause. Believing that only Mennonites are Scriptural when non-Mennonite Christians do much more for the promotion of the Gospel and sound Scriptural education is difficult to accept. The Anabaptist vision that looks back so much is apt to become visionary regarding the future.

Just how negative must Mennonitism be to be a positive factor in a wholesome *Weltanschauung?* Mennonite schools in their aspiration for sound scholarship and recognition find it difficult to stay with the fundamentals of Scripture as did their fathers. It is much easier to philosophize about non-resistance than believe in it because the Bible as God's inspired Word teaches it. To teach that man through Christ's atoning grace becomes non-resistant is seemingly more difficult than to teach non-resistance on the human level.

MENNONITE ETHICS AND OTHER DENOMINATIONS

Mennonites are in many ways much closer to other denominations than is often admitted. Their ethics are just as liable to be wrong without Scriptural support as any other ethics without the Word. Without the Gospel Mennonitism finds itself in endless inconsistencies and difficulties. Their younger members today are inclined to adhere no more to traditions without the Gospel, than any other modern group that finds itself in the throes of present-day civilization. Mennonite philosophy is sound only as long as it is based on dependable Scriptural reasoning. Their ethics by themselves without the Scriptural faith of their fathers are like trees stripped of their foliage in a severe hailstorm.

It is especially hazardous for their ethics to be taught by teachers and ministers who base their teachings on modern religious liberalism. These, warns John Horsch, deny "not only the inspiration and authority of the Scriptures and the deity of Christ, but also the plan of salvation as taught in the Scriptures." "Ritschl," he goes on to say, "reduced the Christian religion to morality, and made morality the center and constructed his theology from the point of view of ethics." Fritz Kuiper thinks that the Mennonite church is especially challenged in our day by the wisdom of the world which undermines their ways. The church cannot afford to ignore that she is the creation of God and not that of world. Ritschl, Schleiermacher, *et. al.*, cannot prescribe Mennonite ethics any more than any other non-Mennonite. Present world conditions demand answers based on the belief that all life comes from God and therefore must be a blessing to all mankind. Where liberalism makes self the center of ethics, the Mennonites, in the words of Kuiper, believe that God manifests the essence of His being in His people. How they present themselves to the rest of mankind is the burning question. Without children a father's real being remains unrehearsed.

It is most definitely not Mennonite to base ethics on a theology independent of Bible authority inspired by God. The anchors for them lie in: (1) man was created by God and as such owes Him complete obedience; (2) Jesus came as His incarnated Son according to the Scriptures; (3) He performed many miracles to confirm His teachings and authority; (4) He died for man's sins on the cross of Calvary; (5) He arose from the dead on the third day as He said that He would; (6) He ascended into heaven; (7) He sent from heaven the Holy Ghost as He had promised; (8) the Holy Ghost now convicts the world of its sin; (9) the Word tells man that when He does not want to be eternally lost he must accept Jesus Christ as his personal Saviour from condemnation and sin, and in full obedience to the Scriptures as the Lord of his daily life. Any other teaching breaks down the very foundations of Mennonite ethics and must result in strange, only so-called Mennonite behavior. "It will become clear" says Horsch, "that working for the personal conversion of man is the most important service you can render to the community and to society."

Due to an increased mingling with non-Mennonites and a constant challenge to re-evaluate his ethics a Mennonite faces the difficulty to ascertain just where to begin his Christian ethics. The non-Mennonite in this connection faces the same difficulty. When a non-Mennonite hears the name "Mennonite," the first things that come to his mind are the unusual clothes of the conservatives, the peculiarities of the Old Colonists, the beards of the Holdemans and the buggies of the Amish. The Mennonites themselves often erroneously believe that their real ethics begin here or with "certain other deeds." The outsider who is ignorant of their deeper ethics is struck only by that which is on the surface.

But this problem of where to begin to place Christian ethics also troubles the non-Mennonite. L. S. Keyser, for instance, is brought to his Christian conclusions by "the product of intelligence in the visible cosmos." Warren C. Young begins where

"God discloses Himself to us." And Emil Brunner resorts to various forms of mediation where man is unable on his own to carry out a consistent behavior. The empirical philosophers begin with experience and the idealists with what remains after all the inferior in their estimation has been eliminated.

For Menno Simons the beginning was the Word, Christ, the new birth and the wisdom of God as He gave it at all times to those who wanted it. He says, a knowledge of the will of God and a consistent Christian behavior do not begin with a "man-made holiness" nor "philosophic cleverness" but by the "precious Word which the Son of God, Christ Jesus, brought to us from the mouth of the Father."

Through the years various emphases of obedience based on the literal interpretation of the Scriptures and "man-made holiness" have become a large factor in Mennonite ethics. These in the works of Menno and Mennonites in our day are unreliable criteria. The beginning of their ethics is in salvation and the decisions the Word offers. Their beginning is the same as that of others who believe in the new-birth experience. What is beyond that is merely tradition and practice and dates back to the religious experiences of earlier Anabaptism. The result of this today expresses itself in two different forms. The first is a training in childhood of the Mennonite way of life, conversion when the guilt of sin makes its appearance, and then, on the basis of the new birth, the teaching of obedience to the Scriptures as understood by that Mennonite group to which the convert happens to belong. The second also begins with the Mennonite way of life, and when the years of understanding have come, there follows the obedience to Biblical truths, but the religious new-birth experience may or may not come anywhere in the process.

MENNONITE ETHICS AND THE WORLD

Mennonite ethics aim to keep lives pure. The only light the world has is that of pure Christians. Never can they do the dark deeds belonging to the world, including all forms of violence and warfare. The light of Jesus Christ must shine from them in every situation of life. They are very conscious of Jesus' words: "Ye are the light of the world."

Temptations must be recognized as originating with Satan.

They come at all times in a Christian's life and it is every individual's own responsibility to resist them. Children must be taught to obey and resist evil. Character is not formed by permitting a child to do as he pleases and afterwards blame others for his own wicked urges and the troubles he may get into. Sin is sin and must be treated as such. With the years of accountability help for complete moral and spiritual restoration in the sight of God through the atonement must be sought through grace and forgiveness in Christ Jesus.

Such ethics of obedience always bring clashes and misunderstanding from an unconverted and intolerant society. Persecution for Christians that separate from the world is just as natural today as it was in the past. Even if it is not as severe, the spirit is the same. Amusements and "good times" are also only for the moment. Joys that resist all stress and strain come only from God. Therefore divine guidance and enlightenment must be sought at all times by the younger from the older. This entails an obedience not taught very much anymore except in the military. But Mennonites as a rule do not come under this, but resort to humility, for they say, "God resisteth the proud and giveth grace to the humble. Therefore humble yourselves under the mighty hand of God that he may exalt you in due time; casting all your care upon him, for he careth for you."

The young who are still inexperienced in the ways of the world are taught to shun the devices it uses to stupefy all who seek satisfaction in its pleasures. They are constantly reminded to be "sober and vigilant because the adversary, the devil, as a roaring lion, walketh about, seeking whom he may devour; whom resist stedfast in the faith, knowing that the same afflictions are accomplished" in others.

The places to obtain proper guidance are the church fellowship and the home. Victory is available for every true believer through full acknowledgment of God's Word, prayer, yieldedness to His will, and the unselfish use of one's talents. "Therefore," says St. Paul, "my beloved brethren, be ye stedfast, unmovable, always abounding in the work of the Lord, forasmuch as ye know that your labour is not in vain in the Lord."

Such abundant assurance from the Scriptures gives the Mennonites unbounded faith and courage. Instead of being "a negative group" as is so often said of them, they are a most positive people with unlimited hope. It is not surprising to hear them often quote Psalm 18:27-32: "For thou wilt save the afflicted people . . . for by thee I have run through a troop; and by my God have I leaped over a wall. As for God, his way is perfect; the word of the Lord is tried. . . . It is God that girdeth me with strength, and maketh my way perfect."

APPENDIXES

APPENDIX I

The wording of this chapter has etymological difficulties. Luther translates *ecclesia, Gemeinde*, not *Kirche*. In the Septuagint the Hebrew word *cahal* is translated "people of God," not a "body called out from the world." In the English New Testament the same word for both concepts is used. (Harold S. Bender, "Church," *ME*, I. 594). Bender continues that in either case the "New Testament concept of the church is that of the body of disciples of Christ, united by faith to Him as Saviour and Lord, regenerated by the Holy Spirit, sharing a fellowship of mutual love and brotherhood with one another, witnessing individually and corporately for Christ in the world. The church is Christ's church, founded by Him, responsible to Him. After several centuries during which it at first maintained more or less its original character and later developed into a hierarchical institute of salvation, the church entered a new phase in which it compromised with the world and became a state church. Thereby it lost most of its original N. T. character and became a great and powerful socio-religious institution. Having at first based its faith, life, and organization on the Bible, it gradually came to base itself largely on its own tradition and the teachings of the Church Fathers, thus making the Church in effect the primary authority, the Scriptures secondary. The Reformation of the 16th century broke off a large segment of the Roman Church in the West, in which the Bible was restored as the sole authority for faith and practice and the N. T. Gospel largely revived, but the medieval concept of the mass state church retained. The Anabaptist movement broke completely with this mass state church of believers," *op. cit.*, I, 594. Wenger in *Glimpses of Mennonite History and Doctrine* also asserts that "the church of the N. T. is called the body of Christ." See Frank C. Peters, in *Your Church and You* (Hillsboro, Kansas: Mennonite Brethren Publishing House, n.d.) p. 11 and Menno Simons, "The New Birth" in *CWMS*, pp. 91-93.

APPENDIX II

(a) Peter Rideman, *Confession of Faith*, Account of Our Religion, Doctrine and Faith, Given by Peter Rideman of the Brothers Whom Men Call Hutterians (Hodder and Stoughton: The Plough Publishing House, 1950), p. 61. This Confession was written by Peter Rideman in prison in 1545. Only three copies of the oldest extant edition (1565) are known to be in existence, one of which is in the British Museum.

(b) *The Schleitheim Confession of Faith* adopted by a Swiss Brethren Conference February 24, 1527. The Seven Articles of Schleitheim had Michael Sattler of Stauffen, Germany, as the chief author, it is believed. Contained in Wenger's *Glimpses of Mennonite History and Doctrine*, p. 210.

(c) Bernhard Rothman, *Restitution rechter und gesunder christlicher Lehre*, eine Wiedertäuferschrift von Bernhard Rothman (Münster 1534) (Flugschriften aus der Reformationszeit; Halle a.S.: Max Niemeyer, 1888), VII, *passim*.

(d) Lydia Müller, "Glaubenszeugnisse oberdeutschen Taufgesinnter," *Quellen und Forschungen zur Reformationsgeschichte*, früher Studien zur Kultur und Geschichte der Reformation (Leipzig: M. Heinsius Nachfolger, 1938), p. xxi

(f) "Die wahre Ethik bringt keine Freude, sie ist Lustlos. Und man handelt weise, wenn man dass für gut hält was gegen die Neigung geht. Tue ich etwas gern und tue ich etwas anderes ungern, so handele ich ethisch zumeist dann richtig wenn ich das tue, was ich ungern tue. Denn alle Ethik ist ja an das 'entwerden' gebunden." Erich D. Seeberg in *Luthers Theologie in ihren Grundzügen* (zeite Auflage; Stuttgart), p. 31.

(g) Friesen in *Die Alt-Evangelische Mennonitische Brüderschaft in Russland* on p. 29 writes: "Noch war aber das formale Einigungswerk nicht recht kräftig, noch nicht ausgebaut. Da kamen endlosen Dogmen- und Formenstreit vom warmen Herzensglauben zum Teil abgewöhnte und dem Formel- und Katechismusglauben, der trockenen "Rechtgläubigkeit" (jeder Gruppe nach ihrer Art).

(h) The "Confession" is translated from the first Dutch imprint edited by S. Cramer and F. Pijper, *Bibliotheca Reformatoria Neerlandica* (The Hague, 1910), VII, 121-138. Goshen College has a photo copy. Its review appeared in the *Mennonite Quarterly Review*, XXII (1948), 120-122 by Leonard Verduin. The "Confession" was written shortly before 1560. For a time it was kept secret by Obbe's exiled companions in Rostock. When it made its way to a Reformed "seeker of the truth" in Holland, it first circulated in manuscript copies. In 1584, it was finally published by Cornelius Claesz. Another Dutch edition appeared in 1609. When the "Confession" was first published, it was seized upon by the enemies of the Mennonites to demonstrate the gross errors and insidious threats which they found imminent in Anabaptism. Many followers of Menno Simons condemned it as a fraud. The "Confession" is not without error or miscalculation since it was written some twenty years after the events described. See *SAW* p. 206.

(i) Jacob Hutter, "Brief Jacob Hutters an den Landeshauptmann in Mähren," *Glaubenszeugnisse oberdeutschen Taufgesinnter*, herausgegeben von Dr. Lydia Müller in *Quellen und Forschungen zur Reformationsgeschichte*, XX, I, 160.

Schiemer's Franciscan experiences are carried over to become Anabaptist ethics when he says: "Ja, so ich Got recht erkennt, so wurd ich mich im geist und seel so hoch erfreien, das dise freü wurd aussdringen in den Leib, das auch der leib gantz unentpfindlich, enleidlich, untödtlich, und glorificiert wurde. . . . Wer sich nun Got also ergibt under das creütz, der ist ein kind Gottes. Es ist aber noch nit genug, er muess sich auch absündern von allen denen, die sich Christo nit wollen ergöben, und muess lieb und gemeinschaft halten mit allen denen, die sich Got also ergeben. . . ." Leonhard Schiemers, "Schriften," in Lydia Müller's *Quellen. . .*, XX, I, 67.

(j) "Ich glaub dem Wort Gottes einfältiklich aus Gnad, nit aus kunst." Harold S. Bender, *Conrad Grebel . . .* , p. iv. "Die erste Gov ist Weissheit/aus Gottes Forcht gekommen/die underscheidet das Gute von dem Boesen/ . . . dass wir von seiner Voelli empfangen Gnad und Warhiet/dardurch wir das evige Licht und Gott selber erkennen/ . . . ." Sebastiani Franck, *Ein Verantwortung/und Reputation. Auf zween Send-Briefen/. Kuertzlich aus der Heil.Schrifft verfasset durch* (title page missing).

". . . het woord bestemming staat onuitwischbaar geschreven in het hart des menschen. . . ." and without it man is "een geesteloos wezen." I. J. L. C. de Bussy, *Ethisch Idealisme* (Amsterdam: J. H. de Bussy, 1875, pp. 20, 21.

(k) "Die Nachfolge Jesu und das durch die zu erstrebende Gottesreich war und blieb das höchste Gut." Samuel Geiser, *Die Taufgesinnten-Gemeinden*, herausgegeben im Auftrag der

Konferenz der Altevangelischen Taufgesinnten-Gemeinden (Mennoniten) der Schweiz (Karlsruhe, Baden; Druck und Verlag: Heinrich Schneider, 1931), p. 19; "Das Leben mit Christus in der Nachfolge," und "Die Jugend in der Nachfolge Christi," in Vorträge und Verhandlungen der Sechsten Mennonitischen Weltkonferenz, *Das Evangelium von Jesus Christus in der Welt*. H. S. Bender Präsident, Theo. Glück, Sekretär (Karlsruhe: Druck und Verlag: Heinrich Schneider, 1957), pp. 19, 130.

(l) "Socinus der Neffe arbeitete in Polen an der Gewinnung unserer Väter, und hat auch gewiss viele gewonnen, wie man aus der allgemeinen Kirchengeschichte schliessen muss, was aber unsere mennonitischen Specialwerkchen wenig oder garnicht berühren, indem sie, nach Abschluss der Verfolgunsperiode, fast nur immer mit dem Erlangen und Verlieren von Wohn-und Gewerberecht, von Privilegien und wirtschaftlicher Tüchtigkeit unserer Väter sich beschäftigen und inm allgemeinen begeisterten. Ausdrücken die hohe Frömmigkeit, Glaubenstreue und Sittlichkeit derselben rühmen, so dass der naive Leser immer meinen muss, vor hundert Jahren da seien die Väter lauter Heilige und Märtyrer gewesen." Peter M. Friesen, *Die Alt-Evangelische Mennonitische Brüderschaft in Russland* (1789-1910) *im Rahmen der mennonitischen Gesamtgeschichte* (Halbstadt, Taurien, Russland: Verlagsgesellschaft "Raduga," 1911), pp. 29, 30.

(m) "Dat *aethos* afstamt van *ethos,* was het vrij algemeene gevoelen der oude Grieken, en is ook zeer aannemelijk, aangezien gewoonte de eigenaardigheden, waarvan de natuur ons de beginselen en kiemen ingeplant heeft, tot ontwikkeling brengt." S. Hoekstra, *Zedenleer* (Amsterdam: P. N. Van Kampen & Zoon, 1894), I, 10.

(n) "De moreele mensch kan nog uit den grond zijns harten bidden: "leid ons niet in verzoeking." Hij is nog tot veel kwaad in staat. . . . Wie ernstig uit eigen ervering weet, wat het zeggen wil verzocht te worden, hij zal ook weten hoeveel kracht er noodig is om den duivel te weerstaan. Die kracht heeft de moreele mensch niet. . . . is eigenlijk slechts de zinnelijke mensch. . . ." De Bussy, *op. cit.,* p. 29.

"De moreele mensch antwoordt slechts door reflexbewegingen aan de indrukken der buitenwereld; hij handelt automatisch. De zedelijke mensch heeft een nieuw levensbeginsel in zich opgenomen; daar hij een doel hoeft, dat buiten hem zelven ligt, en waartoe hij zich zelven moet bepalen, handelt hij autocratisch. De eerste handelt zonder smart, de laatste met smart (zelfverloochening)." *Ibid.,* p. 57.

Appendix II

(o) "Luther sah ein Hauptgebrechen der scholastischen Theologie in der Herrschaft der aristotelischen Philosophie. Der Geist des Pelagianismus von welchem er die römische Kirche und ihre Theologie verderbt sah, schien ihm aus jener Philosophie immer neu Nahrung zu ziehen. . . . Für die ethischen Gebiete der christlichen Lehre war jene Herrschaft um so verhängnissvoller, je mehr sich hier das specifisch Christliche mit dem natürlich Menschlichen, also das Theologische mit dem Philosophischen berührt. Luther . . . . war Alles daran gelegen, das eigenthümliche Wesen des Christlichen in seiner ungemischten Reinheit und Eigenthümlichkeit wieder festzustellen und zur Geltung zu bringen." Ernst Luthardt, *Die Ethik Luthers* (Zweite verbesserte Auflage; Leipzig: Dörffling und Franke, 1875), pp. 12, 13.

". . . die *Grammatici, Idalechtici, Rhetores und Philosophi* werden die heilige Schrift verfälschen und aus derselben und ihrer Kunst ein Gemenge machen: da man doch ein jegliches sollte lassen an seinen Ort bleiben, wie und dazu es von Gott geordnet ist, nicht ineinander bräuen. Die Thologia soll Kaiserin sein, die Philosophia und andere gute Künste sollen derselben Dienerin sein; nicht sie regieren und meistern, wie Servetus, Campanus und andere Schwärmer thun." Martin Luther, *Sämmtliche Schriften*. Colloguia oder Tischreden (Neu revidierte Stereotypausgabe; St. Louis, Missouri: Concordia Publishing House, 1887), XXII, 254.

"Die Gerechtigkeit unsrer Werke bestehet nicht in Anfechtungen und Todesnöthen, ja, sie legt denen die sich darauf verlassen das Herzeleid an. Nichts auf Erden macht den Menschen gewiss . . . allein das Erkenntniss Christi. . . . Für weiblisch und kindisch hielt man es früher, auf der Kanzel Christum zu nennen. Scotus, Bonaventura, Occam, Aristoteles und Plato regierten. . . . Der Propheten und Apostel Namen ward niemals gedacht, noch ihre Schriften angezogen, sondern aller Prediger Regel und Weise zu predigen war diese; zum ersten, ein Thema. Spruch und Frage aus dem Scoto oder Aristotele, dem heidnischen Meister, vorhalten. . . . Die heilige Schrift war gar zugedeckt. . . . Wer den Sohn Gottes hat, der hat das ewige Leben. . . . Darum soll es der Sohn Gottes allein sein. . . ." *Ibid.*, pp. 321-53.

(p) "Darum merckt eben auff, was Gott denen träuet, die seinem Wort und Befehl mit Ungehorsam widerstehen, und die ihre Lehre nicht aus Gottes Wort, sondern aus Menschen und dem bitteren Wasserbrunnen, der verführischen Lehre, zusammen fassen, damit sie so manche Seele verführen und umbringen. . . . Da sind viele die sich des Glaubens rühmen, und Evangelisch seyn wollen, welche man allein aus den

Wercken spüren muss, Röm. 2; Matth. 7. Dass ihr diss mit Verstand, gegen den lautern unbefleckten Spiegel (Göttliches Worts) wollet beschauen, ob es dem unsträfflichen Leben Jesu Christi auch gemäss sey, Jacob. 1. Röm. 8. Michael Sattler, "Send-Brieff an eine Gemeinde Gottes: Samt Kurtzem und wahrhafftigem Anzeigen/wie er Seine Lehr, zu Rotenburg am Neckar, mit seinem Blut bezeuget hat. Anno 1527"; Zum zweyten mal gedruckt, Im Jahr 1702. *Güldene Aepffel in Silbern Schalen, Oder Schöne und nützliche Worte und Warheiten Zur Gottseligkeit;* n.d., pp. 103-04.

(q) "Durch die Erleuchtung des Heiligen Geistes, mit viel Lesen und Nachdencken der Schrift, durch Gottes gnädige Gunst und Gabe erlanget, und nicht durch den Dienst und Mittel der verführischen Secten, wie man mir nachgievt." Menno Simons, *Ein Fundament und Klare Anweisung von der seligmachenden Lehre unsers Herrn Jesus Christi,* aus Gottes Wort kurz begriffen. Aus der Niederländischen Sprache in die Hochdeutsche gebracht und übersezt, mit etlichen andern lehrhaften Büchlein, von dem Author dieses Fundaments auch geschrieben und gemacht; so vor dieser zeit besonders sind gedruckt gewesen; nun aber auch hierbey gefügt und gestellt, und also zu einem gemeinen Handbuch geordnet und gemacht (Gedruckt in Europa im Jahr 1575; Pennsylvania gedruckt im Jahr Christi 1794), p. 4.

"Nun sind aber die Gläubigen oder Gerechten aus Gott geboren, Joh. 1:13, die Werke aber gebären niemand, sondern Gott allein; darum machen sie auch niemand gerecht." Luther, *Sämmtliche Schriften,* XXII, p. 449.

"Ich habe angefangen in dem Namen des Herrn, das Wort einer wahren Busse von der Canzel öffentlich zu lehren; das Volck auf den schmalen Weg zu weisen; alle Sünden und Gottlosigkeiten, dazu alle Abgötterey und falschen Gottesdienst, mit Kraft der Schrift zu bestrafen. . . . Also hat mich der gnädige Gott, durch die milde Gunst seiner grossen Gnade an mir elendigen Sünder vollzogen, in meinem Herzen zum ersten gerühret, ein neues Gemüth gegeben in seiner Furcht erniedriget, zum Theil mich selbsten lernen kennen. . . ." Menno Simons, *Ein Fundament und klare Anweisung von der Seligmachenden Lehre unseres Herrn Jesu Christi, op. cit.,* p. 6.

"Christo und sein Wort bereit stunden, ein busfertiges Leben in der Furcht ihres Gottes führeten, ihrem Nächsten in der Liebe dieneten, das Creuze trugen, aller Menschen Wohlfahrt und Heil gerechtigkeit und Bosheit schrecketen, u.s.w.". *Ibid.,* p. 9.

"... in reiner Furcht Gottes unterthäniglich recht nachkommen...." *Ibid.*, p. 10.

"... de nach deinem Wort, in Frieden fahren...." *Ibid.*, p. 14.

"... dem alten gottlosen Wesen müssen absterben.... *Ibid.*, p. 20.

"Schicket euch unterthänig zu seyn des Herrn Wort und Willen, so werdet ihr Mitgenossen, Bürger, Kinder und Erben des neuen, himmlischen Jerusalems seyn; frey von allen euren Feinden, Höll, Sünd, Tod und Teufel, so ihr nur nach dem Geist wandelt, und nicht nach dem Fleisch, Röm. 8. *Qui credit filio Dei, habet vitam aeternam*, John 3." *Ibid.*, pp. 8-30.

(r) Martin Luther, *Luthers Werke*, herausgegeben von Pfarrer Dr. D. Buchwald, *et al.* (Volksausgabe in Acht Bänden, Erste Folge, Reformatorische Schriften Band II; Berlin: C. A. Schwetschke und Sohn, 1888), II, 444. "Darum ist niemand des Papstes Ueberlieferungen verpflichtet, und er hat kein Recht gehört zu werden, ausser wenn er des Evangelium und Christum lehrt, und er selbst darf nichts anderes lehren als den Glauben mit all seiner Freiheit."

(s) "Der Humanismus ist seinem Ursprung nach keine akademische Richtung. Seine wurzeln breit und tief in Schicht, die der Mittelalterliche Geist bisher hatte brachliegen lassen, und diese werden nich nur die wissenschaftlichen Studien mit neuem Säften nähren, sondern auf viel weiterm geistigen Felde Keine zur Entfaltung bringen, die einen ungeahnten kulturellen Brotertrag verhiessen." Verner Näf, *Vadian und Seine Stadt St. Gallen.* Erster Band: bis 1518 in *Humanist in Wien* (St. Gallen: Fehr'sche Buchhandlung St. Gallen Satz und Druck: Buchdruckerei N. Tschudy & Co., St. Gallen, 1944), p. 119.

(t) There is no evidence of any direct connection between the Anabaptist brotherhood and the Brethren of the Common Life. The latter adhered to the Catholic doctrine and always remained loyal to it. W. J. Kühler, Dutch Mennonite historian, held, however, that the soil for the Anabaptist movement in Holland was prepared in part by the Brethren. Christian Neff, "The Brethren of the Common Life," *The Mennonite Encyclopedia*, I, 426.

(u) Menno Simons, "Foundation of Christian Doctrine," *CWMS*, pp. 187, 188. Here the discussion runs much the same as in Luther's "The Babylonian Captivity of the Church," in the *Works of Martin Luther*, Philadelphia edition: Philadelphia: Muhlenberg Press), pp. 170-297.

(v) Namentlich aber hatte die nach Ostern 1528 zum ersten Male versammelte Synode der zücherischen Geistlichkeit denselven Zweck hinsichtlich der Geistlichen selbst. Wenn wir hören, welche Sittenverderbniss unter ihnen, wie nachher besonders bei den Chorherren und bei den Mönchen zu Rüti, an den Tag trat und von nun an durch öffentliche Censur an den Synoden bekämpft werden musst, so werden wir uns des Aergernisses nicht mehr wundern, das ernstere Gemüther nahmen. An der Synode werden alle Laster von einer Anzahl Gemeinden über ihre Prädicanten eingeklagt. Den Pfarrer von Steinmaur entfernte man wegen Ehebruchs; Wetzikon gab schriftlich ein, "dass der Pfarrer verlümbdet, dass er ein dieb sey"; Wangen berichtet, der Pfarrer sei ein Trinker und Spieler; von dem Pfarrer zu Wald heisst es: "Hat sich nünz erfunden, dann dass er winig werd und zuo ziten mit den puren schlat"; von Rollenbutz zu Bülach: er gehe wenig an die Predigt der andern Geistlichen, sei geizig, "hochbertig," ziehe seine Kinder übel, unzüchtig; er musste daher in die Stadt kommen und studieren. Herr Benedict von Landenberg zu Bärentsweil ist der Rede überwiesen; er habe nach Befehl Neiner Herren ein Weib genommen, "und hiessend si in noch eins nemen, so wöllt er's tuon." Die Pfarrer von Russikon, Zell, Wildberg werden wegen Trinkens, Wirthens und wegen Schlaghändeln "caputuliert," ähnlich der von Turbenthal, der von Laufen wegen Geiz, der von Ottenbach, ein Trinker und Schläger, weil er seine Frau geschlagen und übel mishandelt habe...." Emil Egli, *Die Züricher Wiedertäufer* zur Reformationszeit nach den Quellen des Staatsarchivs (Züricher Druck und Verlag von Friedrich Schulthess, 1878), p. 75.

(w) Leite mich nach deinem Rath, der wohl wunderlich geschiehet, aber endlich in der That auf die schönste Wohlfahrt siehet: denn du führst es wohl hinaus, sieht es gleich verkehrt aus. Mag es doch indessen hier wunderlich mit mir ergehen, dennoch bleib' ich stets in dir, dennoch will ich feste stehen. Ich muss, Trotz sei aller Pain! dennoch, dennoch selig sein." Mennonitischen Verlagshandlung, *Gesangbuch,* eine Sammlung geistlicher Lieder zur Allgemeinen Erbauung und zum Lobe Gottes (Dritte amerikanische Ausgabe, Elkhart, Indiana: Herausgegeben von der Mennonitischen Verlagshandlung, 1918), p. 788.

(x) "Etliche schöne Christliche Gesang, wie sie in der Gefengkniss zu Passau im Schloss von der Schweitzer durch Gottes gnad geticht und gesungen worden" (n.p. 1564). The title of the *Ausbund,* compiled only nineteen years later, showed that the social atmosphere was conducive to the production of this type of literature. It read: "Ausbund Etlicher Schöner Christlicher Gesang, wie die in der Gefengnuss zu

Appendix II

Passau im Schloss von den Schweitzern, und auch von andern recht-gläubigen Christen hin und her gedicht worden. Allen und jeden Christen, welcher Religion sie auch seyen, unparteilich und fast nützlich zu brauchen" (n.p. 1583), Bender, "The Hymnology of the Anabaptists," *MQR, op. cit.*, p. 7.

(y) "First of all, what is meant by the term 'Mysticism'? One of its eminent exponents is the Quaker Rufus M. Jones. Dr. Jones defines mysticism as "a direct way of vital intercourse and correspondence between God and man" *(Pathways to the Reality of God,* Macmillan, 1931, p. 23). According to this definition the particular type of mysticism held by Jones does not recognize human depravity and the need of a divine Mediator. Indeed Dr. Jones says flatly that men are just as capable of finding God as they are of finding "harmony, or beauty, or moral goodness, or truth" (p. 49). He states also that what we find in the mystic is not a supernatural happening; it is apparently the result of a human exertion, made by a religious genius (p. 45). Now it must be evident to every Christian thinker that the type of mysticism represented by this Quaker is far from the Kingdom indeed. If a man is not a lost sinner in need of a Mediator to approach a holy God he is in no wise to be recognized as a New Testament Christian. Also see John C. Wenger, "Christianity and Mysticism," *The Christian Ministry*, I (October, 1948), 207.

(z) *Güldene Aepffel in Silbern Schalen,* Oder Schöne und nützliche Worte und Warheiten Zur Gottseligkeit: Christliche Glaubens-Bekentnuss/Der friedliebenden und förnemlich (unter dem Namen der *Menonisten*) wohlbekannten Christen/Wie auch Etliche Christliche Gebätt derselben Glaubens-Bekenner (Gedruckt im Jahr 1742, n.p.), p. 18. "En deze is enkel en alleen afhankelijk van de plaats waar een mens woont: aan de zijde der wereld, of aan de zijde van God. En dit, en dit alleen is ook de waarachtige oorzaak van al dat grote lijden, dat als een zware druk hangt over het leven der Westerse Wereld."

(1) Matthiä Cervas von Rottennem, "Eilff auserlesene Send-Brieffe, welche er vor und in seinem Gefägnüss an seine Verwandten nach dem Geist und Fleisch geschrieben, und die darinnen enthaltene Warheit endlich mit seinem Blut besiegelt hat; Wie auch Conrad Kochs von Leuenburg. Eines Blutzeugens des Zeugnüss Christi, Zwey andere Brieffe, Samt einer schönen Schluss-Rede, Welche Wegen ihrer Fürtrefflichkeit zur Ehre Gottes und des Nächsten Heyl aufs neue übersehen und aufgeleget worden Im Jahr Christi 1702 in *Güldene Aepffel In Silbern Schalen.* Oder Schöne und nütz-

liche Worte und Warheiten Zur Gottseligkeit." (Written by hand in the front of the book, "wurde geschrieben 1527, zum zweiten male wurde es im Jahre 1702 gedruckt." n.p.), IV, 119.

(2) Michael Sattler, "Send-Brieff an eine Gemeinde Gottes: Samt Kurtzem und wahrhafftigem Anzeigen Wie er Seine Lehr, zu Rotenburg am Neckar, mit seinem Blut bezeuget hat." Anno 1527 Zum zweyten mal gedruckt, im Jahr 1702, In *Güldene Aepffel In Silbern Schalen, op. cit.* p. 35.

(3) "Een profitelijk ende troostelick Boecxken uanden Gheloue ende hoope, wat dat oprechte Gheloue is. Ende welcke ghenade dye mensche doer dat Gheloue mach vercrijgen. Noch een Boecxken van die Liefde die God tot ons heft. met noch een devote Contemplatie van dye Bruyt Christi," Cramer en Pijper, *op. cit.*, IV, 525, 577.

APPENDIX III

(a)

Es glänzet der Christen inwendiges Leben,
Obgleich sie von aussen die Sonne verbrannt,
Was ihnen der König des Himmels gegeben,
Ist keinem als ihnen nur selber bekannt,
Was niemand verspüret,
Was niemand cerühret,
Hat ihre erleuchteten Sinne gezieret.
(H. Franz, *Choralbuch*, p. 54.)

O, heilger Geist,
Du Brunnquell aller Güter,
Du Freudenöhl der christlichen Gemüther,
Füll unser Herz mit Deiner Himmelskraft,
Du ein'ger Geber reiner Gottesliebe,
Leit' unsern Gang, regiere unsre Triebe
Zu Deinem Lob in dieser Pilgrimschaft.
(H. Franz, *Choralbuch*, p. 25.)

Herr, Dein Wort, die edle Gabe,
Diesen Schatz erhalte mir,
Denn ich zieh ihn aller Habe
Und dem grössten Reichtum für.
Wenn Dein Wort nicht mehr soll gelten,
Worauf soll der Glaube ruhn?
Mir ist's nicht um tausend Welten,
Aber um Dein Wort zu tun.

Halleluja, Ja und Amen!
Herr, Du wollest auf mich sehn,
Dass ich mög in Deinem Namen
Fest bei Deinem Worte stehn
Lass mich eifrig sein beflissen,
Dir zu dienen früh un spat,
Und zugleich zu Deinen Füssen
Sitzen, wie Maria tat.

Allgemeinen Konferenz der Mennonitengemeinschaft Nordamerikas, *Gesangbuch der Mennoniten* (Erste Auflage; Newton, Kansas: Board of Publication of the General Conference of the Mennonite Church of North America (this was not printed in the book but stated orally by the office) c.1942), p. 6.

Lass mich, Jesu! deinem Worte
Vollen Glauben stellen zu;
Denn es ist die rechte Pforte
Zu der süssen Seelenruh'.
Niemand kann den Trost ergründen,
Der in deinem Wort zu finden.

Mennonitischen Verlagshandlung, *Gesangbuch*, eine Sammlung geistlicher Lieder zur Allgemeinen Erbauung und zum Lobe Gottes (Dritte amerikanische Ausgabe; Elkart, Indiana: Herausgegeben von der Mennonitischen Verlagshandlung, 1889), p. 106.

(b) Friesen repeatedly refers to the quarreling and bickering among the Mennonites over rules and ordinances, sometimes very insignificant. He says: "Die herrschenden Lehren und die religiös-sittlichen Anschauungen oder Vorurteile sind weit mehr charakterbildend bei den Mennoniten, als die Umgebung. Das sehen wir besonders an dem fast unbeweglichen konservativen Wesen der Mennoniten in der Schweiz und in Nordamerika. Sie haben sich aus religiös-sittlichen Ursachen in diesen freien und hochkultivierten Ländern weit schärfer abgeschlossen als die Mennoniten in Russland. Das gilt besonders von den Amerikanischen "Altmennoniten" und "Amischen," die überwiegend schweizerischen Ursprungs sind. Doch auch von unsern aus Russland nach Amerika ausgewanderten Mennoniten kann man kühn behaupten dass sie konservativer und abgeschlossener sind, als ihre in Russland zurückgebliebenen Confessionsgenossen. Es wanderten eben die Konservatisten (anfänglich) aus, und so entwikeln sie sich, oder richtiger, bleiben sie auch drüben." Friesen, writing in Russia about the Mennonites in America, seems to have at a greater distance a remarkably true perspective. Peter M. Friesen, *Die Alt-Evangelische Mennonitische Brüderschaft.* . . . *op. cit.*, pp. 61-82 and other places.

(c) Wiebe laments that the members do not support the ministers in demanding obedience to tradition. He is one of those conservatives about whom Friesen informs us above. Wiebe writes: Ach wenn nun die Gemeinde oder die Brüder treue Glieder waren und für ihre Aeltesten und Lehrer beteten, und ihnen zur Seite ständen. . . . Sie wollen zwar Glieder in der Kirche sein, aber hinter dem Rücken sind sie mit den Weltweisen und ihrer Lehre eins" (p. 50). "Der böse Feind hat noch eine Wurzel in die Gemeinden hineingelegt, und diese Wurzel ist der Hochmut. . ." (p. 50). "Hoffart und Kleiderpracht nimmt so zu, dass man die sogenannten Mennoniten von den Landeskindern nicht mehr unterscheiden kann, gerade gegen des Herrn und der Apostel Lehre" (p. 51).

"Der Gottesdienst ist verfälscht . . . dass er von der Einfalt keines Lehrmeisters bedarf. . . (p. 53): Gerhard Wiebe, *Ursachen und Geschichte der Auswanderung aus Russland nach Amerika* (Winnipeg, Manitoba, Canada: Druckerei des "Nordwesten," 1898), *passim*.

(d) The *Gesangbuch in Mennoniten Gemeinden für Kirche und Haus* was published for the churches of West Prussia. This book went at least through four editions, the fourth in 1901. It was republished in Danzig in 1873. This book has many songs that are also in the *Gesangbuch in welchem eine Sammlung geistreiche Lieder befindlich,* 9th ed. Elbing. The hymnbook of the Prussian Mennonites was taken by the Prussians to Russia where it was republished in Odessa, 1844. The above numbers are taken from this book. Both hymns are of a true traditional stock.

About the *Ausbund* we read in the *Handbook of the Mennonite Hymnary,* Newton, 1949, p. xxx: "Ausbund, Das ist: Etliche schöne Christliche Lieder, wie sie in dem Gefängnis zu Passau in dem Schlosz von den Schweizer-Brüdern und von andern rechtglaubigen Christen hin und her gedichtet worden."

"At least twelve editions have been printed in Europe, the last one in Basel, 1838. Its use was confined to the South Germans and Swiss Mennonites. Reprinted in America and still in use by the Amish, the *Ausbund* has the distinction of being the oldest hymn book officially in use by any church in America."

APPENDIX IV

Mennonites normally have eleven steps in the process of redemption and human response.

(1) The beginning of the Christian life is only in Christ Jesus, John 6:44; Eph. 2:8. God can save none against his will, John 5:40; John 7:17. The first work of the Holy Spirit is to convict of sin, John 16:8-9.

(2) Upon conviction of sin follows repentance. This means a change in thoughts, forsaking sin and living for God, II Chron. 7:14; I Thess. 1:9. There must be repentance, for sin is wrong and offensive to God, Ps. 51:4. All are guilty and all must repent, Acts 17:30; 2:38; 3:19; Luke 13:3. The goodness of God should lead to repentance, Rom. 2:3-4.

(3) Faith is a necessary condition for salvation, Mark 16:16: Christ is the divine Saviour and must be personally trusted. It includes a knowledge of the gospel and its acceptance, Rom. 10:14; Heb. 11:6; Acts 16:31. It comes by hearing, Rom. 10:7. Never can it be earned, Eph. 2:8-10; John 3:36. Faith and true repentance always exist together.

(4) The proofs of faith are confession and restitution, Prov. 28:13; Luke 19:8. Our faithful confession has the promise of forgiveness, I John 1:9. Salvation is based upon confession, Rom. 10:9-10; Matt. 10:32; Luke 12:8. God dwells in them who confess, I John 4:15. Confession and restitution is voluntary.

(5) This change results in a new life of the sinner, II Cor. 5:17. Where there was death before there is new life, Eph. 2:1.

(6) This regeneration, or the New Birth makes the believer a partaker of the divine nature, II Peter 1:4. Because it makes a person a new creature and gives him a divine nature it is called regeneration, Titus 3:5; Gal. 6:15; Joh 3:3. It is worked in man by God Himself, I Peter 1:3, 23; John 3:5-6; II Cor. 10:5. This no one can avoid and become a child of God, John 3:3, 5. Water baptism does not bring it about, Acts 10:44, 47. Water is mentioned in that the Word makes clean through the Holy Ghost, John 3:5; Titus 3:5; Rom. 6:4; Eph. 5:26. This is not understood without the Holy Ghost, John 3:8; 14:16. The new life is the evidence of a new heart, I John 2:4, 29.

(7) God gives further evidence to the sinner that he is free from guilt through justification, Rom. 4:5; II Cor. 5:21.

Appendix IV

This comes with no merit of our own, Rom. 3:24-25; Gal. 2:16. No good works of our own are good enough to stand before God, Ps. 143:2; Isa. 64:6. But such faith will reveal good works, Gal. 5:6; James 2:17; Eph. 2:10. Justification gives us blessings of peace with God and freedom from the bondage of sin, Rom. 5:1; Rom. 8:16; John 8:36; Heb. 12:14; II Cor. 7:1.

(8) The sinner further receives the adoption as a child of God, I John 3:1-2; Gal. 4:5; II Chron. 7:14. We can now know that we are sons of God, I John 3:1-2. (Here not all Mennonite branches agree fully). Testing takes place in our sonship, Heb. 12:7.

(9) The converted is to grow in his Christian life, Phil. 3:12-13. This growth is in grace, II Peter 3:18, and requires watchfulness, and effort, Phil. 2:12; Eph. 6:11; I Peter 2:2. The believer should live a peaceable and holy life, I Pet. 1:15. There is a possibility and great danger that the Christian may fall into sin, Rom. 6:6; James 4:4; Heb. 3:12-19. The Holy Spirit, the Word, and prayer help in this life, Rom. 2:2; Ps. 119:9-11; Rom. 8:26; John 14:14; Acts 9:20-22.

(10) The church of God is composed of such believers, Heb. 12:23; Gal. 3:26.

(11) Every such believer ought to be baptized, Acts 2:38; Matt. 10:32-33. This means being baptized in the Trinity, Matt. 28:19. Those who have given proof of real repentance are fit subjects for baptism, Acts 2:38. Baptism is a solemn vow of loyalty to Christ, Col. 3:1-3.

All Mennonite statements of their *Fundamentals of Faith*, in the main state these points with more or less individual emphasis. See Board of Home Missions of Southern District Conference of the Mennonite Brethren Church (P. C. Hiebert, H. R. Wiens, A. W. Epp), *Fundamentals of Faith* (Third edition: Hillsboro, Kansas: Mennonite Brethren Publishing House, 1954), pp. 34-46 and *passim*.

BIBLIOGRAPHY

A. PRIMARY SOURCES

A. B. "Kasper von Schwenkfeld und die Correspondenz der Schwenkfelder mit der holländischen mennonitischen Societät in den Jahren 1725. Aus dem Archiv der Mennoniten-Gemeinde zu Amsterdam, "*Geschichte der Mennoniten*. Compiled by K. Daniel Cassel. Philadelphia: J. Kohler, 1880. Pp. 365-84.

Anastasi j. Ioannis. "Von dem waren Leib Christi. Dar in ein yeder Christ die Päbstliche irthumb und Abgöttereien mit dem Meszbrot kan erkennen. Wider die Jhesuijten vnd andere, 1561." *Bibliotheca Reformatoria Neerlandica*, IV, 461-90.

Ausbund, Das ist: Etliche schöne Christliche Lieder, wie sie in dem Gefängnis zu Passau in dem Schloss von den Schweizer-Brüdern und von andern rechtglaubigen Christen hin und her gedichtet worden. 1570, n.p.

Barth, Karl. *Evangelium und Gesetz*. Munich, Germany: Kaiser Publishing Company, n.d.

Bible, Holy. Authorized Version.

Braght, J. Thieleman van, compiler. *The Bloody Theatre or Martyrs' Mirror*. Compiled from authentic chronicles and testimonies. Published in the Dutch language. Translated into German. Revised by I. Daniel Rupp. Lancaster County, Pennsylvania: David Miller, Near Lampeter Square, 1837.

———, compiler. *The Bloody Theatre or Martyrs' Mirror*. Translated from the oiginal Dutch Edition of 1669 by Joseph F. Sohm. Scottdale, Pennsylvania: Mennonite Publishing House, 1938.

Brunner, Emil. *The Mediator*. Philadelphia: The Westminster Press, 1957.

Bussy, de I. J. L. C. *Ethisch Idealisme*. Amsterdam: J. H. De Bussy, 1875.

Calvin, John. *A Compend of the Institutes of the Christian Religion*. Edited by Hugh Thomson Kerr. Philadelphia: Presbyterian Board of Education, 1939.

Cervas, Matthiä von Rottennem. "Eilff auserlesene Send-Brieffe," *Güldene Aepffel In Silbern Schalen, Oder Schöne und nützliche Worte und Warheiten Zur Gottseligkeit*. Geschrieben 1527, gedruckt 1702, n.p. Pp. 1-167.

Cramer, S. and F. P. Pijper, editors. *Bibliotheca Reformatoria Neerlandica*. 10 vols. 's-Gravenhage: Martinus Nijhoff, 1906.

Denck, Hans. "Whether God Is the Cause of Evil." Augsburg, 1926. *Spiritual and Anabaptist Writers*. Edited by George Hunston Williams and Angel M. Mergel. Library of Christian Classics, XXV. Philadelphia: The Westminster Press, 1957. Pp. 88-111.

"Dordrecht Confession of Faith, The." *Glimpses of Mennonite History and Doctrine*. Third edition. Scottdale, Pennsylvania: Herald Press, 1949. Pp. 214-28.

Erasmus Desiderius. *The Praise of Folly*. With a Short Life of the Author by Hendrik van Loon of Rotterdam. New York: Walter J. Black, 1942.

Erasmus, Des. of Rotterdam. *Querela Pacis*. Translated by Jose Chapiro under the title "Peace Protests!" *Erasmus and Our Struggle for Peace*. Boston: The Beacon Press, 1950. Pp. 125-35.

Evangelical Mennonite Brethren. *Constitution and Confession of Faith.*
Revised. Mountain Lake, Minnesota: The Evangelical Mennonite Brethren, 1950.
———, *1958 Annual Report of the 64th Annual Conference Session, June 4-8, 1958.* Omaha: Evangelical Mennonite Brethren Headquarters, 1958.
Evangelical Mennonite Church. *Church Manual.* Revised and adopted at the Annual Conference at Upland, Indiana, 1947.
Evangelium von Jesus Christus in der Welt, Das. Vorträge und Verhandlungen der Sechsten Mennonitischen Weltkonferenz vom 10. bis 16. August 1957 in Karlsruhe, Deutschland. Druck und Verlag: Heinrich Schneider, Karlsruhe, 1958.

Franck, Sebastian. "A Letter to John Campanus." *Spiritual and Anabaptist Writers* in *Library of Christian Classics Series,* XXV, 1957. Pp. 147-160.
———, *Ein Verantwortung/ und Reputation. Auf zween Send-Brief/. Kiertzlich aus der Heil.* Schrifft verfasset durch Dietrich Philip. (Title page missing.
Friedmann, Robert. "Reason and Obedience: An Old Anabaptist Letter of Peter Walpot (1571) and Its Meaning." *The Mennonite Quarterly Review,* XIX (January, 1945), 27-40.

Gesangbuch. Eine Sammlung geistlicher Lieder zur allgemeinen Erbauung und zum Lobe Gottes. Durchgesehene amerikanische Ausgabe, Elkhart, Indiana: Herausgegeben von der Mennonitischen Verlagshandlung, 1918.
Grebel, Conrad. "A Letter of Conrad Grebel to Vadian." *Glimpses of Mennonite History and Doctrine.* Scottdale, Pennsylvania: Herald Press, 1949. Pp. 202-03.
———, "Letters to Thomas Müntzer," *Spiritual and Anabaptist Writers,* of the *Library of Christian Classics.* XXVI. Philadelphia: The Westminster Press, 1957. Pp. 49-70.
Güldene Aepffel In Silbern Schalen, Oder Schöne und nützliche Worte und Warheiten Zur Gottseligkeit: Christliche Glaubens-Bekantnuss/Der Friedliebenden und fürnemlich (unter dem Namen der Mennoniten) wohlbekannten Christen/ Wie auch Etliche Christliche Gebätt derselben Glaubens-Bekenner. Gedruckt im Jahr 1742, n.p.

Hoekstra, S. *Zedenleer.* No. vols. Amsterdam: P. N. Van Kampen & Zoon, 1894.
Holdeman, Johannes. *Der Alte Grund und Fundament aus Gottes Wort gefasst und geschrieben.* Lancaster, Pennsylvania: Gedruckt für den Verfasser von Johann Sär's Söhnen, 1862.
Huizinga, J. *Verzamelde Werken Biografie.* Haarlem: H. D. Tjeenk Willink & Zoon N. V., 1950.
Hutter, Jacob. "Brief Jacob Hutters an den Landeshauptmann in Mähren," *Glaubenszeugnisse oberdeutscher Taufgesinnter. Quellen und Forschungen zur Reformationsgeschichte* (früher Studien zur Kultur und Geschichte der Reformation). I. 1938. 148-90.

Kant, Immanuel. *Eternal Peace.* Translated by W. Hastie with an introduction by Edwin D. Mead. Boston: The World Peace Foundation, 1914.
———, *Kritik der praktischen Vernunft.* Gesammelte Schriften, Bk. V. Reimer Verlag, 1908.
———, *Kritik der reinen Vernunft.* Text der Ausgabe 1781 mit Beifügung sämmtlicher Abweichungen der Ausgabe 1787. Herausgegeben von Karl Kehrbach. Zweite verbesserte Auflage. Leipzig: Druck und Verlag von Philipp Reclam jun., 1878.
Kierkegaard, Soren. *Either-Or.* II. Translated by David and Lilean Swanson. Princeton, New Jersey: Princeton University Press, 1944.

Kleingemeinde Diener-Konferenz vom 23. bis zum 28. Oktober 1937 in Meade, Kans.
Kornelsen, G. G., Reimer, K. J. B., Toews, J. G., et al. *Das 60-jährige Jubiläum (1874-1934)*. Beiträge zur mennonitischen Geschichte. Heft I. Steinbach, Manitoba, Canada: Warte-Verlag, 1934.
Luther, Martin. *Luthers Werke*. Herausgegeben von Pfarrer D. Dr. Buchwald, et al., Volksausgabe in Acht Bänden. Erste Folge: *Reformatorische Schriften*. Berlin: C. A. Schwetschke und Sohn, 1898.
———, *Sämmtliche Schriften*. Zweiundzwanzigster Band. *Colloguia oder Tischreden*. Neue revidirte Stereotypausgabe. St. Louis, Mo.: Concordia Publishing House, 1887.
———, *Works of Martin Luther*. The Philadelphia Edition. Philadelphia: Muhlenberg Press, 1930. Vols. I to VI.
Mann, W. J. *Hallesche Nachrichten*. Allentown, Pennsylvania: Verlag von Brohst, Diehl & Co., 1886.
Mennonite Brethren Church of North America. *Confession of Faith*. Translated by H. F. Toews. American Edition. Hillsboro, Kansas: Mennonite Brethren Publishing House, n.d. (after 1916).
Mennonite Brethren Church Board of Home Missions, P. C. Hiebert, H. R. Wiens, A. W. Epp, *Fundamentals of Faith in Question and Answer Form*. Third edition. Hillsboro, Kansas: Mennonite Brethren Publishing House, 1954.
Mennonite Church Polity. S. F. Coffman, editor. Scottdale, Pennsylvania: Mennonite Publishing House, 1944.
Müller, Lydia. *Glaubenszeugnisse ober-deutscher Taufgesinnter*. Quellen und Forschungen zur Reformationsgeschichte (früher Studien zur Kultur und Geschichte der Reformation). Leipzig: N. M. Heinsius Nachfolger, 1938.
Müntzer, Thomas. "Sermon Before the Princes," *Spiritual and Anabaptist Writers*, Library of Christian Classics. XXV, 1957. 41-46.
Pestalozzi, Carl. *Heinrich Bullinger*, Elberfeld: Verlag von L. L. Friderichs, 1858.
Philips, Dietrich. *Enchiridion oder Handbüchlein, von der Christlichen Lehre und Religion*. Translated into German. Dritte Amerikanische Auflage. Elkhart, Indiana: Gedruckt und herausgegeben von John F. Funk und Brud, 1872.
———, *Enchiridion oder Handbuechlein, von der Christlichen Lehre und Religion*. Uebersezt in hochdeutsche Sprache, Lancaster: Gedruckt bey Joseph Ehrenfried, 1811.
Philips, Obbe. "Bekenntnisse," *Bibliotheca Reformatoria Neerlandica*. VII, 1906. Pp. 109-38.
Rideman, Peter. *Confession of Faith. Accounts of Our Religion, Doctrine and Faith, Given by Peter Rideman of the Brothers Whom Men Call Hutterians*. Hodder and Stoughton: The Plough Publishing House, 1950.
Ris, Cornelius. *Mennonite Articles of Faith*. A translation. Reprinted by the Committee on Doctrine and Conduct of the General Conference of the Mennonite Church of North America. Berne, Indiana: Mennonite Book Concern, 1946.
Rol, Henrick. "Die Slotel van dat Secreet des Nachtmaels onses Heren Jesu Christi, welcke ontsluyt dat rechte verstant, dat daer verborgen is. Geschreuen doer eynen Henrick Rol, om des Geloofs wille, anno 1536 verbrant tot Maestricht. Al nu verbetert ende grondelick wederom gestelt na die eerste waerheyt, also de leser lichtelick kan bevinden. Ende is gedylt in dry stucken." *Bibliotheca Reformatoria Neerlandica*. V, 1906. 41-94.

——, "Een profitelijk ende troostelick Boecxken vanden Gheloue ende Hoope, wat dat oprechte Gheloue is. Ende Welcke ghenade dye mensche doer dat Gheloue mach vercrijgen. Noch een Boecxken van die Liefde die God tot ons heeft. Met noch een deuote Contemplatie van dye Bruyt Christi." *Bibliotheca Reformatoria Neerlandica*. IV. 1906. 521-592.

Roosen, Gerhard. *Unschuld und Gegen-Bericht der Evangelischen Taufgesinneten Christen/ so Mennisten genandt werden/ des Menno Simonis Wehmütige und Christliche Entschuldigung/ Menno Simonis Ausgang aus dem Pabstthum/ Menno Simonis Glaubens-Bekänntniss von der heiligen Gottheit und Göttlichen Dreyeinigkeitl Appendix Wegen des Menno Simonis Lebens-Lauff und dessen Ende. Evangelisches Glaubens-Bekändtniss der Tauff-gesinnten Christen.* Predigt. Hamburg: Gedruckt bey Sigismund Hoffman/1702.

Rotmann, Bernhard. *Restitution rechter und gesunder christlicher Lehre.* Eine Wiedertäufer-schrift von Bernhard Rotmann. (Münster, 1534) Flugschriften aus der Reformationszeit. VII. Halle a.S.: Max Riemeyer, 1888.

Sattler, Michael. "Send-Brieff An eine Gemeinde Gottes: Samt Kurtzem und wahrhafftigem Anzeigen Wie er Seine Lehr zu Rotenburg am Neckar, mit seinem Blut bezeuget hat. Anno 1527." Zum zweyten mal gedruckt, Im Jahr 1702. In *Güldene Aepffel In Silbern Schalen, Oder Schöne und nützliche Worte und Warheiten Zur Gottseligkeit*: n.p. Pp. 1-236.

Schiemers, Leonhard. "Schriften," *Glaubenszeugnisse oberdeutscher Taufgesinnter* in *Quellen und Forchungen zur Reformationsgeschichte*. I. 43-80.

Schlaffers, Hans. "Ein Kurzer Unterricht zum Anfang Eines Recht Christlichen Lebens durch Unseren Lieben Brueder Und Zeugen Jesu Christi Hans Schlaffer," *Glaubenszeugnisse oberdeutscher Taufgesinnter* in *Quellen und Forschungen zur Reformationsgeschichte*. I. 1938. 83-110.

Schlatter, D. A. *Das Christliche Dogma.* Zweite Auflage. Stuttgart: Calwer Vereinsbuchhandlung, 1923.

"Schleitheim Confession of Faith, The." *Glimpses of Mennonite History and Doctrine*, 1949. Pp. 210-15.

Simons, Menno. *The Complete Works of Menno Simons.* Translated from the original Dutch or Holland. First Part; Elkhart, Indiana: Published by John F. Funk and Brother, 1871.

——, *The Complete Writings of Menno Simons, c.1496-1561.* Translated from the Dutch by Leonard Verduin and edited by John Christian Wenger, with a biography by Harold S. Bender. Scottdale, Pennsylvania. Herald Press, 1956.

——, *Ein Fundament und Klare Anweisung von der seligmachenden Lehre unsers Herrn Jesu Christi.* Ins deutsche Übersetzt und zu einem gemeinem Handbuch geordnet und gemacht. Gedruckt in Europa in Jahr 1575. Pennsylvanian, gedruckt im Jahr Christi 1794.

Stadler, Ulrich. "Cherished Instructions on Sin, Excommunication, and the Community of Goods," *Spiritual and Anabaptist Writers in Library of Christian Classics*, 1957. Pp. 274-84.

——, "Schriften," *Glaubenszeugnisse oberdeutschen Taufgesinnter*. In *Quellen und Forschungen zur Reformationsgeschichte*. I, 1938.

Unruh, H. Benjamin. "Die Botschaft des Evangeliums in unserer Zeit," *Botschaft und Nachfolge*. Edited by Theo. Glück. Karlsruhe: Evangelische Sortiments- und Verlagsbuchhandlung Flügel & Co. Nachfolger, 1947. Pp. 14-28.

Veluano, Auth. Ioan. Anastasio. "Der Leken Wechwyser," *Bibliotheca Reformatoria Neerlandica*. IV. 1906. 123-376.

Wiebe, Gerhard. *Ursache und Geschichte der Auswanderung aus Russland nach Amerika.* Winnipeg, Manitoba, Canada: Druckerei des "Nordwesten," 1898.

Williams, George H. and Angel M. Mergal, editors. *Spiritual and Anabaptist Writers* in *Library of Christian Classics*. Philadelphia: The Westminster Press, 1957.

B. SECONDARY SOURCES

Aiken, Henry D. *The Age of Ideology.* A Mento Bk. New York: The New American Library, New York, 1956.
Aulen, Gustaf. *Christus Victor.* Translated by A. G. Hebert. American edition. New York: The Macmillan Company, 1956.
———, *The Faith of the Christian Church.* Translated from the fourth Swedish edition by Eric H. Wahstrom and Everet Arden. Philadelphia: The Muhlenberg Press, 1948.
Baillie, John, Jh. T. McNeill, Henry P. Van Dusen. "Introductions," *Spiritual and Anabaptist Writers.* In *Library of Christian Classics.* XXV. 1957. Pp. 19-38; 39-40; 47-48; 71-72; 87; 112-13; 136-37; 145-46; 161-62; 182-83; 204-05; 226-27; 261-62; 272-73; 320-321; 330-34; 351-56.
Bainton, Roland H. *The Age of the Reformation.* New York: D. Van Nostrand Company, Inc. 1956.
———, *The Reformation of the Sixteenth Century.* Boston: The Beacon Press, 1952.
———, *The Travail of Religious Liberty.* Nine Biographical Studies. Philadelphia: The Westminster Press, c.1951.
Bancroft, H. Emery, arranger and compiler. *Christian Theology.* Johnson City, New York; Johnson City Publishing Company, 1946.
Bax, Belfort, E. *Rise and Fall of the Anabaptists.* Part III of *The Social Side of the Reformation in Germany.* London: Swan Sonnenschein & Co., Ltd., 1903.
Beckerath, Gerhard von. *Die Wirtschaftliche Bedeutung der Krefelder Mennoniten und Ihrer Vorfahren im 17. and 18. Jahrhundert.* Fakultät der Rheinischen Friedrich-Wilhelms-Universität zu Bonn, 1951.
Beckmann, Joachim. Hans Kulp, Peter Brunner, Walter Reindell, *P. Gott d. an Sonn und Festagen.* Guttersloh: C. Bertelsmann Verlag, 1949.
Bender, Harold S. *The Anabaptist Vision.* Reprinted from *The Mennonite Quarterly Review,* April, 1944. Scottdale, Pennsylvania: Mennonite Publishing House, 1955. Pp. 3-23.
———, "Das Anliegen des Täufermennonitentums innerhalb der Reformationsbewegung," *Botschaft und Nachfolge.* 1947. Pp. 64-74.
———, "A Brief Biography of Menno Simons," *The Complete Writings of Menno Simons c.1496-1561.* I. 1955. 1-29.
———, "Church," *The Mennonite Encyclopedia.* I. c.1956. 594-97.
———, *Conrad Grebel c.1498-1526 the Founder of the Swiss Brethren Sometimes Called Anabaptists.* Scottdale, Pennsylvania: Herald Press, c.1950.
———, "Eschatology," *The Mennonite Encyclopedia.* II. 1956. 247-48.
———, "The Hymnology of the Anabaptists," *The Mennonite Quarterly Review,* XXXI (January, 1956), 5-10.
———, "The Pacifism of the Sixteenth Century Anabaptism," *The Mennonite Quarterly Review,* XXX (January, 1956), 5-18.
Berkouwer, G. C. *Modern Uncertainty and Christian Faith.* Grand Rapids, Michigan: Wm. B. Eerdmans Publishing Co., 1953.
Bliss, William Root. *Side Glimpses from the Colonial Meeting-House.* Boston: Houghton, Mifflin and Company. The Riverside Press, Cambridge, 1896.
Binnerts, A. Sz. *Wat is ons "Doopsgezind"?* No. 36 in *Geschriftjes ten Behoeve van de Doopsgezinden in de Verstrooiing.* 1897.
Bohn, Ernest J. *Christian Peace According to the New Testament Peace Teachings Outside the Gospels.* Peace Committee of the General Con-

ference of the Mennonite Church of North America, Souderton, Pennsylvania, 1938.
Bohnoeffer, Dietrich. *Ethics.* Edited by Eberhard Bethge. New York: The Macmillan Company, 1955.
Brockhaus. "Menno Simons," in *Konversations-Lexikon.* 14. Auflage. Edited by F. A. Brockhaus. XI. Leipzig: F. A. Brockhaus, 1894. 770.
Brons, Anna *Ursprung, Entwickelung und Schicksale der altevangelischen Taufgesinnten oder Mennoniten in kurzen Zügen übersichtlich dargestellt.* Dritte Auflage, neu bearbeitet von E. M. ten Cate, Apeldoorn (Holland). Amsterdam: van Baerlestraat, Verlag von Johannes Müller, Boekhandel, c.1912.
Brunk, George R., Jr. *Ready Scriptural Reasons.* Scottdale, Pennsylvania: Herald Press, 1954.
Byington, Ezra, Hoyt. *The Puritans in England and New England.* Boston: Roberts Brothers, 1896.

Cattepoel, Dirk. "Christusbotschaft und Wissenschaft," In *Botschaft und Nachfolge.* 1947. Pp. 29-45.
Century Dictionary and Cyclopedia, The. Prepared under the superintendency of William Dwight Whitney and Benjamin E. Smith. XII. Revised and enlarged. New York: The Century Co., 1911.
Chapiro, Jose. *Erasmus and Our Struggle for Peace.* Boston: The Beacon Press, 1950.
Charles, Howard and Jesse W. Hoover. *Before You Decide.* Akron, Pennsylvania: Mennonite Central Committee, 1948.
Compton, Wilson Martingale. "Otelia Augsburger Compton," *Mennonite Life.* XI (October, 1956), 176-79.
Coulton, G. O. *Mediaeval Faith and Symbolism. Part I of Art and the Reformation.* New York: Harper & Brothers, Torchbook edition, 1958.
Craandijk, J. *Iets uit de Geschiedenis der Nederlandsche Doopsgezinden.* Arnhem: Karel F. Misset, 1889.
Crous, Ernst. "Franciscans," *The Mennonite Encyclopedia.* II. 1956. 363.
———, "Nonresistance," *The Mennonite Encyclopedia.* I. 897-907.

Dickinson, Edward. *Music in the History of the Western Church.* New York: Charles Scribner's Sons, 1902.
Dodd, C. H. *The Meaning of Paul for Today.* New York: Living Age Books. New York: Meridian Books, 1957.
Dosker, Henry Elias. *The Dutch Anabaptists.* Philadelphia: The Judson Press, c.1921.
Dyck, Peter J. "The MCC Atomium in Europe." *The Mennonite Weekly Review.* XXXVI (August 7, 1958), p. 4.

"Editorial," *The Mennonite Quarterly Review.* XXXVI (July 17, 1958), p. 6, c. 1.
"Editorial," *The Mennonite Quarterly Review,* III. (April, 1929), 91-98.
Egli, Emil. *Die Züricher Wiedertäufer zur Reformationszeit.* Nach den Quellen des Staatsarchivs. Zürich: Druck und Verlag von Friedrich Schulthess, 1878.
Elert, Werner. *The Christian Ethos.* Translated by Carl J. Schindler. Philadelphia: Muhlenberg Press, 1949.
Ellwood, Charless A. *A History of Social Philosophy.* New York: Prentice-Hall, Inc., 1938.
"Eucharistic Piety," *Tabernacle and Purgatory.* LI (April, 1956), pp. 355-357.
Evans, Austin Patterson. *An Episode in the Struggle for Religious Freedom: The Sectaries of Nuremberg 1524-1528.* New York: Columbia University Press, 1924.

Fellman, Walter. "Ethik," *Mennonitisches Lexikon.* I. 1913. 612-13.
Forell W. George. *Ethics of Decision.* Philadelphia: The Muhlenberg Press, c.1955.
Franz, H. compiler. *Choralbuch.* Erste amerikanische Auflage. Elkhart, Indiana: Mennonitische Verlagshandlnng, 1878.
Frerichs, O. E. "Menno Simons," *Geschriftjes ten Behoeve van de Doopsgezinden in de Verstrooiing.* No. 8. 1897.
Fretz, J. Winfield. *Christian Mutual Aid.* Section for Mennonite Aid Publication Number 3. Akron, Pennsylvania: The Mennonite Central Committee, 1947.
Friedman, Robert. "Anabaptists," *The Mennonite Encyclopedia.* I. 1956. 114-16.
———, "Ausbund," *The Mennonite Encyclopedia.* I. 1956. 391-92.
———, *Mennonite Piety.* Through the Centuries Its Genius and Its Literature. Goshen College, Goshen, Indiana: The Mennonite Historical Society, 1949.
Friesen, Peter M. *Die Alt-Evangelische Mennonitische Bruederschaft in Russland (1789-1910) im Rahmen der mennonitischen Gesamtgeschichte.* Halbstadt, Taurien, Russland: Verlagsgesellschaft "Raduga," 1911.
Fritz, F. "Die Wiedertaeufer und der wuerttembergische Pietismus," *Blaetter fuer wuerttembergische Kirchengeschichte.* Neue Folge. Im Auftrag des Vereins fuer wuerttembergische Kirchengeschichte herausgegeben von Julius Rauscher. Stuttgart: Druck und Verlag von Chr. Scheufele. II. 1939.

Geberding, E. H. *The Lutheran Pastor.* Reprint. Philadelphia: Muhlenberg Press, 1955.
Geiser, Samuel. *Die Taufgesinnten-Gemeinden.* Herausgegeben im Auftrag der Konferenz der Altevangelischen Taufgesinnten-Gemeinden (Mennoniten) der Schweiz, Karlsruhe (Baden) Karlstrasse 26: Druck und Verlag: Heinrich Schneider, 1931.

Händiges, Emil. "Humanism," *The Mennonite Encyclopedia.* II. 1956. 841-43.
———, *Seid eurer Väter wert!* Ein Gedenkblatt zum 400-jährigen Jubiläum der Taufgesinnten oder Mennoniten. Am 25. Januar 1924. Herausgegeben von der Konferenz d. Südd. Mennoniten e.P., Ludwigshafen a. Rhein. Karlsruhe i.P.P. Buch- und Kunstdruckerei Heinrich Schneider, 1925.
———, *Was ist mennonitisch?* Vortrag auf der Konferenz der Pfaelisch-Hessischen Mennonitengemeinden zu Eppstein. Sonderdruck aus den Mennonitischen Blaettern. Elbing: Reinhold Kuehn, 1930.
Haller, William. *The Rise of Puritanism.* Harper Torchbooks, first edition. New York: Harper & Brothers, Publishes, 1957.
Harder, J. "Das Mennonitentum als gemeindliche und gesellschaftliche Erscheinung," *Der Mennonit.* Internationales mennonitisches Gemeindeblatt, II (Juni 1948), Karlsruhe: Buchdruckerei Heinrich Schneider.
Hatch, Edwin. *The Influence of Greek Ideas on Christianity.* Harper Torchbooks, first edition. New York: Harper & Brother Publishers, 1957.
Heering, G. J. *The Fall of Christianity.* Translated from the Dutch by J. W. Thompson. First American Edition 1943. New York: Fellowship Publications.
Hege, Hans. "Der Christ im täglichen Leben," *Botschaft und Nachfolge.* 1947. Pp. 45-63.
Hershberger, Guy F. *Mennonites and Their Heritage.* Number V in series of *Christian Relationships to State and Community.* Second edition. Akron, Pennsylvania: The Mennonite Central Committee, 1942.
———, editor. *The Recovery of the Anabaptist Vision.* Scottdale, Pa.: Herald Press, c.1957.

Bibliography

———, *War, Peace, and Nonresistance.* Scottdale, Pa.: Herald Press, 1953.
Hesta, L. "De tegenwoordige toestand onzer Broederschap in Nederland," *Geschriftjes ten Behoeve van de Doopsgezinden in de Verstrooing.* No. 2. 1897.
Heussi, Karl und Hermann Mulert. *Atlas zur Kirchengeschichte.* Tübingen: Verlag von J. C. B. Mohr (Paul Sieback), 1905.
Hiebert, P. G. "Church of God in Christ, Mennonite," *The Mennonite Encyclopedia.* 1956. Pp. 598-600.
Hillerbrand, Jans J. "The Anabaptist View of the State," *The Mennonite Quarterly Review.* XXXII (April, 1958), 83-111.
Hoekstra, S. *Beginselen en Leer der Oude Doopsgezinden,* vergeleken met die van de overige Protestanten. Amsterdam: P. N. Van Kampen, 1863.
Hordern, William. *A Layman's Guide to Protestant Theology.* New York: The Macmillan Company, 1957.
Horsch, John. *Mennonites in Europe.* Second edition, slightly revised. Scottdale, Pa.: Mennonite Publishing House, 1950.
———, *Menno Simons.* Scottdale, Pa.: Mennonite Publishing House, 1916.
———, *The Mennonites, Their History, Faith and Practice.* Elkhart, Indiana: Mennonite Publishing Company, 1893.
———, *Modern Religious Liberalism.* Scottdale, Pa.: Fundamental Truth Depot, 1921.
Horst, B. Irvin. *A Ministry of Goodwill.* I. Akron, Pa.: Mennonite Central Committee, 1950.
Horst, John, editor. W. C. Herschberger, Joseph N. Nissley, members of a Committee appointed by the Southwestern Pennsylvania Mennonite Conference. *Instructions to Beginners in Christian Life.* Fourth Printing. Scottdale, Pa.: Mennonite Publishing House, 1947.
Horton, Walter Marschall. *Christian Theology: An Ecumenical Approach.* Revised and Enlarged Edition. New York: Harper & Brothers Publishers, 1958.
Hostetler, John S. *Mennonite Life.* Fifth edition. Scottdale, Pa.: Herald Press, 1956.
Hostetler, Lester, co-editor. *Handbook to the Mennonite Hymnary.* Newton, Kansas: General Conference of the Mennonite Church of North America Board of Publications, 1949.
Hostetler, John H. *An Invitation to Faith.* Second Printing. Scottdale, Pa. Herald Press, 1958.
"How the Mennonites Helped," *The Wichita Beacon.* July 5, 1958, p. 4, col. 3.
Hulme, E. William. *Counselling and Theology.* Philadelphia: Muhlenberg Press, 1956.
Hunzinger, Abraham. *Das Religons- Kirchen- und Schul-Wesen der Mennoniten oder Taufgesinnte.* American edition. Pennsylvania: Milford Square, 1862.
Hyma, Albert. *World History.* A Christian Interpretation. Revised edition. Grand Rapids, Michigan: Wm. B. Eerdmans Publishing Company, 1952.

Intelligenzblatt für Crefeld und die umliegende Gegend (1837, 16. Aug.), aus der Reise des Marschalls Herzogs V. Ragusa, Stuttgart, 1837, "Die Mennoniten in der Krim," *Die Heimat.* Jahrgang 21, Heft 1-2. 1950. pp. 37-38.

Jones, T. Ilion. *A Historical Approach to Evangelical Worship.* New York: Abingdon Press, 1954.

Kauffman, Daniel. *The Two Standards.* Scottdale, Pa.: Mennonite Publishing House, 1924.

Keizer, G. "De geestelijke ontwapening der Christenheid in haar geschiedenis geschetst," *Geestelijk Werloos of Weerbaar?* Samengesteld door J. H. De Goede Jr. Amsterdam: Uitgevers-Mij Holland, n.d. Pp. 1-74.
Keller, Amalie. "Scholar with a Mission," *Mennonite Life*. VIII (October, 1953), 159-161.
Kepler, Thomas, S. *The Table Talks of Martin Luther*. New York — Cleveland: The World Publishing Co., 1952.
Keyser, Leander S. *The Philosophy of Christianity*. Burlington, Iowa: The Lutheran Literary Board, 1928.
Kielstra, Tj. "Hans Denck, 1498-1527," *Geschriftjes ten Behoeve van de Doopsgezinden in de Verstrooiing*. No. 3. 1897.
Köhler, Walther. *Reformation und Ketzerprozess*. Sammlung Gemeinverständlicher Vorträge und Schriften aus dem Gebiet der Theologie und Religionsgeschichte No. 22. Tübingen und Leipzig: Verlag von J. C. P. Mohr (Paul Siebeck), 1901.
Koolmann, E. ten Doornkaat. "Isaak Jan le Cosquino de Bussy," *Mennonitisches Lexikon*. I. 1937. 305-07.
Krahn, Cornelius. *Menno Simons (1496-1561)*. Ein Beitrag zur Geschichte und Theologie der Taufgesinnten. Karlsruhe: Druck und Verlag: Heinrich Schneider, 1936.
Kreider, Robert. "Anabaptism and Humanism," *Mennonite Quarterly Review*. XXI (April, 1952), 129-141.
Kuhn, Walter. "Catholicism and Anabaptism," in *The Mennonite Encyclopedia*. I, 534.

Langenwalter, J. H. *Christ's Headship of the Church According to Anabaptist Leaders Whose Followers Became Mennonites*. Berne, Indiana: Mennonite Book Concern, 1917.
Latourette, Kenneth Scott. *A History of Christianity*. New York: Harper & Brothers, c.1953.
Lehman, C. K. "Eternal Security," 1956. *Mennonite Encyclopedia*. I. 253-54.
Lentz, Harold H. *Reformation Crossroads. A Comparison of the Theology of Luther and Melanchthon*. Minneapolis, Minnesota: Augsburg Publishing House, 1958.
Letts, Harold C., editor. *The Lutheran Heritage*. Vol. II of *Christian Social Responsibility, a Symposium in Three Volumes*. Philadelphia: Muhlenberg Press, c.1957.
Linden, Otto zur, Friedrich. *Melchior Hofmann, ein Prophet der Wiedertaeufer mit neun Beilagen*. Haarlem, De Erven F. Bohn, 1885.
Lindsay, T. M. "Anabaptists," *Encyclopaedia Britannica*. Edited by T. S. Baynes. Ninth edition. XXV. I. Chicago: R. S. Peale Company 1892. Pp. 786-87.
Littell, Franklin, Hamlin. *The Anabaptist View of the Church*. Second edition, revised and enlarged. Boston: Starr King Press, 1958.
Loserth, Johann. *Doctor Balthsar Hubmaier und die Anfänge der Wiedertaufe in Mähren*. Herausgegeben von der historisch-statistischen Section der k. k. mähr. Gesellschaft zur Beförderung der Landwirtschaft, der Natur- und Landeskunde. Brün: Verlag der hist.-statist. Section. Druck von Rudolf M. Rohrer, 1893.
Luthardt, Ernst, Chr. *Die Ethik Luthers*. Zweite verbesserte Auflage. Leipzig: Dörffling und Franke, 1875.

Mackintosh, Hugh Ross. *Types of Modern Theology*. Schleiermacher to Barth. Reprinted. London: Nisbet and Co., Ltd., 1954.
Manhardt, H. G. "Corpus Schwenkfeldianorum," in *Geschichte der Mennoniten* compiled by Cassel, K. Daniel. Philadelphia: J. Kohler, Nr. 911 Arch-Strasse, 1890. Pp. 361-64.

Bibliography

Meisinger, Karl August. *Erasmus von Rotterdam.* 2. Auflage. Veröffentlichungen des Instituts für Reformationsforschung E. V. München Nr. 1. Berlin: Albert Nauck & Co., 1948.
Mennonite Encyclopedia. Edited by Harold S. Bender and C. Henry Smith. Scottdale, Pa.: Mennonite Publishing House, c.1956.
Mennonitisches Lexikon. Herausgegeben von Christian Hege und Christian Neff. Frankfurt a.M. und Weierhof (Pfalz), 1913ff.
Minear, Paul Sevier. *Eyes of Faith.* Philadelphia: The Westminster Press, 1954.
Moerikofer, J. C. *Ulrich Zwingli.* Erster Theil. Leipzig: Verlag von S. Hirzel, 1867.
Mueller, Theodore John, *Christian Dogmatics.* St. Louis, Mo.: Concordia Publishing House, 1955.
Muralt, von Leonhard. *Glaube und Lehre der Schweizerischen Wiedertaeufer in der Reformationszeit.* Zuerich: Kommissionsverlag Beer & Co., 1938.
Mussolini, Benito. *John Huss.* Translated by Clifford Parker. New York: Albert & Charles Boni, 1929.

Näf, Verner. Vadian und Seine Stadt St. Gallen. Erster Band: bis 1518 in *Humanist in Wien.* St. Gallen: Fehr'sche Buchhandlung St. Gallen Satz und Druck: Buchdruckerei H. Tschudy & Co., St. Gallen, c.1944.
Nash, S. Henry. "Ethics," *New Schaff-Herzog Encyclopedia of Religious Knowledge,* edited by Samuel McAuley, Jackson Charles, Colbrook Sherman, George Williams Gilmore. Grand Rapids, Michigan: Baker Book House, 1950, IV, 185.
Neff, Christian. "Albigenses," *The Mennonite Encyclopedia.* 1956. P. 34.
———, "Ban," *The Mennonite Encyclopedia.* I. 1958. 219-23.
———, "The Brethren of the Common Life," *The Mennonite Encyclopedia.* III. 1956. 425-26.
———, and Walter Fellmann. "Denk (Denck), Hans," *The Mennonite Encyclopedia.* III. 1956. 32-35.
———, "Desiderius Erasmus," *The Mennonite Encyclopedia,* 1956. Pp. 239-40.
———, "Georg (Cajacob) Blaurock," *The Mennonite Encyclopedia,* Vol. II, 1956. Pp. 354-59.
———,' "Konrad Grebel," *Mennonitisches Lexikon.* II. 1937. Pp. 162-172.
Nestler, Hermann. *Die Wiedertäuferbewegung in Regensburg. Ein Ausschnitt aus der Regensburger Reformationsgeschichte.* Regensburg: Druck und Verlag von Josef Habbel 1926. Zweiter Teil: Die Wiedertäuferakten des Regensburger Stadtarchivs. Pp. 45-140.
Newman, Albert Henry. *A Manual of Church History.* Modern Church History. Revised and enlarged. Eighteenth Printing. Philadelphia: The American Baptist Publication Society, 1944.
Nichols, Robert Hastings. *The Growth of the Christian Church.* Revised edition. Philadelphia: The Westminster Press, 1941.
Niebuhr, Richard H. *The Social Sources of Denominationalism.* Living Age Books New York: Meridian Books, 1957.
Nippold, Friedrich. Beiträge vermehrt und herausgegeben. *Berner Beiträge zur Geschichte der Schweizerischen Reformationskirchen.* Bern: Druck und Verlag von K. J. Wyss, 1884.
Noonan, John P. *Ethics.* Chicago Loyola University Press, 1947.

Oates, E. Wayne. *The Religious Dimensions of Personality.* New York: Association Press, 1957.
Oehninger, Friedrich. *Geschichte des Christentums in seinem Gang durch die Jahrhunderte.* Elftes bis zwanzigstes Tausend. Konstanz: Verlag von Carl Hirsch, 1897.

Pannabecker, S. F. "Conversion," *The Mennonite Encyclopedia.* X. 1905. 704-05.

Pflug-Hartung, Julius von. Herausgegeben in verbindung mit Joh. Haller, Georg von Below, Walter Friedensburg, Jakob Wille, Walter Köhler und Otto Harnack. *Im Morgenrot der Reformation.* Stuttgart: Wilhelm Verlag, n.d.
Plantinga, B. P. *Secretaris der Vereeniging voor de Verstroodide Doopsgezinden. Geschriftjes ten Behoeve van de Doopsgezinden in de Verstrooiing.* XVI. Haarlem, Holland, 1911.
Preuschen, Erwin. "Eusebius of Caesarea," *The Schaff-Herzog Encyclopedia of Religious Knowledge.* IV. Grand Rapids, Michigan: Baker Book House, 1952. Pp. 208-11.

Qualben, Lars P. *A History of the Christian Church.* Revised and enlarged. New York: Thomas Nelson and Sons, 1942.
Quiring, Horst. "Cathars," *The Mennonite Encyclopedia.* I. 1956. 531-32.

Ramaker, A. J. "Hymns and Hymn Writers Among the Anabaptists of the Sixteenth Century." *The Mennonite Quarterly Review,* III, (April, 1929). 93-132.
Reed, D. Luther. *The Lutheran Liturgy.* Fourth printing. Philadelphia: Muhlenberg Press, 1947.
Rembert, Karl. *Die "Wiedertäufer" im Herzogtum Jülich.* Berlin: R. Gaertners Verlagsbuchhandlung Hermann Reyfelder, 1899.
Reu, Michael Johann and Paul H. Buehring, *Christian Ethics.* Columbus, Ohio: The Lutheran Book Concern, 1935.
Rian, Edwin H. *Christianity and American Education.* Second Printing. San Antonio, Texas: The Baylor Company, 1951.
Roland Albert. "The Waldensians — Their Heroic Story," *Mennonite Life.* V (April, 1950), 14-18.
Rouse, Ruthe and Stephen Charles Neill, editors. *A History of the Ecumenical Movement, 1517-1948.* Philadelphia: The Westminster Press, 1954.

Sawatzky, H. *Templer mennonitischer Herkunft.* Vol. 11/1955 of *Historische Schriftenreihe des Echo-Verlags.* Winnipeg, Manitoba, Canada: Echo-Verlag, 1955.
Schrag, Menno. *Mennonite Weekly Review Calendar for 1958.* Newton, Kansas: Herald Publishing Company, 1958.
Schultz, G. P. *Short Talks on Live Themes.* Scottdale, Pa.: Mennonite Publishing House, 1924.
Schweitzer, Albert. *An Anthology.* Edited by Charles R. Jay. Boston: Beacon Press, 1947.
———, *The Philosophy of Civilization.* Translated by C. T. Campion. First America edition. New York: The Macmillan Company, 1957.
Seeberg, Erich, D. *Luthers Theologie in ihren Grundzügen.* Zweite Auflage. Stuttgart: W. Kohlhammer Verlag, 1950.
Seeberg, Reinhold. *History of Doctrines.* Vol. I. History of Doctrines in the Ancient Church. Translated by Charles E. Hay. Grand Rapids, Michigan: Baker Book House, 1954.
Shelly, Maynard, editor. *Studies in Church Discipline.* Newton, Kansas: Mennonite Publication Office, c.1958.
Shenk, Coffman. Review of "The Eternal Why" by L. Fuerbringer in *The Christian Ministry.* II (April 1949), 127.
Sihler, E. G. "Humanism," *New Schaff-Herzog Encyclopedia of Religious Knowledge.* Editors Samuel Macauley Jackson, Lefferts A. Loetscher. Grand Rapids, Michigan: Baker Book House, 1950. Pp. 401-03.
Skillin, Edward S. "Editorial," *The Commonweal,* LXVII (Dec. 27, 1957), 236-29.
Smart, James D. *The Teaching Ministry of the Church.* Philadelphia: The Westminster Press, 1954.

Smissen, Carl H. A. van der. *Kurzgefasste Geschichte und Glaubenslehre der Altevangelischen Taufgesinnten oder Mennoniten.* Summerfield, Illinois: Im Selbstverlag des Verfassers, 1895.
Smith, C. Henry. "Baptiste," *The Mennonite Encyclopedia.* II. 1956. 228-30.
———, *The Education of a Mennonite Country Boy.* Bluffton, Ohio: n.p. 1943.
———, *The Story of the Mennonites.* Berne, Indiana: Mennonite Book Concern, c.1941.
Smith, Preserved. *Erasmus, A Study of His Life, Ideals and Place in History.* New York: Harper & Brothers, Publishers, 1923.
Smith, T. V. "Ethics," *Encyclopedia of the Social Sciences.* Vol. V. Edited by Edwin R. A. Seligman and Alvin Johnson. New York: The Macmillan Company, 1938. 602-06.
Smyth, Newman. *Christian Ethics.* New York: Charles Scribner's Sons, 1892.
Snider, Benton J. *Modern Philosophy.* St. Louis: Sigma Publishing Co., 1904.
Spinka, Matthew, editor. XIV. *Advocates of Reform.* In the *Library of Christian Classics.* Philadelphia: Westminster Press, 1953.
Springer, Nelson P. *Mennonite Quarterly Review* Cumulative Index Volumes 26-30 (1952-1956). Supplement to index for volumes 1-25 published in January, 1952: Goshen, Indiana: Mennonite Historical Society, 1956.
———, *Mennonite Quarterly Review.* Cumulative Index Volumes 1-25 (1927-1951), Reprinted from *The Mennonite Quarterly Review,* January, 1952; Goshen, Indiana: Mennonite Historical Society, 1952.
Stagner, Ross. *Psychology of Personality.* Second edition. New York: McGraw-Hill Book Company, Inc., 1948.
Sweet, William Warren. *The Story of Religion in America.* New York: Harper & Brothers, Publishers, 1950.

Terstegen, Gerhard. *Religion in Geschichte und Gegenwart.* Stuttgart: D. F. Riegersche Buchhandlung, 1844. Band II.
Thomte, Reidar. *Kierkegaard's Philosophy of Religion.* Second Printing. Princeton: Princeton University Press, 1949.
Thompson, Dorothy. "Queer People," Reprint from the January issue of *Ladie's Home Journal.* Philadelphia, Pennsylvania: The Curtis Publishing Company, Independence Square, 1952.
Tillich, Paul. *Biblical Religion and the Search for Ultimate Reality.* Chicago: The University of Chicago Press, 1955.
———, "The Relation of Religion and Health," *Religion and Health.* Edited by Simon Doniger. A Symposium, Reflection Book. New York: Association Press, 1958.
Troeltsch, Ernst. *The Social Teaching of the Christian Churches.* Translated by Clive Wyon. Second impression. London: George Allen & Unwin Lt., 1949.
Tumbült, Georg. *Die Wiedertäufer.* Vol. VII of *Monographen zur Weltgeschichte.* In Verbindung mit Anderen herausgegeben von Od. Heyck. Leipzig: Verlag von Welhagen & Klasing, 1899.

"Unit XII, The Nonconformed Life," *Program Builder.* VII (October-December, 1951), pp. 245-59.

Vos, K. and Van der Zipp, K. "Erasmus, Desiderius," *The Mennonite Encyclopedia,* II, 239-40.
———, "Geschriftjes," No. 28 *Onze Doopsgezinde Sociëteiten,* 1897.
Waard, De, S. "Het Ontstaan Onzer Broederschap," *Geschriftjes ten Behoeve van de Doopsgezinden in de Verstrooiing.* No. 3. 1897.

Wace, Henry. *Principles of the Reformation.* New York: American Tract Society, n.d.
Wach, Joachim. *Sociology of Religion.* Phoenix Books. Chicago: The University of Chicago Press, 1944.
Walker, Williston. *A History of the Christian Church.* New York: Charles Scribner's Sons, 1945.
———, *The Reformation in Ten Books of Church History.* Edited by John Fulton, Vol. IX. New York: Charles Scribner's Sons, 1902.
Walther, C. F. W. *Law and Gospel.* Reproduced from the German edition of 1897 by W. H. T. Dau. St. Louis, Missouri: Concordia Publishing House, 1928.
Waltner, Erland. "The Anabaptist Conception of the Church," *The Mennonite Quarterly Review.* XXV (Jan. 1951), 5-19.
Wand, J. W. C. *A History of the Modern Church.* Reprinted. London: Methuen and Co., Ltd., 1957.
Watson, Philip S. *Let God Be God!* An Interpretation of the Theology of Martin Luther. London: The Epworth Press, 1947.
Weber, Otto. *Karl Barth's Church Dogmatics.* Translated by Arthur C. Cochrane. Philadelphia: The Westminster Press, 1953.
Webster, A. Merriam. *New Collegiate Dictionary.* Second edition. Springfield, Mass.: G. & C. Merriam Co., Publishers, 1951.
Wenger, F. H. "Holdeman," *The Mennonite Encyclopedia,* 1956. Pp. 788-89.
Wenger, John C. "Christianity and Mysticism," *The Christian Ministry* I (Oct., 1948), 207-212.
———, *Glimpses of Mennonite History and Doctrine.* Third edition. Scottdale, Pennsylvania: Herald Press, 1949.
———, *Introduction to Theology.* Second edition (Revised). Scottdale, Pa.: Herald Press, 1956.
———, "Notes," The Complete Writings of Menno Simons, 1956.
———, *Who are Mennonites?* Scottdale, Pa.: Herald Press, n.d.
"Wiedertäufer," *Meyers grosses Konservations-Lexikon.* Sechste gänzlich neubearbeitete und vermehrte Auflage; Leipzig und Wien. Bibliographisches Institut, 1909. Vol. XX, 596.
Williams, Daniel Day. *What Present-Day Theologians Are Thinking.* New York: Harper & Brothers, Publishers, 1952.
Williams, George Huntston, and Angel M. Mergel, editors. *Spiritual and Anabaptist Writers.* Vol. XXV of *The Library of Christian Classics.* Philadelphia: The Westminster Press, 1957.
Windelband, Wilhelm. *A History of Philosophy.* Vol. I. First Harper Torchbook edition. New York: Harper & Brothers, Publishers, 1958.
Wiswedel, Wilhelm. "The Inner and the Outer Word," *The Mennonite Quarterly Review.* XXVI (July, 1952), 171-92.
Wray, E. J. "Free Will," *The Mennonite Encyclopedia.* Scottdale, Pa.: Mennonite Publishing House, 1956. Pp. 386-89.
Yoder, Edeard. "Conrad Greber as a Humanist," *Mennonite Quarterly Review.* III (April, 29), 132-46.
Young, Warren C. *A Christian Approach to Philosophy.* Wheaton, Illinois: Van Kampen Press, 1954.
Zimmermann, Wilhelm. *Der Grosse Deutsche Bauernkrieg.* Volksausgabe. Berlin: Dietz Verlag, 1952.
Zipp, N. van der. "Rembrandt van Rijn 1606-1956," *Mennonite Life.* XI (October, 1956), 145-151.
Zwemer, M. Samuel. *Sons of Adam.* Grand Rapids, Michigan: Baker Book House, 1951.

INDEX

A

Accountability — 230, 236
Action — 36
Adjustments — 58, 59
Adulteration — 87
Albigenses — 79
Alexander — 62
Ambivalence — 100, 209
Ambrose — 76, 85
Amish — 28, 39, 42, 48, 82, 136, 149, 161, 198
Anabaptism — 17
Anabaptism, third type — 197
Anabaptists — 27, 31
   Evangelical — 61
   Half-way — 64
   Latent — 54-56
   Leaders — 117-121
   Patent — 56-58
   Personalities — 200
   Pre-Reformation — 54
   Submission — 214
Anarchism — 193
Anglicans — 15
Annihilate — 9
Antiquity — 60
Apostolic Church — 36, 43, 49, 107, 192
Apostolic succession — 28
Apocalyptic — 22, 51
Aristotle — 27, 98
Armenian — 89
Art — 105, 140
Artisans — 142
Artlessness — 128
Asceticism — 4
Assisi, Francis of — 109, 166
Assurance — 40
Athanasius — 62
Atonement — 95, 205, 224
Atoning reach — 95-97
Augustine — 76, 104
Aulen, Gustave — 6, 14, 97
Ausbund — 149, 215
Austria — 73
Awakening — 137
   Great — 123

B

Bainton, Ronald — 106
Ban — 186, 195
Baptism — 18, 27, 47, 79, 174, 194
   Adult — 191
   Again — 55
   Age — 135
   Immersion — 48
   Mode — 28
Baptists — 24, 28, 29
Barth — 130, 131, 139, 162
Basic concepts — 81
Bauer — 134
Baum, J. W. — 6
Bavaria — 73
Beards — 83
Becker, Edwards — 126
Behavior — 49
Belonging — 221, 222, 225
Bender, Harold S. — 3, 4, 21, 55, 102, 121, 124, 149
Berne — 126
Bias — 221
Biblicism — 4, 49, 84, 158, 228
Bible — 4, 14, 204
Biblical ethic — 59
Biblical faith — 174
Biblical interpretation — 86
Biblicists — 109
Bigots — 73, 88
Binnerts, A. — 3
Blanke, Fritz — 55
Blaurock, Georg — 23, 57, 59, 73, 77, 119
Bonhoeffer — 4, 78, 131
Born again — 96, 210
Braght, Thielman J. van — 54, 76
Brethren — 23

Brethren of the Common Life — 70,
  85, 112, 121
Brotherhood — 50, 94
Bruderhof — 126, 190
Brunner, Emil — 94
Bullinger, Heinrich — 185
Butzer — 50

C

Calixt, Ernst — 97
Calvinists — 206
Calvin, John — 50, 103, 125, 132, 136,
  182, 184
Carnality — 47
Castelberger, Andreas — 106
Categorical imperative — 78, 92
Cathars — 79
Catholics — 167
  Church — 128
  Decision — 74-76
  Ethics — 70-76
  Roman — 4, 7, 8, 12, 35, 39, 43,
    126
Cemetery — 159
Ceremonialism — 43
Ceremonies — 112, 168, 213
Chaco — 180
Challenges — 7, 8
Character — 87
Cheltchizki, Peter — 74
Chiliasm — 136
Chiliacism — 19, 116
Christianity — 85
Christocentric — 116
Christology — 42
Chrysostom — 76
Church — 51
  Body of believers — 51
  Buildings — 159
  Corinthian — 43
  Early — 51, 77, 106
  Fall — 50
  Membership — 41, 145
  Primitive — 116, 128, 132, 131
  Protestant — 29
  Pure — 42, 79
  Purity — 51, 200, 202
  State — 39, 45, 202
  True — 23, 28, 42, 50-53

Churchianity — 226
Circumceilians — 79
Citizenship — 213
Civil — 18
  Disobedience — 18
  Government — 67
Clannishness — 203
Clarean — 118
Clergy — 50
Clothes — 211
Coexistence — 45, 63
Colonial meeting house — 86
Commitment — 87
Communion — 153, 230
  Closed — 159
Communication — 210
Communists — 61
Communities — 161
Community — 42
Compromise — 4
Compton, Otelia Augsburger — 147
Compton, Otelia Augsburger — 147
Conception of sin — 79
Conclusion — 221
Concreteness — 154
Conduct — 4, 37, 39, 81, 87, 203
Conferences — 207
Confession — 18
Congregation — 17
Conscience — 17, 30, 97
Conscientious objection — 69, 94, 208,
  214
Conservative branches — 42
  Mennonites — 139, 161
Conservatism — 207, 218
Cosmopolitan — 119
Constantine — 50
Contemplation — 153
Covenant — 41
Conversion — 45, 94, 153, 202
Co-operation — 30, 38
Crandijk — 5
Criterion — 53
Cujus regio ejus religio — 52
Culture — 28, 41, 42, 60, 104, 134,
  209
Cultus — 4, 225
Custom — 6
Cyprian — 62, 79

Index 271

D

De Bussy — 7, 57, 81
Decision— 74
Deed — 37, 39, 199
Definitions — 17-32
Deknatel, Johannes — 54, 89
Denial — 122
Denk, Hans — 5, 45, 74, 88, 107, 152, 161
Dennert, Jacob — 89
Denomination — 207, 210
Denominationalism — 228
Deportment — 7, 41, 83, 203
Depravity — 139, 206
Deprivations — 9
De Ries, Hans, — 89
Descendants — 76
Destiny — 227
Deventer — 110
De Waard, S. — 52
Dialetics — 169
Dichotomy — 133
Differences — 25
Disaster organization — 228
Discernment — 78
Discipleship — 124, 217, 231
Discipline — 88
Disobedience — 18
Dispersion — 41-61
Disputations — 37, 86
Dissenters — 114
Divine imperative — 209
Divisions — 39
Doctrine — 3, 41
Doubt — 38
Dogma — 50, 88
Dogmatism — 226, 230
Dominican Monks — 71
Donatists — 10, 79
Doopsgezind — 3, 7, 14, 210
Doopers — 44, 167
Dosker, Henry Elias — 20, 101
Draft dodgers — 69
Dunkers — 126
Dutch — 20
Dutch Mennonites — 54
Duty — 209

E

Earthly — 79
Eberhard, Arnold — 126
Ecclesiastical — 54
Ecclesiasticism — 103
Eckhart, Meister — 64
Economic conditions — 79, 88, 186
Ecumenicals — 144
Edicts — 22, 29
Edwards, Jonathan — 123
Egli, Emil — 129
Either-or Philosophy — 87
Elert, Werner — 37, 44, 95
Embellishments — 40
Emigrations — 207, 209, 226
Emphasis, positive — 39
Empiricism — 235
End — 5
Endurance — 207
Enlightenment — 105
Enthusiasm — 58
Entwertung — 64
Epictetus — 83, 84
Erasmus — 60, 67, 70, 85, 108-113, 181
Errors — 56
Eschatalogical — 51
Eschatology — 197-199
Eternal security — 206
Ethico-conversion — 207
Ethics — 3, 4, 5, 7, 9, 49, 232, 234
  Application — 179-199
  Denominations — 233
  Difficulties — 231
  Faith — 9-12, 14
  Standards — 223
  Vigor — 227
Etiology — 203
Etymology — 74
Eusebius — 62, 68, 121
Evangelicals — 75, 98, 115
Evangelical — 20, 24
  Anabaptists — 20, 24
  Mennonites — 228
  Mennonite Brethren — 180
  Principles — 155
Evil — 107
Example — 43
Excommunication — 203, 205
Exemptions — 209
Existentialists — 194
Exterior religion — 191

F

Faith — 98, 112, 201, 202
Fanaticism — 155
Fanatics — 22, 57
Fashionable society — 83
Fasts — 213
Fatalistic — 141
Fathers — 62, 107
Fear — 81
Fellowship — 231
  Saints — 43
  Spiritual — 44
Fichte — 46
Finney, Charles G. — 164
Foot-washing — 153, 230
Foreknowledge — 212
Forell, George — 9, 28, 46
Formalism — 127
Fortitude — 202
Forward reach — 93-95
Franciscan Monastery — 62, 73
Franciscans — 161
Francke — 138
Frank, Sebastian — 11, 57, 61, 103, 151
Free Churches — 50
Freedom — 95, 168
Freedom of conscience — 191
Freedom of will — 107, 111, 113, 132
Free will — 88
Fretz, Winfield J. — 89
Friedman, Robert — 129
Friesen, Peter M. — 21, 42, 88, 184
Frugality — 209
Fuerbringer, L. — 131
Fundamentalism — 225

G

Geiser, Samuel — 43
Gesangbuch — 215
General Conference — 9
Gnostics — 87
God — 164
  Awareness — 164
  Glorifying — 82
  Spirit — 175
Goebel, Max — 123
Good and evil — 84
Grace — 81, 150
Grandeur — 92
Great Awakening — 123
Grebel, Conrad — 8, 23, 53, 73, 81, 85, 101, 106, 116, 117, 150, 152
Gregory VII — 76
Groups — 26, 79, 205
Guidance — 60, 217
Guides — 222

H

Händiges — 56, 101, 122
Halle — 127, 131
Hatch, Edwin — 37
Headcovering — 205
Hegel — 46, 91, 93
Hell — 100
Heretics — 55, 77, 109
Herring, G. J. — 67
Herschberger, Guy — 67
Hetzer — 107
Hierarchy — 44, 49
Hoekstra, S. — 7, 22, 25, 26, 36, 40, 47, 91, 154, 179
Hofmann, Melchior — 136
Hofmanschen — 25
Holdeman, John — 180, 205, 211, 213
Holdemans — 234
Holiness — 25, 142
Holiness, man-made — 235
Holy Spirit — 40, 41
Homogeneous — 19
Honesty — 209
Horsch, John — 135
Hubmaier, Balthasar — 29, 38, 107, 161
Humanism — 60, 106
Humanists — 60, 67
Human life, value of — 227
Human need — 227
Humanistic teaching — 113-117
"Huns" — 209
Huss, John — 56, 68, 74
Hussites — 74
Hutterites — 23, 28, 42, 73, 82, 116, 161, 190
Hymn Books — 47
Hymns — 147, 215
Hypocrisy — 204

Index

I

Iconoclasts — 188
Idealism — 91
Ideals — 12-14, 17, 192
Idiosyncrasies — 19
Image worship — 76
"Imitation of Christ" — 111, 217
Incarnation — 15, 72
Individual worth — 44, 79
Inhibition — 38
Initial Christianity — 106
Inner consciousness — 100
  Greatness — 202
  Light — 74, 91, 153, 165, 171, 172
  Man — 90
Inspiration of Bible — 16, 22, 204, 209
Insurrectionism — 153
Intellect — 40
Interpretation, allegorical — 116
  Bible — 86
  History — 78
Intimacy — 86
Intolerance — 88
Isolationism — 49
I-W Service — 143

J

James, Epistle of — 179
Jerome — 62, 76
Jesuits — 123
Joachimites — 51
Jones, Rufus M. — 109, 151
Joris, David — 25, 135, 155
Justification — 90, 98, 104
Juvenile delinquency — 216

K

Kant, Immanuel — 45, 46, 48, 78, 91, 92, 132
Karlstadt — 146
Kauffman, Daniel — 96
Keyser, Leander — 78
Kierkegaard — 7, 211
Kingdom — 145
Kingship — 113
Klaingemeinde — 173
Köhler, Walter — 102
Kurtz, Johann Heinrich — 30
Kyrie — 160

L

Laentantius — 66
Laity — 50, 124
Languages — 74, 107
Latin — 117
Latourette, Kenneth — 57
Left wing — 20
Legalism — 203, 209, 226
Leiden, John of — 27
Liberalism — 155, 233
Liberty of conscience — 73, 74, 75
Literal — 6, 36, 192, 235
Litigation — 36
Littell, Franklin — 102, 197
Liturgy — 160
Locke, John — 96, 97
Lord's return — 197
Lord's Supper — 41, 142, 158, 168
Louvain — 101
Love — 58
Luther, Martin — 48, 52, 65, 77, 98, 99, 104, 111, 125
Lutheranism — 149
Lutherans — 26, 48

M

Mackintosh, Hugh Ross — 89
Magistracy — 17, 29
Man, a mystical being — 165
Man, worth of — 46, 48-50
Man, natural — 67
Manichaean — 79, 164
Mantz, Felix — 107, 119
Marpeck — 59, 110
Marriage — 129
Martyrs — 8
Martyrdom — 24
Martyr hymnal — 148
Marxist — 194
Mass — 76
Materialists — 47
Maximilian — 66
Mediaeval — 37, 70, 144, 192
Mediator — 92, 109, 122
Melanchthon — 98, 104
Members — 44
Mennonite — 31, 45

Artists — 146
Brethren — 3, 48, 97, 162
Central Committee — 143, 182, 210, 229
Encyclopedia — 150
Old Colony — 180, 234
Related — 39
Mennonitism — 3, 23, 31
Menno Simons — 5, 7, 10, 19, 20, 26, 38, 58, 62, 63, 64, 77, 79, 90, 99, 105, 121, 157, 167, 194, 203
Menno Simon and sects — 195
Merit — 115
Metaphysics — 15, 37
Meusel, Karl — 23
Meyer, Sebastian — 71
Military service — 201
Millennium — 136, 198
Ministers — 61, 173
Minority — 48
Missionary — 51
Monasteries — 127
Monasticism — 121
Moral consciousness — 90
   Earnestness — 79
   Law — 67, 132
   Perfection — 84
   Purpose — 82
   Reformation — 83, 116
   Support — 77
Morality — 35, 41
Morals — 50
Moravians — 123
Moslems — 67
Mother of Christ — 59
Motivation — 162
Motives — 22, 137-140, 229
Münsterites — 10, 19, 22, 23, 51, 104, 151, 206
Müntzer, Thomas — 8, 75
Muralt — 6, 55
Mussolini, Benito — 109
Mutual Aid — 61, 89, 116, 210
Mutuality — 192
Mysticism — 75, 126, 150-176
   Leaders of — 152
   Mediaeval — 75
   Pagan — 163
Mystical — 13
   Practical achievement — 166
Mystics — 64, 155

N

Nachfolge (Obedience) — 40, 63, 81, 100, 127, 201, 212
Naive — 88
Name calling — 18, 36
Narrow way — 90
Nächstenliebe — 44
Neff, Christian — 79, 102, 111
Neo-platonism — 68
Niebuhr, Richard — 105
Nicea — 64
Nicene Creed — 12
Noncomformity — 30, 49, 131
Nonparticipants — 209
Nonresistance — 13, 25, 36, 61, 66, 74, 158, 161, 185
Norm of concepts — 83-86
Norm of purity — 87
Norms — 4, 9, 25, 44, 74, 105, 117, 119

O

Obedience — 17, 35, 40, 41, 59, 86, 211-218
Objective — 40
Obliquity — 203
Oecolampadius — 107
Oehninger, Friedrich — 57
Old Catholicism — 61
Opinions — 86
Orders, Catholic — 70
Ordinances — 203
Origen — 62
Original sin — 116, 165
Orthodox — 131
Ostentatiousness — 145
Outward expression — 55
Overcoming — 159

P

Pacifism — 114, 118
Pacifists — 29, 69
Paganism — 83
Pantheism — 89, 164
Paradise — 209
Paraguay — 126
Parliament — 29

Index 275

Passions — 67
Pastor, Adam — 11
Patience — 206
Patriotism — 119
Paul, Apostle — 44, 63, 65
Pauline urge — 208
Peace — 7, 113
  Efforts — 209
  Organizations — 207
  World — 229
Peasants — 80, 119, 210
  War — 19, 57
Peculiarities — 28, 228
Pelagianism — 112, 162, 203
Pennance — 11, 201
Pentecostal Assemblies — 180
Persecution — 6, 22, 35, 63, 86
Personal faith — 79
Philips, Dietrich — 10, 31, 60, 111, 146, 151, 223
Philips, Obbe — 19, 22, 61, 81
Philosophy — 11, 45, 81-100, 87
Pietism — 4, 123-149
Pietistic examples — 146-149
  Influences — 133
Piety — 43, 79, 88
Pleasures — 51
Polemics — 126
Political — 50
  Conditions — 81
Positivism — 227
Practise — 86
Prayers — 214, 217
Prayer Book — 11
Predestination — 115, 116, 143, 170
Pre-reformers — 64
Prestige — 203
Pride — 198, 200
Priests — 73
Priesthood — 79
Principles — 36, 98
Professionalism — 50
Propagation of faith — 207
Prophets — 93
Protestantism — 40
Providence — 117
Psychology — 221
Purification — 182
Puritans — 28, 29, 134

Q

Quakers — 29
Qualben, Lars — 151, 186
Quarreling — 203
Quibbling — 88
Quietism — 39, 103, 205-207

R

Race — 42
Racial qualities — 28
Radicalism — 12, 25, 80, 155, 158, 183-195
Radicals — 21, 50, 57
Rationalism — 51, 88, 120, 141
Rationalization — 40, 91
Realism — 47
Realistic — 140
Rebellion — 18, 22
Reciprocity — 15
Re-creation — 210
Redemption — 40
Reformation — 50, 54, 55
Reformed — 26, 48, 144
Regeneration — 17, 42
Relationship — 13, 39
Relief — 180
Religious experience — 210
Rembrandt — 146
Ritschl, A. — 15
Ritual — 40, 43, 79, 89, 94
Remonstrants — 114
Renaissance — 46, 60, 70, 115
Renunciation — 88, 206
Repentance — 72, 104
Resistants — 39
Restoration — 49, 114
Restrictions — 9
Retrogression — 227
Reublin, Wilhelm — 70
Revelation — 89
Revolutionists — 39
Righteousness — 201, 224
Robes, clerical — 159
Romans 7 and 8 — 120
Roosevelt, Franklin D. — 221
Rothman, Bernt — 51
Russian Revolution — 228

S

Sacraments — 19, 51, 61, 95, 191
Saints — 51
Salvation — 98, 183
Salzburg — 73
Sattler, Michael — 98
Savonarola — 56
Schaff-Herzog — 82
Schiemer, Leonhard — 73
Schismaticism — 88
Schlaffer, Hans — 73
Schleiermacher, Friedrich — 91
Schleitheim Confession of Faith — 52, 89, 189
Scholarship — 140
Scholastics — 97, 98
Schools, state controlled — 209
Schweitzer, Albert — 82, 227
Schwenkfelders — 126, 151, 157, 238
Scriptures — 38, 163, 168, 173, 183
   Authority — 35-37
   Interpretation — 75
   Spirit of — 40
Sebastian, Frank — 86
Seclusion — 6
Secret societies — 36
Sectarianism — 115, 195-197
Sects — 44
Secularization — 76, 193, 217
Security — 206
Seeberg, Erich — 64
Seneca — 113
Separateness — 17, 30, 36, 42-46
Sermon on the Mount — 11, 28, 36, 58, 78, 80, 84, 100, 120, 139, 158, 211, 223, 227
Servet, Michel — 103
Sharing — 45
Shunning — 43, 71, 193, 205
Simplicity — 140, 156, 182
Singing — 192
Sin — 116
   Original — 116, 165
   Washing away — 47
Smith, Henry C. — 28
Smith, Preserved — 112
Sobriety — 209
Social — 7, 9
   Conditions — 80
   Direction — 189

   Intercourse — 84
   Religious — 55
   Status — 128
   Upheavals — 62
Socialism — 186
Society — 14, 17, 207
Socinian — 88
Socinians — 207
Speculation — 37
Spener, Jacob — 128, 138
Spinoza — 122
Spirit — 38
Spiritualism — 23
Spiritual restoration — 236
Spiritualize — 158
Spontaneousness — 88
Spurgeon — 89
Stability — 89
Stadler, Ulrich — 60
Standards — 20, 204, 223-225
Stewards — 231
Stewardship — 142
Stillen im Lande — 63
Stoics — 5, 83, 86
Subjectivity — 7, 45, 46
Swearing of oaths — 36
Swiss Brethren — 79, 106, 111, 117, 181, 190, 202
Symbols — 76, 141
Synthesis — 48

T

Templars — 180, 223
Temptations — 236
Tersteegen, Gerhard — 137
Tertullian — 62, 63, 212
Theologians — 14, 43
Theological — 37
   Controversy — 79
   Ethics — 97-100
   Natural — 37
Thomas à Kempis — 85
Thompson, Dorothy — 108
Tillich, Paul — 37
Tolerance — 45, 191
Tradition — 6, 50, 99
Transcendence — 154
Transubstantiation — 76
Trinity — 70, 212
Troeltsch, Ernst — 93, 196

Index

U

Urchristentum — 44
Urgemeinde — 48
Unity — 43
Unruh, B. H. — 39
Upward reach to God — 90-93
Urbanity — 210

V

Vadian of Vienna — 110, 118
Vadian, Joachim — 116
Vigilance — 225
Village — 210
Virtue — 45
Vision — 16, 58
Vives, Ludocius — 114
Voluntarism — 50, 61, 108, 193
Voluntary service — 143
Von Rottenem, Matthia Cerval — 40
Vos, K. — 102

W

Wach, Joachim — 27, 31
Waldenses — 9, 55, 76, 136, 161
Waldo, Peter — 39, 56
Walker, Williston — 110
Walther, Zacharias — 64
War — 69, 79, 92, 93
Waterlanders — 88
Wedel, Theodore — 180
Weltanschauung — 6, 48, 101, 223, 226, 227
Wenger, John C. — 35, 89
Wiedertäufer — 21, 24, 206
Will — 115
William the Silent — 6
Windelband, Wilhelm — 91
Wisdom — 81, 87
Withdrawal — 6, 43, 73, 74, 229
Whitfield, George — 123
World Council of Churches — 181
Worldly Power — 144
World, the — 43, 48, 192, 210, 235
  Transformation — 132
Wars — 208, 226, 228
Worms — 107
Worship — 35, 42, 202
Wüst — 135
Wycliff, John — 56, 75

Z

Zinzendorf, Count — 138
Zipp, van der — 147
Zwickau Prophets — 146
Zwingli — 29, 37, 49, 52, 79, 94, 106, 111, 117, 125

www.ingramcontent.com/pod-product-compliance
Lightning Source LLC
Chambersburg PA
CBHW050340230426
43663CB00010B/1930